AF324318

Risk Control Theory
of
Online Transactions

Risk Control Theory
of
Online Transactions

Changjun Jiang

Tongji University, China

Wangyang Yu

Shaanxi Normal University, China

SCIENCE PRESS

World Scientific

Published by

World Scientific Publishing Co. Pte. Ltd.

5 Toh Tuck Link, Singapore 596224

USA office: 27 Warren Street, Suite 401-402, Hackensack, NJ 07601

UK office: 57 Shelton Street, Covent Garden, London WC2H 9HE

Library of Congress Cataloging-in-Publication Data
Names: Jiang, Changjun, author. | Yu, Wangyang, author.
Title: Risk control theory of online transactions / Changjun Jiang, Tongji University, China,
    Wangyang Yu, Shaanxi Normal University, China.
Other titles: Wang luo jiao yi feng xian kong zhi li lun. English
Description: Singapore ; Hackensack, NJ : World Scientific, [2022] |
    "Originally published in Chinese as [Wang luo jiao yi feng xian kong zhi li lun] by
    China Science Publishing & Media Ltd. Copyright © China Science Publishing &
    Media Ltd., 2018" -- Title page verso. | Includes bibliographical references and index.
Identifiers: LCCN 2021038194 | ISBN 9789811241161 (hardcover) |
    ISBN 9789811241178 (ebook) | ISBN 9789811241185 (ebook other)
Subjects: LCSH: Electronic commerce. | Finance--Data processing. | Electronic funds transfers
Classification: LCC HF5548.32 .J52713 2022 | DDC 381/.142--dc23
LC record available at https://lccn.loc.gov/2021038194

British Library Cataloguing-in-Publication Data
A catalogue record for this book is available from the British Library.

网络交易风险控制理论
Originally published in Chinese by China Science Publishing & Media Ltd.
Copyright © China Science Publishing & Media Ltd., 2018

For any available supplementary material, please visit
https://www.worldscientific.com/worldscibooks/10.1142/12393#t=suppl

Desk Editors: Aanand Jayaraman/Steven Patt

Typeset by Stallion Press
Email: enquiries@stallionpress.com

Foreword

With the rapid development of the Internet, China's online transactions and other emerging industries have developed rapidly and gradually become an important part of the stability and sustainable development of the national economy. However, compared with the rapid development of the industry, the key technologies of online transactions in China are still lagging, and the regulatory capabilities and means are insufficient. In recent years, online transactions have been subjected to malicious attacks, Trojan horse hijacking, phishing, and credit card fraud. Various types of transaction fraud, smuggling tax evasion, and other illegal business practices have emerged in an endless stream.

The traditional transaction risk control is mainly based on the legal system, and it is realized by supervision and monitoring under the corresponding legal constraints. However, limited by the imperfect development of new forms and the lack of research data reserve, some legal norms are difficult to meet, so new technologies have emerged, such as transaction authentication mechanisms, third-party trusteeship mechanisms, and participants' cognitive ability classification mechanism, the geographical classification mechanism in transactions and so on. Through the subdivision of transaction participant information, detailed transaction rules are formulated for different scenarios to achieve risk control. However, the online transaction security threat characterized by "fraud" is difficult to guard against the existing risk prevention and control technologies with identity authentication as the core, rule detection as the means, and defense attack as the target.

Professor Changjun Jiang led the research and development team of Tongji University to propose the behavior certification technology of online transaction risk prevention and control, and established the element path and standard specification of user behavior data mining. By collecting and analyzing the clues left by users in the system, "behavior texture" and "transaction mode" which represent the characteristics and habits of the users are constructed, the behavior authentication mechanism based on the model is designed, the technical bottleneck of poor real-time performance and low release rate of the online transaction rules is broken, and the problem of high identification and strong real time of the transaction fraud is effectively overcome. Relevant achievements were published in important academic journals domestic and abroad, and were highly appraised by international peer experts.

This book is the embodiment of the authors' research results. It is also the first academic monograph facilitating the study of online transaction risk control theory based on the information subject. At the same time, the book also has important reference value for the study and research of Internet financial risk control, and it is hereby recommended to readers in the relevant fields.

Wu Jiangxing
Academician of the Chinese Academy of Engineering
Shanghai, China

Preface

This book mainly introduces the risk control technologies of online transaction processes, applies the traditional security technologies and advanced behavior authentication methods to the trustworthy guarantee of online transaction systems, and promotes the development of the trustworthy online transaction theory and technologies. The book consists of eight chapters, which respectively introduce the research background and significance of online transaction risk control technologies, the online transaction system modeling, risk prevention, control technology and online monitoring technology in detail, and emphatically highlight the risk prevention and control of user behaviors with identity authentication as the core and the behavior certification methods of software systems. Finally, the book focuses on the related development of credit information technologies and case studies of the online transaction system. This book can be used as a reference by researchers in the fields of computer science and technology, and online transaction risk prevention and control.

Online transaction has become one of the important parts of the new economy and finance, with great strategic significance to the sustainable and healthy development of the national economy. At the same time, transaction payment fraud also presents an explosive growth trend. The online transaction crime gradually presents the scale and the systematization characteristics. In the face of the gradually formed black-gray industrial chain, the security of online transaction has become increasingly complex, and the credibility of the online transaction process and behavior has become more and more prominent, thus gradually becoming a bottleneck for the development of online transactions. A trusted online transaction system not only needs a mature and appropriate theoretical basis but also relies on the authentication and analysis platform of online transactions realized by advanced information technologies and improves the security management level and management efficiency of the online transaction.

From the perspective of information technology, this book introduces the theory and related technology of risk prevention and control of the online transaction; focuses on the method of behavior authentication into the credible guarantee of the online transaction for the first time; and carries out the application research of behavior authentication technology in the online transaction system. After years of research and development, it has been supported by the Shanghai municipal government, the National Foundation of China and the Ministry of Science and Technology, and has formed a whole set of theories and methods for risk prevention and control of online transaction systems and developed large-scale online transaction risk prevention and control system platform, which is carried out during the application demonstration in prestigious companies.

The research on the risk control technology of online transactions not only establishes the behavior authentication theory and business process-oriented modeling and analysis technology but also promotes the research on the trusted online transaction process. The focus is on the development of large-scale online transaction risk prevention and control platform to achieve large-scale, real-time monitoring and management of online transactions, with the aim of achieving a more secure online transaction process for the users by building a solid line of defense, a not so credible deal is also expected to be applied in the future to the Internet in the field of financial engineering, free trade zone offshore settlement, and more.

This book mainly introduces the modeling of the online transaction system, risk prevention and control of software system, risk prevention, and control of user behavior, online monitoring of online transaction system, credit analysis, and other technologies. The research team has published dozens of SCI, EI and other academic achievements, obtained dozens of patents, and trained more than 20 doctors, masters and postdocs. Research achievements related to risk prevention and control of online transactions have won the first prize of Shanghai Science and Technology Progress and the second prize of National Science and Technology Progress.

In the process of writing this book, we have received great support from doctoral students, master's students, and postdoctoral fellows under the guidance of Professor Jiang Changjun, and we thank them for providing the relevant materials for this book.

Thanks also to academician Wu Jiangxing for putting forward many valuable opinions on this manuscript and writing a Foreword to this book.

Thanks for the enthusiastic support and help from the teachers, doctoral students, master's students, and postdoctoral fellows of the Key Laboratory of Embedded System and Service Computing, Ministry of Education, Tongji University.

This book is suitable not only for graduate students and related researchers in the field of information technology but also for people in the field of trusted software and online transaction.

Due to the limited time and level of work, there might be some inevitable omissions and shortcomings in the book, and the readers are requested to correct these errors as required.

About the Authors

Changjun Jiang is Professor and Doctoral Supervisor, winner of the National Science Fund for Distinguished Young Scholars, and Chief Scientist of the 973 Project. In 1986 and 1991, he obtained a bachelor's degree in computational mathematics, and a master's degree in computer software and theory from Shandong University of Science and Technology. In 1995, he obtained a Ph.D. in control theory and engineering from the Institute of Automation, Chinese Academy of Sciences. In 1997, he finished the work as postdoctoral fellow at the Institute of Computing Technology, Chinese Academy of Sciences. From 2008 to 2015, he served as the Vice President of Tongji University. From 2015 to 2019, he was the President of Donghua University. From 2019 to 2021, he was the Vice President of Tongji University. He is currently the Director of Key Laboratory of Embedded Systems and Service Computing, Tongji University, Ministry of Education, and the Director of the service platform of Shanghai Electronic Transaction and Information Knowledge Service. Main academic positions include Member of the Advisory Committee of the Information Science Department of the National Natural Science Foundation of China (2014–2016), Vice Chairman of the Chinese Association for Artificial Intelligence (2015–2019),

Chief Supervisor of the Chinese Association for Artificial Intelligence (2019–), Managing Director of the Chinese Association of Automation (2006–), Director of the Network Information Service Committee of the Chinese Association of Automation (2015–), Member of a council in China Computer Federation, Vice Chairman of China Cloud System Industry Innovation Strategy Alliance (2014–), Vice Chairman of Shanghai Association for Science and Technology (2012–), Vice Chairman of IEEE Shanghai Branch (2007–), Fellow of Chinese Association for Artificial Intelligence (CAAI Fellow, 2017–), Fellow of the British Institute of Engineering and Technology (IET Fellow, 2014–), was awarded the Honorary Professor of Brunel University (2016–). He is the Editorial Board Member of leading journals, including *Big Data Mining and Analytics*, *Chinese Journal of Computer*, *Journal of Software*, *Acta Electronica Sinica*, *Journal of Artificial Intelligence*, *Journal of Applied Science*, and *Journal of Computer Research and Development*. He has served as the Chairman of many international academic conferences and as Chairman of the Program Committee more than 20 times. At present, he has been carrying out cooperative research with the City University of Hong Kong, University of Macau, France Higher Telecom, University of Aldo, Argonne Laboratory, University of Coronado, New Jersey Institute of Technology, Texas Tech University and Kiel University.

His main research interests include network concurrency theory, network risk prevention and control, network computing environment and network information service. He is the Chief Scientist of "Model and Mechanism Research of Information Service", a National Key Research and Development Program (973). He has presided over more than 10 projects, such as the Major Research Program of National Natural Science Foundation of China, Key Project of National Natural Science Foundation of China, 863 Project, and International Key Scientific and Technological Cooperation Project. He has published more than 300 papers in *Science China*, *ACM Transactions on Embedded Computing Systems*, *ACM Transactions on Autonomous and Adaptive Systems*, *IEEE Transactions on Computers*, *IEEE Transactions on Parallel and Distributed Systems*, *IEEE Transactions on Mobile Computing*, *IEEE Transactions on Services Computing*, *IEEE Transactions on Automation Science and Engineering*, *IEEE Transactions on Systems, Man and Cybernetics* and other prestigious publications and conference proceedings. The papers were cited by domestic and foreign counterparts more than 2800 times. He has independently completed two books, published by Chinese Science Press (*Publishing Fund of Chinese Academy of Sciences*) and Chinese Higher Education Press (*Outstanding Doctoral Dissertation Publication Fund of the Ministry of Education*). He has obtained 60 Chinese national invention patents, Australian innovation patents, 19 international PCT patents, and 17 industrial technical standards. The two concluding evaluations of General Projects of the National Natural Science Foundation of China are "excellent". The concluding evaluations of his 973 Project, Major Integrated Project, and Key Project of the National Natural Science Foundation of China are all "excellent".

His research results obtained the following awards: the 2016 National Science and Technology Progress Second Prize (No. 1), the 2013 National Science and Technology Progress Second Prize (No. 1), the 2010 National Technology Invention Second Prize (No. 1), 5 first prizes of the provincial- and ministerial-level awards (nature science, technology invention, scientific and technological progress). Besides, he also won the following: The First National Hundred Excellent Doctoral Thesis, the International Discrete Event Dynamic System (DEDS), Ho Pan Qingyi Award (once every two years, each time rewarding 1–2 outstanding authors), the 2010 Best Paper Award of *International Journal of Distributed Systems and Technologies* (IJDST), the 11th IET Innovation Awards, the 15th ACM MobiHoc Best Paper Awards (domestic scholars the first time). One of the graduate students who have been instructed by Jiang has been nominated for the National Outstanding Doctoral Thesis, another one obtained the CCF Outstanding Doctoral Thesis, and five obtained the Shanghai Outstanding Doctoral Thesis. In 2007, he was the leader of the "Embedded Service Computing" team and received the Excellent Innovation Team Prize from the Ministry of Education of China.

Wangyang Yu is Associate Professor at the School of Computer Science of Shaanxi Normal University. He graduated from the School of Telecommunications of Tongji University in 2013. From December 2016 to November 2017, he is a visiting scholar of the University of Derby in the UK. He is in charge of several national and provincial projects, including the National Natural Science Foundation of China. He has published more than 30 papers in prestigious domestic and international publications and conferences, such as *IEEE Transactions on Automation Science and Engineering* and *IEEE Transactions on Systems, Man, and Cybernetics*. His main research interests include Petri net theory and applications, trustworthy software and online transaction system.

Contents

Chapter 1

Introduction

1.1 Introduction

In recent years, with the development of network technologies, as well as the support of the relevant policies of "Internet plus", the online transaction as a new business model has developed very rapidly. According to the statistics of the China Internet network information center, shopping users reached 467 million as of December 2016 [1]. Group buying, online payment, Internet finance, and online travel have all grown. However, the security and credibility of online transactions have become increasingly prominent concerns. Among the website systems of various industries, e-commerce websites have the highest proportion of high-risk factors, which is 26% [2]. In 2014, 80 million Internet users, accounting for 12.6% of the total Internet users, suffered security problems due to online consumption. 49.0% of Internet users said the Internet is not very safe or that it is very unsafe [3]. Domestic and foreign major e-commerce websites also frequently appear in a variety of technical problems, business problems, security incidents, and so on [4]. For example, many open-source e-commerce systems and third-party payment platforms have process defects [5–7]; In 2012, the security risks of a third-party payment platform resulted in the loss of users' funds [8]; The defect of a B2C top-up platform makes the business website suffer heavy losses [9]; In 2013, "authorized payment" and new forms of transaction hijacking appeared [10]; In 2014, various security problems exposed by major e-commerce platforms have also brought new threats to online shopping, and it has become a new trend to use the interface between server program and application program to carry out malicious behaviors [2]. At the same time, in recent years, phishing as a typical social engineering method has been endangering the healthy development of online transactions.

In the dynamic and open network environment, the cooperation among distributed online transaction systems is realized through the business interaction of participants. The online transaction system has various structures, with many participants, such as banks, third-party payment platforms, buyer clients, shopping websites, and so on. Transaction participants interact and communicate with each other through application open interfaces (API, web service interface, SaaS-software as a service, CaaS-cash as a service), combining their complex business processes into complete, loosely-coupled, more complex hybrid Web applications. In the open network environment, this integration and interaction bring more uncertainties, which create new security challenges. Among different participants and sessions, the interaction is complex, the business logic is found to be inconsistent, and the internal data state is often uncoordinated. The complex linkage of data flow, control flow, and capital flow among business processes can lead to very serious problems, such as violation of transaction attributes and huge economic losses. The complex human factors, combined with the different main bodies of the business processes among different sessions, mean a malicious user can still obtain illegal interests by discovering the logic errors brought by the interaction among the client and the server business, even if all the traditional security requirements are met (information integrity, access control, security policy, etc.).

The entities and modes of the online transaction process are constantly changing, and the open and dynamic network environment also makes the environment faced by the online transaction system complex and diverse. According to Ai Rui consulting statistics, the number of third-party service providers in Tmall and Taobao has exceeded 2800. Alibaba even proposed "Stone Tower" and "Ali Wireless Baichuan Project" to enhance cooperation with third-party businesses [11]. The diversified system structure and the participation of many roles make the process of cooperation among different participants complex, and the security risk is bound to increase. Therefore, there is a trusted hidden danger in the process design and construction of the online transaction software system, which will lead to the unpredictable behavior of the online transaction system with the business process as the core.

As we all know, online transactions have become an important part of the national economy and national industry in China as well as globally, and promise to be extremely critical to life and economic development in the future information age.

1.2 Internet Development

The network applications of China have developed rapidly since Internet access was introduced to China. The continuous improvement of Internet infrastructure construction, the continuous introduction of favorable policies, and the penetration of the Internet into various industries together promote the continuous growth of the scale of Internet users. In the first half of 2016, the state council and other relevant departments issued guidelines on "Internet plus government services", "Internet plus circulation", and "Internet plus manufacturing", promoting the integration of the Internet with various industries. In the future, as the infrastructure of the information society, the Internet will further exert a profound impact on the development of China's politics, economy, culture, society, and other fields [12].

In 2016, China's personal Internet applications maintained steady development, and the user scale was on the rise, with online takeaway and Internet medical care being the two applications with the fastest growth rate, reaching 83.7% and 28%, respectively [1]. Online shopping also maintained a rapid growth rate of 8.3% in half a year. Most applications for the mobile phone have maintained rapid growth, among which the scale of mobile online takeaway users has the most obvious growth, with a half-year growth rate of 40.5%. Meanwhile, the half-year growth rate of mobile online payment and shopping is close to 20%. While promoting consumption upgrading, the government has increased regulations on cross-border e-commerce and other related industries. Online shopping platforms have expanded from shopping consumption mode to service consumption mode [12].

Internet financial applications maintained a growth trend in 2016. The growth rate of online payment and Internet financial management users was 9.3% and 12.3%, respectively [12]. With the rapid development of e-commerce applications, online payment manufacturers continue to expand and enrich the offline consumption payment scene, and implement all kinds of marketing strategies to open the social relationship chain, driving the transformation of non-online payment users; The scale of Internet financial management users continues to expand; The increasing number of financial products and the continuous improvement of product user experience drive the public to gradually develop the habit of online financial management. Platform, scene, and intelligence have become the new direction of Internet financial management.

In 2016, the number of users of all kinds of Internet public service applications increased, and the number of users of online education, online taxi booking, and online government affairs services exceeded 100 million, showing obvious characteristics of diversification and mobility. The field of online education has been continuously refined, the user boundary has been continuously expanded, and the service has been developing in the direction of diversification. Meanwhile, the personalized learning scene provided by mobile education, as well as the functional advantages such as the touch and voice output of mobile devices, have promoted it to become the mainstream of online education. In the field of online car rental, based on the huge market demand and the increasingly perfect technology application, the scale of the industry continues to expand; In the field of online government affairs, government websites are combined with government Weibo, WeChat, and the client to give full play to the carrier role of Internet and information technology and optimize the user experience of government services [12].

As for the number of Internet users, as of December 2016, China had 731 million Internet users, adding 42.99 million new Internet users in the whole year, with a growth rate of 6.2%. The Internet penetration rate was 53.2%, 2.9% points higher than at the end of 2015. More than the global average of 3.1% points and the Asian average of 7.6% points. China's Internet population is already the size of Europe's. China has 695 million mobile Internet users, with 75.5 million more than at the end of 2015. Internet users are further concentrating on mobile devices. With the continuous improvement of the mobile communication network environment and the further popularization of smartphones, mobile Internet applications have penetrated all kinds of life demands of users [1].

1.3 The Present Situation of the Online Transaction

After two decades of development and continuous optimization of the market, e-commerce giants Alibaba, JD.com, VIPSHOP, and others have been listed in the United States. On the one hand, e-commerce continues to develop from comprehensive online shopping to sub-sectors such as maternal and infant, cross-border, and rural areas. On the other hand, the combination of online and offline, the integration of enterprises, and the application of big data technology all symbolize the ecological development of e-commerce in China. Meanwhile, enterprises keep opening the ecological entrance, products, services, and scenarios, and reintegrate the resources in their ecological system [13].

As of December 2016, the scale of shopping users in China has reached 460 million, accounting for 63.8% of Internet users, with a growth rate of 12.9%. The shopping market in China still maintains a fast and steady growth trend. Among them, the scale of shopping users in China's mobile network reaches 441 million, accounting for 63.4% of mobile Internet users, with an annual growth rate of 29.8%. As the main entrance of O2O, the popularity of mobile terminal plays a direct role in guaranteeing the development of O2O and is the user base for carrying out various forms of online and offline integration. In 2016, the number of Internet users buying Internet financial products reached 98.9 million, an increase of 8.63 million users compared with at the end of 2015, and the utilization rate of Internet users was 13.5%, an increase of 0.4 percentage points compared with at the end of 2015. After several years of the rapid development of the Internet financial management market, the number of financial products is increasing, the user experience continues to improve, and the online financial management habits of netizens have initially formed. By December 2016, the number of online payment users in China had reached 475 million, an increase of 58.31 million or 14% over the end of 2015. The proportion of online payment users in China increased from 60.5% to 64.9%. Among them, the scale of mobile payment users has grown rapidly, reaching 469 million, with an annual growth rate of 31.2%. The proportion of Internet users using mobile online payment has increased from 57.7% to 67.5% [1].

By December 2016, the number of Internet users who had booked airline tickets, hotels, train tickets, or holiday products online had reached 299 million, an increase of 3.96 million or 15.3% over the end of 2015. Online booking of train tickets, air tickets, hotels, and holiday products accounted for 34.0%, 15.9%, 17.2%, and 7.4%, respectively. Among them, 262 million Internet users booked air tickets, hotels, train tickets, and holiday products through mobile phones, up 51.89 million or 24.7% from the end of 2015. The proportion of Chinese netizens using mobile phones to book online travel increased from 33.9% to 37.7% [1].

The latest data from Ai Rui consulting shows that the transaction scale of China's e-commerce market in 2016Q3 is 5.2 trillion yuan, up 30.8% year-on-year, and 12.9% month-on-month. Among them, mobile online shopping increased by 56.1% year-on-year, which became an important force to promote the development of the e-commerce market. Besides, the year-on-year growth of the B2B market of 13.7% and online travel of 28.4% jointly drive the growth of the e-commerce market transaction scale. The online shopping industry is becoming increasingly mature. In addition to constantly expanding categories, optimizing logistics, and after-sales service, e-commerce enterprises are also actively developing cross-border online shopping and developing rural e-commerce through submerging channels. Some enterprises aim at maternal and child, medical care, home decoration, and other vertical e-commerce fields deeply, these will become the network shopping market development new promotion point. The concentration of the mobile online shopping market is very high. Ali Wireless, VIPSHOP, JD.com, SUNING, Gome, and other enterprises have also vigorously developed mobile terminals, and the proportion of mobile terminals has increased, resulting in fierce market competition [14].

From macro policies to enterprise promotion, the government and enterprises work together to promote consumption upgrading. The 13th five-year plan defines the direction of consumption upgrading from the top-level design. It emphasizes the expanding service consumption to drive the upgrading of consumption structure and guide consumption to develop in the direction of intelligence, environmental protection, intensification, and quality. As the product of the combination of traditional retail and information consumption, shopping conforms to the development trend of new consumption upgrading. At the same time, the e-commerce platform marketing mode is diversified and upgraded, extending from shopping consumption mode to service consumption mode. For example, introduce media elements in a PC terminal and mobile terminal to conduct interest shopping, and expand the function of e-commerce media; Explore video e-commerce shopping guide mode, and take short videos and live broadcast as carriers to deeply explore the economic value of web celebrity effect [12].

1.4 Online Transaction Risk

The security risk of online transaction software systems is also highlighted with the rapid development of Internet. Many e-commerce software technologies are not mature and reliable; there are security vulnerabilities that are easily exploited by outside intruders, resulting in huge economic losses. According to the statistics of relevant data, the economic losses caused by network security problems in the United States reached nearly 10 billion dollars every year, and the domestic situation is not optimistic [15]. In 2010, more than 100 million users had encountered at least one security threat against shopping, which brought direct economic losses of more than 15 billion yuan, and the average economic losses of online shopping users increased from 80 yuan in 2009 to about 150 yuan [16]. According to the statistics of the China Internet network information center (CNNIC), in the first half of 2011, 8% of Internet users suffered economic losses when shopping online, and the group size reached 38.8 million [17]. Besides, online shopping Trojans and phishing sites also seriously threaten the security of online shopping. According to the statistics of Jinshan Network Cloud Security Center in 2011, thousands of online shopping Trojans are monitored every day, and there are more phishing websites. Compared with the same period last year, the number of server hosts and intercepted visits to phishing sites has increased by as much as 10 times [18]. In the second quarter of 2016, 360 Internet security center intercepted 375,000 new phishing websites, accounting for 16.2% of fake shopping websites and 8.7% of fake banks. There were 862 cases of fraudulent shopping, accounting for 15.8%, 658 cases of online game trading, accounting for 12.0%, 654 cases of virtual goods, accounting for 12.0%, and 497 cases of financial planning, accounting for 9.1% [19].

Typical cases emerge in the process of online transactions [20]. In 2010, a new attack mode for online transactions emerged: transaction hijacking [10]. While the normal transaction is proceeding, a hacker use the legitimate identity of an user to make a background transaction, and the recipient account belongs to the hacker. If the user is about to pay, via the payment link, the normal transaction is hijacked to the hacker background transaction, to pay the user's money to the hacker account. Hackers have formed a complete industrial chain of online shopping security threats, the trend of group warfare is more and more obvious, with more risk factors for online shopping, as fraud techniques emerge endlessly, rendering the security situation very serious. Even the highly secure banking system has had repeated problems. In recent years, APT attacks on banks, securities, and other financial industries have continuously appeared. On February 5, 2016, the Bangladesh Central Bank was attacked by hackers, which resulted in the theft of $81 million [21]. According to the big data analysis of 360 Internet security center, fake shopping phishing websites of singles' day in 2016 are more sophisticated, and a large number of phishing websites are made by hacking into regular government or large enterprise websites, which greatly increases the difficulty of security software protection. Not only that, the total number of newly added phishing websites intercepted on November 11, 2016, increased by 18.7% compared with that on November 11, 2015. 360liwang.com received 532 online fraud reports from users across the country, with an average loss of 9,282.8 yuan. The vulnerability threat of financial industry websites is more complicated. Many high-risk vulnerabilities have been exposed not only in traditional financial fields such as banking and insurance, but also in the emerging field of third-party payment and Internet P2P [22].

In today's online transaction system, the defects and logic errors that lead to interactive behavior security problems exist in the design stage and application layer of the business process. The detection of defects and logic errors in the trading process in the system model design stage can ensure the security and reliability of online transaction business process design. If errors are discovered after the implementation of the system, the modification and remediation of the existing system will be expensive and may cause irreparable losses. In the stage of system design, it is necessary to use formal methods for modeling and analysis. Based on strict mathematical definition and analysis, problems can be found and solved to the greatest extent. Not only known defects can be found, but also unknown defects can be found, which greatly improves the completeness of the system. Therefore, the business process model and analysis method of online transactions based on formal methods are the important research subject facing the interaction behavior security research.

1.5 Risk Response Measures

Given the risk prevention problem of online transaction systems, domestic and foreign scholars and industry have done a lot of research on business process modeling and validation, as well as business system security.

In recent years, process-driven information system construction has been more and more widely used, and the business process model plays an important role in the understanding and accurate design of a software system. Herein, business process restructuring and optimization have always been an important research direction [23]. Domestic and foreign scholars have done a lot of research on business process execution language, process mining, process instance representation, and functional correctness verification [24–28]. To aid this, Petri net, one of the formal tools, is widely used to describe business processes and solve the deadlock problem caused by incompatible interactive behaviors in web service composition [29, 30]. Petri net was proposed to study the responsibilities and obligations in collaboration with online transaction systems [43]. They can also be used to optimize the control of the system to ensure reasonable resource allocation and smooth execution of the process [31–34]. The modeling method of the business process lays a solid foundation for the modeling of the online transaction system.

For the security of business systems, domestic and foreign scholars have studied how to integrate security policies into collaborative business processes to ensure access control authority and information security of different roles [35, 36]. Some scholars have studied access control and information security in business processes. Information leakage in the process of accessibility detection based on Petri nets are to ensure the security of sensitive data [37]. Some scholars also introduce signatures into business processes to ensure information integrity and data privacy, or describe and define the security attributes of business processes, to facilitate the design and development of systems with security in mind, and try to guarantee the security of business systems from the perspective of software development [37–41]. Starting from the security policy, this research group explored the behavior of mutual simulation of different interactive systems based on the Petri net model, discussed whether two systems with different behavioral security policies and the same function are equivalent, and used formal methods to describe the behavioral equivalence of two security-oriented interactive systems [42]. Meanwhile, referring to the relevant characteristics of the colored Petri net and the predicate net, the EBPN model (E-commerce Business Process Nets) is proposed to depict the data attributes and malicious behaviors of the e-commerce business process, and to be able to find verification errors and logic defects in the business process [44–46].

In the industry, the integration of traditional security technology into the transaction process is also a common practice to ensure the security of user payment. For example, the secure sockets layer (SSL) protocol and secure electronic transaction (SET) protocol are commonly adopted by online transaction platforms as the underlying protocols [47]. In addition to SSL, the main third-party payment companies also adopt OTP and PKI systems to ensure the safety of online payments. The above technologies and methods are mainly aimed at traditional security issues such as identity authentication, security policy, and protocol and access control. These classical security measures undoubtedly play an important role in the protection of the online transaction process. However, the interactive behavioral security problem in online transaction systems emerges from subjects' behavioral interactions. Under the premise of legitimate identity and authority, users can carry out malicious behaviors within the scope permitted by the system behavior.

For the prevention and control of phishing, the industry, and academia at home and abroad also, have relevant studies [48–51]. In the industry, there are ways to deploy digital certificates such as SSL server certificates, GlobalSign-EVSSL certificates, and so on. Some black and whitelisting approaches, such as IE7.0, Earth-Link's Scam2Block, PhishGuard, Netcraft, and Google SafeBrowsing on Firefox, all use it. Ali Wangwang, Tencent QQ, Jinshan Shield, 360net Shield, Yi Bao payment, and other enterprises have also launched the corresponding anti-phishing system. In the academic world, there are mainly methods for email protocol vulnerability, methods for comparing web page similarity, methods based on the document-oriented model comparison, methods for judging sender reliability, and URL detection methods. These technologies and methods mainly use the black and whitelist method, page comparison, and URL detection technology, which is similar to the traditional antivirus software using signature code antivirus. However, the blacklist has certain limitations, which cannot prevent new phishing attacks, let alone deal with the high technology of cross-site phishing.

After the deployment and debugging of the e-commerce trading system, online monitoring should be carried out in its actual operation process to monitor users' trading behaviors in real-time and deal with illegal activities. Existing online monitoring technologies mainly include interceptor-based, AOP (Aspect Oriented Programming)-based, monitoring API-based, exception handling-based, and other online monitoring technologies. At present, another monitoring technology is adopted in the operation process of a networked software system: abnormal behavior monitoring and processing [52, 53]. The abnormal behavior monitoring and processing mechanism provides a method to deal with abnormal situations when the system or program is running and provides the modes that can be adopted by the abnormal behavior monitoring and processing mechanism: unconditional transfer pattern, interrupt pattern, retry pattern, and recovery pattern. This mechanism has not only been applied in advanced programming languages but also, in recent years, researchers have begun to introduce exception handling and recovery mechanism in system fault-tolerant design, workflow system design and execution, web service, or component interaction. This mechanism is an effective means to improve software reliability and provides some support in fault detection and online fault tolerance.

Online data mining of user behaviors is an important method for the timely detection of fraud incidents [54, 55]. At present, the mining technology of user behavior information is mainly to model a class of users, abstract a class of users' preferences or consumption habits, and other behavioral characteristics. With the growth of users' personalized demands in the e-commerce system, the research of modeling users' individual behaviors, preferences, and other characteristics has gradually attracted people's attention. On the one hand, this method can provide users with more accurate services, and on the other hand, it can prevent fraud based on users' previous behaviors.

1.6   Chapter Summary

To sum up, with the rapid development of the Internet and online transactions, the risk prevention of online transactions has become a new security problem to be solved urgently in the online transaction system. In the open network environment, the complete online transaction business process involves multiple participating entities, and the multi-session mechanism also makes the interaction behavior in the business process more complex. The diversified system structure of the online transaction and the participation of many roles make the security risk inevitably increase. Therefore, how to accurately describe the multi-agent and multi-session business process, effectively analyze the transaction data, and finally achieve effective risk prevention and control are important challenges at present. Domestic and foreign research on this issue is still in the development stage; therefore, the research in this field is expected to achieve innovative results.

References

[1] China Internet Network Information Center (CNNIC). The 39th Statistical Report on Internet Development in China, (2017). http://www.cac.gov.cn/2017-01/22/c_1120352022.htm.

[2] 360 Internet Security Center. 2014 Chinese Website Security Report, (2015). https://www.docin.com/p-1117710380.html.

[3] China Internet Network Information Center (CNNIC). The 35th Statistical Report on Internet Development in China, (2015). http://www.cac.gov.cn/2015-02/03/c_1114222357.htm.

[4] 360 Internet Security Center. 2016 China Internet Security Report, (2017). https://bbs.360.cn/thread-14837467-1-1.html.

[5] Wang, R., Chen, S., Wang, X. F. *et al.* How to Shop for Free Online — Security Analysis of Cahi-as-a-Service Based Web Stores. In *32th IEEE Symposium on Security and Privacy (S&P)*, IEEE, Oakland, USA, pp. 465–480 (2011).

[6] Chen, E. Y., Chen, S., Qadeer, S. *et al.* Securing Multiparty Online Services via Certification of Symbolic Transactions. In *36th IEEE Symposium on Security and Privacy (S&P)*, IEEE, San Jose, USA, pp. 833–849 (2015).

[7] Sun, F. Q., Xu, L., and Su, Z. D. Detecting Logic Vulnerabilities in E-Commerce Applications. In *21st Network and Distributed System Security Symposium (NDSS)*, Internet Society, San Diego, USA, pp. 1–16 (2014).

[8] Inventory 2012 Payment Security. http://www.ebrun.com/20130107/64953_all.shtml.

[9] Jingdongloopholes. https://baike.baidu.com/item/%E4%BA%AC%E4%B8%9C%E%BC%8F%E6%B4%9e/6169452.

[10] Transaction Hijacking Trojan. http://baike.baidu.com/view/4952320.html? from Taglist.

[11] Ai Rui. China E-Commerce Software Industry Research Report, (2015). http://report.iresearch.cn/report_pdf.aspx?id=2491.

[12] China Internet Network Information Center (CNNIC). The 38th Statistical Report on Internet Development in China, (2016). http://www.cac.gov.cn/2016-08/03/c_1119326372.htm.

[13] Ai Rui Consulting. China E-Commerce Vitality Report, (2016). http://report.iresearch.cn/report_pdf.aspx?id=2691.

[14] Ai Rui Consulting. 2016Q3 China E-Commerce Core Data, (2016). http://report.iresearch.cn/content/2016/11/265616.shtml.

[15] Try to Talk About E-Commerce Faces: A Number of Network Security Problems. http://b2b.toocle.com/detail, 6008854 HTML.

[16] In 2010, China's Online Shopping Security Report. http://www.infosec.org.cn/news/news_view.php?Newsid=14139201.

[17] China Internet Network Information Center (CNNIC). The 28th China Internet Network Development Statistics Report, (2011). http://tech.163.com/special/cnnic28.

[18] In The First Half of 2011 China's Online Shopping Security Report. http://www.ijinshan.com/download/2011zgwlgwaQBG.PDF, 2011.

[19] 360 Company. Research Report on the Trend of Online Fraud in the Second Quarter of 2016, (2016). http://zt.360.cn/1101061855.php?did=210019970&dtid=1101062366.

[20] Apple itunes Component Application Vulnerabilities. https://Cn.Aliy un.Com/Zixun/Content/2_6_822916.Html.

[21] 360 Company. Comprehensive Analysis of Bank SWIFT System Attack Event, (2016). https://blog.csdn.net/qq_27446553/article/det ails/52191394.

[22] 360 Company. 2016 Double 11 China Online Shopping Security Special Report, (2016). https://www.doc88.com/p-40599009542712.html? r=1.

[23] Yousfi, A., de Freitas, A., Dey, A. *et al.* The Use of Ubiquitous Computing for Business Process Improvement. *IEEE Transactions on Services Computing*, 9(4): 621–632 (2015). DOI: 10.1109/TSC.

[24] Hertis, M. and Juric, M. B. An Empirical Analysis of Business Process Execution Language Usage. *IEEE Transactions on Software Engineering*, 40(8): 738–757 (2014).

[25] Kunze, M., Weidlich, M., and Weske, M. Querying Process Models by Behavior Inclusion. *Software and Systems Modeling*, 14(3): 1105–1125 (2015).

[26] Appice, A. and Malerba, D. A Co-Training Strategy for Multiple View Clustering in Process Mining. *IEEE Transactions on Services Computing*, 9(6): 832–845 (2015). DOI: 10.1109/TSC.2015 2430327.

[27] Song, L., Wen, L. J., Jian, M, *et al.* Decomposition of Process Representation Graph Based on Completely Finite Prefix. *Journal of Tsinghua University: Natural Science Edition*, 54(4): 490–494 (2014).

[28] Zhang, C., Duan, Z. H., Tian, C. *et al.* Modeling, Verification and Testing of Interactive Behavior of Distributed Software Systems. *Computer Research and Development*, 52(7): 1604–1619 (2015).

[29] Van der Aalst, W. M. P. Service Mining: Using Process Mining to Discover, Check, and Improve Service Behavior. *IEEE Transactions on Services Computing*, 6(4): 525–535 (2013).

[30] Du, Y. H., Li, X. T., and Xiong, P. C. A Petri Net Approach to Mediation-Aided Composition of Web Services. *IEEE Transactions on Automation Science and Engineering*, 9(2): 429–435 (2012).

[31] Jiao, L. and Lu, W. M. Petri Net System Integration and Conservation Based on Shared Location. *Acta Computer Sinica*, 30(3): 352–360 (2007). (in Chinese with English abstract).

[32] Bi, J., Zhu, Z. L., and Fan, Y. H. Behavior Compatibility Analysis and Optimal Control Strategy in Web Service Portfolio. *Acta Electronica Sinica*, 39(12): 2842–2849 (2011).

[33] Zeng, Q. T., Lu, F. M., Liu, C. *et al.* Modeling and Verification for Cross-Department Collaborative Business Processes Using Extended Petri Nets. *IEEE Transactions on Systems, Man, and Cybernetics: Systems*, 45(2): 349–362 (2015).

[34] Wang, J., Hu, H., Yu, P. *et al.* Cross-organizational Process Modeling Combined with Public View and Object Petri Nets. *Computer Science and Exploration*, 8(1): 18–27 (2014).

[35] Badr, Y., Biennier, F., and Tata, S. The Integration of Corporate Security Strategies in Collaborative Business Processes. *IEEE Transactions on Services Computing*, 4(3): 243–254 (2011).

[36] Li, X. and Xue, Y. A Survey on Server-Side Approaches to Securing Web Applications. *ACM Computing Surveys (CSUR)*, 46(4): Article no. 54 (1–29) (2014).

[37] Accorsi, R., Lehmann, A., and Lohmann, N. Information Leak Detection in Business Process Models: Theory, Application, and Tool Support. *Information Systems*, 47: 244–257 (2015).

[38] Hoon, W. L., Kerschbaum, F., and Wang, X. H. Workflow Signatures for Business Process Around. *IEEE the Transactions on Dependable and Secure Computing*, 9(5): 756–769 (2012).

[39] Ben, O. L., Angin, P., Weffers, H. *et al.* Extending the Agile Development Process to Develop Acceptably Secure Software. *IEEE the Transactions on Dependable and Secure Computing*, 11(6): 497–509 (2014).

[40] Bu, N., Liu, Y. L., Lian, Y. F. *et al.* Modeling and Analysis Method of Network Security System Based on UML. *Computer Research and Development*, 51(7): 1578–1593 (2014).

[41] Bentounsi, M., Benbernou, S., and Atallah, M. J. Security — Aware Business Process as a Service by Hiding Provenance. *The Computer Standards and Interfaces*, 44: 220–233 (2016).

[42] Liu, G. J. and Jiang, C. J. Secure Bisimulation for Interactive Systems. *Lecture Notes in Computer Science*, 9530: 625–639 (2015).

[43] Du, Y. Y., Jiang, C. J., Zhou, M. C. *et al.* Modeling and Monitoring of E-Commerce Workflows. *Information Science*, 179(7): 995–1006 (2009).

[44] Yu, W. Y., Yan, C. G., Ding, Z. J. *et al.* Modeling and Validating E-Commerce Business Process Based on Petri Nets. *IEEE Transactions on Systems, Man, and Cybernetics: Systems*, 44(3): 327–341 (2014).

[45] Yu, W. Y., Yan, C. G., Ding, Z. J. *et al.* Modeling and Verification of Online Shopping Business Processes by Considering Malicious Behavior Patterns. *IEEE Transactions on Automation Science and Engineering*, 13(2): 647–662 (2016).

[46] Yu, W. Y., Yan, C. G., Ding, Z. J. *et al.* Analyzing E-Commerce Business Process Nets via Incidence Matrix and Reduction. *IEEE Transactions on Systems, Man, and Cybernetics: Systems*, 48(1): 130–134 (2016). DOI: 10.1109/TSMC.2016.2598287.

[47] Xiao, Y. Y., Su, K. L., Ma, Z. Y. *et al.* Verification and Improvement of SET Payment Protocol Based on Instantiated Spatial Logic. *Journal of Huazhong University of Science and Technology (Natural Science Edition)*, 41(7): 97–102 (2013).

[48] Ren, Q., Mu, Y., and Susilo, W. An Email System for Anti-Phishing. In *Proceedings of the 6th IEEE/ACIS International Conference on Computer and Information Science*, IEEE, Melbourne, Australia, pp. 782–787 (2007).

[49] Ma, L. P., Torney, R., Watters, P. *et al.* Automatically Generating Classifier for Phishing Email Prediction. In *10th International Symposium on Pervasive Systems, Algorithms, and Networks*, IEEE, Kaoshiung, Taiwan (December 14–16, 2009).

[50] Hea, M., Horng, S.-J., Fanc, P. *et al.* An Efficient Phishing Webpage Detector. *Expert Systems with Applications*, 38(10): 12018–12027 (2011).

[51] Zhang, Y., Hong, J., and Cranor, L. Cantina: A Content-Based Approach to Detecting Phishing Web Sites. In *Proceedings of the 16th international conference on World Wide Web*, International World Wide Web Conference Committee (IW3C2), Banff, Alberta, Canada, pp. 639–648 (2007).

[52] Shah, H. B., Gorg, C., and Harrold, M. J. Understanding Exception Handling: Viewpoints of Novices and Experts. *IEEE Transactions on Software Engineering*, 36(02): 150–161 (2010).

[53] Brito, P. H. S., de Lemos, R., Rubira, C. M. F, *et al.* Architecting Fault Tolerance with Exception Handling: Verification and Validation. *Journal of Computer Science and Technology*, 24(02): 212–237 (2009).

[54] Wang, S. A Comprehensive Survey of Data Mining-Based Accounting-Fraud Detection Research. In *2010 International Conference on Intelligent Computation Technology and Automation (ICICTA '10)*, IEEE, Changsha, China, pp. 50–53 (2010).

[55] Wang, Y.-T. and Lee Anthony, J. T. Mining Web Navigation Patterns with a Path Traversal Graph. *Expert Systems with Applications*, 38(6): 7112–7122 (2011).

Chapter 2

Basic Knowledge

2.1 Introduction

With the rapid development of science and technology, human society has entered into the information era. Network technology has undergone a fundamental change, and a large number of new and high technology fields have emerged, including web service, network computing, cloud computing, big data technology, etc. Based on these advanced technologies, many emerging internet industries and related information systems were born, such as online transactions, search engines, online communication, and so on. The behaviors of these systems are very difficult to plan, schedule, and control due to the hugeness and complexity. In that regard, such systems have become challenging research topics in system science and computer science in recent years. Formalized analysis and verification of information systems has become an important research field. Benefiting from the precise mathematical definition and analysis, problems can be readily found and solved. Both the known defects and those unknown can be found, which significantly improves the system completeness. There have been formal models and theories such as automata, Petri net model, business process model, and Markov process during decades of development. Meanwhile, cryptography and dynamic random code are also widely used in online transaction systems.

2.2 Automata

The theory of automata is a discipline developed in the 1950s and gradually developed in the 1970s. Automata is a dynamic mathematical model of the computer and the computing process, which is used to study computer architecture, logic operation, program design, as well as computational complexity theory. As an important foundation of computer science, automata is a widely used software design pattern. It was introduced as an important branch of computer science and was widely used in compiling systems and pattern recognition. Since the 1980s, it has been widely used in control science and system science. Nowadays, the term, automata, is also widely used in other related disciplines with different contents and research objectives. Automata can be divided into deterministic finite automata (DFA), non-deterministic finite automata (NFA), non-deterministic finite automata with ε transfer (FND-ε or ε-NFA), cellular automata, etc. The following are some basic definitions [1–5].

Definition 2.1 $FSM = (\Sigma, Q, \delta, q_0, Q_m)$ is called a finite state automaton, if and only if:

(1) Σ is a finite set of events.
(2) Q is a finite set of states.
(3) $\delta : Q \times \Sigma \to Q$ is a state transition function.
(4) $q_0 \in Q$ is an initial state.
(5) $Q_m \subseteq Q$ is a set of identification states.

Definition 2.2 A four-tuple $G = (N_F, N_T, \Gamma, S_0)$ is called a grammar, if and only if:

(1) N_F, N_T are finite sets, called finalizes and nominalizes, respectively, such that $N_F \cap N_T = \varnothing$.
(2) Γ is a finite set, called the generating set. The production formula is as follows:

$$\alpha\beta\gamma \to \omega,$$

of which:

$$\alpha, \gamma, \omega \in (N_F \cup N_T)^*, \quad \beta \in N_F.$$

(3) $S_0 \in N_F$, S_0 is called the start character.

Definition 2.3 Let the grammar $G = (N_F, N_T, \Gamma, S_0)$, when:

(1) G is called a phrase structure grammar (type 0 grammar), only if the production in Γ is not limited.

(2) $\forall \alpha \to \beta \in \Gamma$, $|\alpha| \leq |\beta|$, G is called a context-dependent grammar (type 1 grammar), denoted as CSG.

(3) $\forall \alpha \to \beta \in \Gamma$, $A \to \beta$, $A \in N_F$, $\beta \in (N_F \cup N_T)$, then G is a context-free grammar (type 1 grammar), denoted as CFG.

(4) $\forall \alpha \to \beta \in \Gamma$, $A \to \delta$, or $A \to \delta B$, $\delta \in N_T^*$, $A \in N_F$, $B \in N_F$, then G is a normal grammar, denoted as RG.

Definition 2.4 Let FSM $= (\Sigma, Q, \delta, q_0, Q_m)$ be a finite state automaton, in which

$$L(\text{FSM}) = \{\sigma | (\sigma \in \Sigma^*) \wedge (\delta(\sigma, q_0) \text{ is defined}\},$$

$$L_m(\text{FSM}) = \{\sigma | (\sigma \in \Sigma^*) \wedge \delta(\sigma, q_0) \in Q_m\}.$$

Then $L(\text{FSM})$ and $L_m(\text{FSM})$ are FSM language and recognition language, respectively.

2.3 Petri Nets

Petri net is an important tool for modeling and analysis of asynchronous concurrent systems. It was first established by the German scientist professor Carl Adam Petri in his doctoral thesis in 1962 and later spread in European and American countries. The significance has been attached to researches in many countries around the world and has become a hotspot in the computer and automation field. The net theory has made great progress and formed a considerable research field since Mr. Petri's pioneering work. Regarding the theory, certain analytical techniques are established, including the equation of state and algebraic analysis techniques, graph analysis techniques based on overlay tree (graph), and inductive analysis techniques based on simplification and decomposition [6–11]. The formal description is as follows:

Definition 2.5 A three-tuple, $N = (P, T; F)$ is a net, when

(1) $P \cup T \neq \varnothing$, $P \cap T = \varnothing$.

(2) $F \subseteq (P \times T) \cup (T \times P)$.

(3) $dom(F) \cup cod(F) = P \cup T$.
$\forall x \in P \cup T$,

$$^\bullet x = \{y | (y \in P \cup T) \wedge ((y, x) \in F)\}$$
$$x^\bullet = \{y | (y \in P \cup T) \wedge ((x, y) \in F)\}$$

They are the pre-set and the post-set of x, respectively.

Definition 2.6 A four-tuple, $PN = (P, T; F, M_0)$, is a Petri net, if and only if:

(1) $N = (P, T; F)$ is a net.
(2) $M: P \to Z$ (the set of non-negative integers) is a marking function, where M_0 is the initial marking (the original state).
(3) Trigger rules:

    (i) For the transition $t \in T$, if $\forall p \in {}^\bullet t : M(p) \geq 1$, then the transition t will be enabled under the marking M, and it is denoted as $M[t >$.

    (ii) The transition t is enabled under the marking M. When t is triggered, there will be a subsequent identification M', and it is denoted as $M[t > M'$.

$$\text{Among then: } M'(p) = \begin{cases} M(p) + 1, & \text{if } p \in t \cdot - \cdot t, \\ M(p) - 1, & \text{if } p \in t \cdot - \cdot t, \\ M(p), & otherwise. \end{cases}$$

Suppose M is a state of PN in the Petri net. If $\exists t_1, t_2 \in T$, making that $M[t_1 > \wedge M[t_2 >$, then

(1) If $M[t_1 > M_1 \to M_1[t_2 > \wedge M[t_2 > M_2 \to M_2[t_1 >$, we say t_1, t_2 is concurrent under M.
(2) If $M[t_1 > M_1 \to \neg M_1[t_2 > \wedge M[t_2 > M_2 \to \neg M_2[t_1 >$, we say t_1, t_2 is a conflict under M.

For M, if $\exists \alpha \subseteq T$, noted ${}^\bullet \alpha = \bigcup_{t \in \alpha} {}^\bullet t$, and $\forall p \in {}^\bullet \alpha : M(p) \geq \sum_{t \in p^\bullet \cap \alpha} 1$, then α is said to be enabled under M, and also α is a concurrent step.

In PN, if $\exists M_1, M_2, \ldots, M_k$, making $\forall 1 \leq i \leq k, \exists t_i \in T : M_i[t_i > M_{i+1}$, we can say the transition sequence $\sigma = t_1 t_2 \cdots t_k$ is enabled under M_1, in other words, M_{k+1} is accessible from M_1, denoted by $M_1[\sigma > M_{k+1}$.

If $R(M_0)$ is all state sets accessible from M_0 off PN, then $R(M_0)$ is called the reachable state sets of PN.

To introduce the algebraic method to analyze Petri nets, the structure of nets can be expressed by matrix and the state of nets can be described by a vector.

The PN structure of a Petri net can be represented by an incidence matrix $C = [c_{ij}]_{n \times m}$, where $m = |P|$, $n = |T|$, and

$$c_{ij} = \begin{cases} 1, & \text{if } p_j \in t_i \cdot - \cdot t_i, \\ -1, & \text{if } p_j \in \cdot t_i - t_i \cdot \\ 0, & \text{otherwise.} \end{cases}$$

A state M of PN can be represented by an m-dimension vector of a non-negative integer, $(M(i) = M(p_i))$, which is still called M.

If $\alpha \in T^*$, $\exists M \in R(M_0)$: $M[\sigma >$, note that $\#(t/\sigma)$ is the number of t occurrences in α, such that

$$X(i) = \#(t_i/\sigma), \quad i \in \{1, 2, \ldots, n\},$$

The vector X is the emission vector of the emission sequence σ. For convenience, $\underline{\sigma}$ is sometimes also the emission vector α.

If $M[\sigma > M', M, M' \in R(M_0), \sigma \in T^*$, we say that

$$M = M + C^T X$$

is an equation of state for PN.

Another analysis method of the Petri net is based on the concept of the reachable graph (or cover-ability tree). For the bounded Petri nets, the set of reachable state (or accessibility marker) $R(M_0)$ is a finite set, so a directed graph $RMG(PN) = (V, E, f)$ can be used to describe the state changes of the net. Among that $V = R(M_0)$, for M_i, $M_j \in R(M_0)$, if $t \in T$, making that $M_i[t > M_j$, there will be a directed edge from M_i to M_j, such that $(M_i, M_j) \in E$, and then put t next to this edge, that is $f((M_i, M_j)) = t_\circ$.

For the unbounded Petri nets, $R(M_0)$ is not a finite set, so we need to introduce the concept of cover-ability tree. The cover-ability tree reflects some rules of the state change of Petri net in the form of a finite tree graph, but also results in the loss of some important information.

The structural properties of Petri nets are used to characterize the structural aspects of the system, its research objects are some properties of the net $N = (P, T; F)$. It can be analyzed using linear algebra due to the state equation of Petri net to research. The main structural properties to be discussed are structural boundedness, conservativeness, repeatability, compatibility, S (T)-invariants, and fairness.

Definition 2.7 A net $N = (P, T; F)$ is called to be structurally bounded, if and only if $PN = (P, T; F, M_0)$ is bounded for any initial state M_0 of N.

Definition 2.8 A net $N = (P, T; F)$ is conserved, if and only if there is a weight function $Y : P \to Z$ (set of non-negative integers) of the position set, so that for any initial state M_0 and any $M \in R(M_0)$ of N, there is $\sum_{i=1}^{m} Y(p_i)M(p_i) = \sum_{i=1}^{m} Y(p_i)M_0(p_i) = \textbf{Constant}$.

Definition 2.9 A net $N = (P, T; F)$ is repeatable, if and only if there is an initial state M_0 and a transition sequence σ, making $M_0[\sigma > M_0$ and for any $t \in T$, there is $\#(t/\sigma) = \infty$.

Definition 2.10 A net $N = (P, T; F)$ is compatible, if and only if there are an initial state M_0 and a transition sequence σ, making $M_0[\sigma > M_0$, and for any $t \in T$, there is $\#(t/\sigma) \geq 1$.

Definition 2.11 A net $N = (P, T; F)$ is called the m-dimensional non-zero and non-negative integer vector Y is an S-invariant of N, if and only if $CY = 0$. Assuming $\|Y\| = \{p_i | p_i \in P \boxplus Y(i) \neq 0\}$, then we say $\|Y\|$ is the pillar of the S-invariant Y of N.

Definition 2.12 A net $N = (P, T; F)$ is called the n-dimensional non-zero and non-negative integer vector X is a T-invariant of N, if and only if $CY = 0$. Assuming $\|X\| = \{t_i | t_i \in T \boxplus X(i) \neq 0\}$, then we say $\|X\|$ is the pillar of the T-invariant X of N.

Definition 2.13 To say the Petri net $PN = (P, T; F, M_0)$ is fair, if and only if:

$$\forall t_1, \ t_2 \in T, \quad \exists k > 0, \ \text{for } \forall M \in R(M_0), \ \forall \sigma \in T^*,$$

all have

$$M[\sigma > \wedge \#(t_i/\sigma) = 0 \to \#(t_j/\sigma) < k, \quad i, j \in \{1, \ 2\}, \ i \neq j.$$

The dynamic properties of Petri nets are used to characterize the dynamic operation of the system. The research objects are some properties related to the initial state M_0 of the $PN = (P, T; F, M_0)$ in the Petri nets. So far, the analysis has generally relied on the reachable graph (or cover-ability tree). The main dynamic properties to be studied are boundedness, liveness, regression, and some linguistic properties.

Definition 2.14 The Petri net of $PN = (P, T; F, M_0)$ is bounded (or safe), if and only if:

$$\forall M \in R(M_0), \quad \forall p \in P, \quad \exists k \geq 0, \quad M(p) \leq k \ (k = 1).$$

Definition 2.15 The Petri net of $PN = (P, T; F, M_0)$ shows liveness, if and only if:

$$\forall t \in T, \ \forall M \in R(M_0), \ \exists M' \in R(M), \quad M'[t > .$$

Definition 2.16 The Petri net $PN = (P, T; F, M_0)$ is regressive, if and only if:

$$\forall M \in R(M_0), \ \exists \sigma \in T^*, \quad M[\sigma > M_0.$$

Definition 2.17 The seven-tuple $HPN = (P, T; F, M_0, \Sigma, h, G_f)$ is a label Petri net, if and only if:

(1) $PN = (P, T; F, M_0)$ is a Petri net.
(2) Σ is a finite character set.
(3) $h: T \to \Sigma$ is an identification function.
(4) $G_f \subseteq R(M_0)$ is a final state set of language.

Definition 2.18 Let $HPN = (P, T; F, M_0, \Sigma, h, G_f)$ be a label Petri net, assuming:

$$L(HPN) = \{h(\sigma) \in \Sigma^* | (\sigma \in T^*) \wedge (M_0[\sigma > M) \wedge (M \in G_f)\}$$

and $L(HPN) = \{h(\sigma) \in \Sigma^* | (\sigma \in T^*) \wedge (M_0[\sigma > M) \wedge (\exists M' \in G_f) \wedge (M \geq M')\}$, then:

(1) $L(HPN)$ is an $L-$Petri net language of HPN.
(2) $L'(HPN)$ is a $G-$Petri net language of HPN.
(3) If $G_f = \{M \in R(M_0) | \forall t \in T : \neg M[t >\}$, then $L(HPN)$ is a $T-$Petri net language of HPN.
(4) If $G_f = R(M_0)$, then $L(HPN)$ is a $P-$Petri net language of HPN.

2.4   Business Flow

With the continuous development of information technology and the continuous advancement of enterprise information, more attention has been paid to system analysis and design based on business flow. Service-Oriented Architecture (SOA) is also one of the research hotspots in recent years. Business flows are capable of service composition, service choreography, and concurrent processing. It emphasizes the enterprise-level end-to-end business process management oriented to service, mainly used for cross-system and cross-department enterprise systems [12]. The key point of business flow management is business sorting and optimization analysis. It focuses on certain aspects, such as business modeling, composition, interface transformation, and management. Meanwhile, it is business-centric, focuses on global business value and service reuse, and can adapt to system business restructuring and optimization. In business flows, processes are more closely associated with business data. Systems can be correlated and coordinated when different services are invoked by process interfaces to ensure transaction integrity. The system interface of business flow is mainly aimed at the external heterogeneous application system and is suitable for the standardized interaction integration and collaboration between enterprise-level systems and other systems [13–16].

The business process management model should have a formal description basis. It should clearly describe the problems, have no ambiguity, and should provide a strictly mathematical basis for the analysis process. As mentioned earlier, the prototype Petri net was put forward by C. A. Petri, a German scientist in the 1960s. In the following decades, Petri net theory has been greatly enriched and widely applied in many research fields, such as protocol engineering, flexible manufacturing system, and business processing, and so on. Petri nets have an intuitive graphical representation, but also a rigorous formal language foundation. Prototype Petri net has three components: transitions, places, and directed arcs to indicate the relationship between two elements. High-level Petri nets all have formal semantic definitions. Besides, a Petri net model with corresponding semantics can describe a business process. Some process modeling methods focus on describing system state changes, such as state automata; some modeling methods are based on events that occur in the system, such as process algebra. Petri nets can explicitly describe system states and events at the same time, which facilitates the understanding and analysis of the system. The model of the Petri net is rich in system analysis techniques, such as invariant (invariance), activity (liveness), boundedness (boundness), security (safety), and so on. The performance of the system can be calculated, such as response time, waiting time, resource utilization, etc. [16].

Business Process Management Initiative (BPMI) introduces two standards, Business Process Modeling Language (BPML) and Business Process Query Language (BPQL), which, respectively, serve as standard interfaces for process modeling and process model access, and also proposes a BPM framework based on this. The system architecture of the Business Process Management System (BPMS) is shown in Figure 2.1.

BPML, the technical framework for BPM modeling, is an XML-based model description language that can describe the business process as a combination of control flow, data flow, and event flow. On that basis, the features, such as business rules, security rules, transaction management, and so on, can be added to business processes. Compared to traditional process modeling languages, it can describe the "end-to-end" process. We can view the process model from the

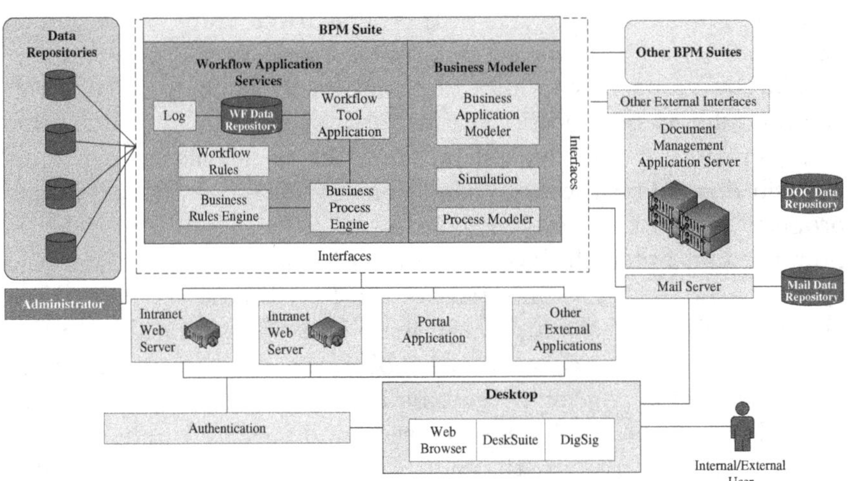

Figure 2.1   System architecture diagrams of BPMS [15].

perspective of multiple actors in this way. Also, BPML uses Pi-Calculus as its mathematical foundation, and this formal description has endowed BPML with strong abilities in consistency checking, deadlock prevention, bottleneck detection, and process optimization [13–16].

2.5   Markov Process

In probability theory and statistics, the Markov process is an important method to study the state space of a discrete event dynamic system, whose mathematical basis is the random process theory. Its original model, the Markov chain, was proposed by the Russian mathematician Markov in 1907 [17–19].

In the process of modeling, the Markov model state has Markov property, which can simplify the complexity of analysis. Among them, discrete-time Markov chain (DTMC) is widely used in behavior analysis of the online transaction system. Taking DTMC as an example, Markov property indicates the following conditional probability relations:

$$\Pr(T_{n+1} = q_{n+1} | T_1 = q_1, T_2 = q_2, \ldots, T_n = q_n)$$
$$= \Pr(T_{n+1} = q_{n+1} | T_n = q_n).$$

In the expression, $T_i, i \in [1, n+1]$ is the current state of the model, and $q_k k \in [1, n+1]$ is the state q_k of the model at the time k.

Markov property simplifies the computational complexity of calculating the state condition probability of the model at the time T_{n+1}, making it only depend on the state q_n at the current time T_n, and depend on the state conditions at $T_1, T_2, \ldots, T_{n-1}$. Markov property is also known as memorylessness. To simplify the calculation, the first-order Markov chain discards the information provided by the $T_1, T_2, \ldots, T_{n-1}$ time state for the T_{n+1} time state, thus reducing the accuracy of conditional probability estimation at T_{n+1} time. However, in the practical application of stochastic process simulation, Markov property can make the building model simple and efficient.

DTMC assumes that time increases gradually by 1 unit, whether it is 1 minute or 1 hour, the model does not care. Therefore, having considered the model's dwell time in each state, continuous-time Markov chain (CTMC) is used to model the stochastic process of unbalanced dwell time, in which the dwell time of each state is fitted by an exponential distribution.

Discrete-time Markov chains are defined by the three-tuple $M = (Q, A, \pi)$, where

- The observable state set of the model is $Q = \{q_1, q_2, \ldots, q_m\}m$, the number of different states in the set (i.e., $m = |Q|$).
- $A \in R^{m \times m}$ is the transition probability matrix of m states in Q, satisfying $\sum A_i. = 1$.
- $\pi \in R^{m \times 1}$ is the probability distribution of the model in state m at the initial moment.

2.6 Hidden Markov Model

Hidden Markov Model (HMM) is a kind of Markov chain, which is used to describe a Markov process with Hidden unknown parameters. HMM adds a layer of hidden state based on the original Markov chain to simulate the effect of unobservable information on the random process. In the normal Markov model, the state is directly visible to the observer; such transition probability of the state is the parameters. However, in HMM, states are not directly visible, but something that can be observed through a sequence of observation vectors. Each observation vector is represented as various states through some probability density distribution, and each observation vector is generated by a state sequence with response probability density distribution. The sequence of output symbols can reflect some information about the state sequence. The difficulty is to determine the implicit parameters of the process from observable parameters, then these parameters can be used for future analysis such as pattern recognition [20].

HMM is a double random process, which has a hidden Markov chain with a certain number of states and a set of display random functions. One of the random processes is a finite-state Markov chain, which describes state transition; another describes the statistical correspondence between states and observed values. Here, the state values and the observed values follow some probability distribution.

Hence, HMM can be represented as a five-tuple, $HMM(\Omega_X, \Omega_O, A, B, \pi)$, of which

- $\Omega_X = \{X_1, \ldots, X_N\}$: is a finite set of HMM implied states, N is the total number of the HMM implied states, S_i is the implicit states of the HMM at the time t, and S_i is an element in the set of Ω_X.
- $\Omega_O = \{O_1, \ldots, O_M\}$: is a finite set of HMM observations, M is the total number of observations that occur, each of which corresponds to a possible output value of the system.
- $A = \{a_{ij}\}, i, j \in [1, n]$: is the state transition probability matrix (here we only consider the first-order HMM), $a_{ij} = P(X_{t+1} = q_j | X_t = q_i)$ represents the probability of transition from state q_i to state q_j at time t in the HMM.
- $B = \{b_{ij}(k)\}$: B is the probability matrix of the distribution of any observation value in the observation probability space of each state in the observation value sequence, in which $b_{ij}(k)$ represents the probability of generating the observation O_k when the HMM moves from state q_i to state q_j. Suppose $X = (X_1, \ldots, X_t)$ represents a sequence of HMM observations, then $b_{ij}(k)$ can be represented as follows: $b_{ij}(k) = P(X_t = O_k | S_{t-1} = q_i, S_t = q_j)$.
- $\pi = \{\pi_1, \ldots, \pi_n\}, \pi_1 = P(X_1 = q_j)$: is the initial state distribution of the HMM, which is the distribution probability of each state in the model at $t = 0$.

Training, decoding, and evaluating are the three basic problems of the HMM. Training refers to giving an observation sequence O to determine the model parameter $\lambda = (A, B, \pi)$ and maximize $P(O|\lambda)$. The dynamic programming idea is used to calculate the various probabilities, which is specifically the forward method and backward method; Decoding refers to the state sequence q that maximizes $P(q|O, \lambda)$ in the case of given λ and O (Viterbi algorithm is commonly used); Evaluating refers to giving the model parameter λ to calculate the probability $P(O|\lambda)$ of the observation value sequence O.

Meanwhile, the Baum–Welch algorithm is often used as the model training algorithm, and the specific algorithm steps are as follows:

(a) Determine the initial model (untrained model) λ_0.
(b) Training the new model λ based on λ_0 and observation sequence O.

(c) If $\log P(X|\lambda) - \log P(X|\lambda_0) < \Delta$, it indicates that the training has achieved the expected effect, and then the algorithm ends.

(d) Otherwise, $\lambda_0 = \lambda$, and continue the work in step 2(b).

2.7 Cryptography

Cryptography is a technique for creating confusion that hopes to turn normal (identifiable) information into unrecognizable information. Cryptography is the general term for "password" in Chinese [21]. The password used to log on to websites, E-mail, and bank accounts is strictly speaking just a "password", or a secret number. Password encryption methods mainly include the RSA algorithm, ECC encryption method, two-square password, four-square password, three-point password, Playfair cipher, and so on [22–28]. Cryptography falls into the following categories:

- One-time password: OTP [29]

Also known as a dynamic password or single-use valid password, refers to the computer system or other digital devices that can only use a password once. During the authentication process, the password validation is one login session or transaction, and the next authentication will be another password (see Section 2.8).

- Personal identification number: PIN [30]

The PIN is data information that identifies the identity of the cardholder in online trading, it is not allowed to appear in clear text in any part of the computer or network system.

- Online PIN verification

This is a cardholder authentication method that sends the encrypted PIN value to the card-issuing line through the authorization request message and verifies the identity of the cardholder by comparing the PIN value in the message with the PIN value of the card-issuing line.

- Message authentication code: MAC

MAC is used to verify the correctness of the source of the message and prevent data from being tampered with or stolen by illegal users.

- Two-factor authentication: 2FA

In addition to a static password, dynamic password, digital certificate, and other technology are adopted, through dual authentication to strengthen the authentication method of identity management.

- Digital certificate [31]

Unforgeable public key information of an entity signed by an authentication center.

- Digital signature [32]

The digital signature is a special encryption algorithm. The data receiver can confirm the source and integrity of data, avoid data being tampered with by any third party, and the data sender can also ensure that data is not tampered with by the receiver.

2.8   Dynamic Random Code

As a form of identity authentication, dynamic random code (also known as one-time password (OTP)) has been currently applied in more and more industries. It has become the mainstream of identity authentication technology and is widely used in the global banking industry. More enterprises are engaged in the research and production of dynamic passwords at home and abroad.

OTP generates an unpredictable combination of random numbers according to a special algorithm, which usually consists of six or eight bits. Each OTP can only be used once, which is widely used in the application of online banking, online games, telecom operators, e-government, enterprise, and other fields. OTP is a secure and convenient account security technology, which can effectively protect the transaction and login authentication security. For static passwords, the most important advantage of OTP is that it is not vulnerable to a replay attack. It avoids some of the drawbacks associated with traditional (static) password authentication; some practical techniques also absorb two-factor authentication, such as a built-in OTP random code password generator or PIN. Currently, the terminals used to generate dynamic passwords are hardware token, SMS password, mobile phone token, software token, etc. The earliest e-bank password generator issued to users by the domestic bank was a hardware token, for example, the Bank of China electronic password card. At present, the most mainstream terminal is the hardware password based on time synchronization, which changes the dynamic password every 60 seconds, and the dynamic password is valid once.

With the rapid development of the mobile internet, the synchronization ability between devices has been greatly improved, and the dynamic password generation technology that used to rely on independent devices has quickly evolved into the SMS dynamic code on phone (also known as SMS password). SMS password is a dynamic password sent by the background system in the form of mobile phone SMS to the user-bound mobile phone, including 6 bits or more random numbers of the dynamic password. The user through the reply to the dynamic password proves authentication to ensure the security of the system. Dynamic password is based on a special algorithm to generate an unpredictable combination of random numbers at intervals, each password can only be used once. For authentication, users must enter a dynamic password in addition to their account and static password. The only path to the normal login or transaction is through system verification, which effectively ensures the legitimacy and uniqueness of the user's identity. The most significant advantage is that as each time the user uses a different password, it is impossible for criminals to impersonate the legitimate user's identity [33–36]. Mobile phone token is a kind of mobile phone client software, which is based on time synchronization. The password generation process does not generate communication and expense. It has the advantages of ease of use, high security, low cost, and no necessary additional equipment. It is an important trend in the development of dynamic password identity authentication in the mobile internet era.

Nowadays, dynamic password authentication mainly consists of three technical models: time-based synchronization, event-based synchronization, and challenge-response (asynchronous)-based mechanisms. The generation of the dynamic password is mainly based on time difference as the synchronization condition between the server and the password generator. When login is needed, a password generator is used to generate a dynamic password. OTP is generally divided into two types: counting usage and timing usage. Counting type can be used unlimited times. Every time it is used, the counter will be increased by one, and then the new password will be generated. Generally, the dynamic password for counting times is based on the HOTP algorithm, its full name is "An HMAC-Based One-Time Password Algorithm", which is a one-time password generation algorithm based on event count. Timing usage can set the valid time of the password, ranging from 30 seconds to two minutes. However, OTP will be abandoned after the authentication, and the next authentication must use a new password, its core algorithm is TOTP, which is short for the "Time-Based One-Time Password Algorithm". The algorithm is based on HOTP, the core of which is to change the movement factor from the event count in HOTP to the time difference [36].

2.9   Chapter Summary

To guarantee the security and credibility of the online transaction system has been a hotspot in recent years. This chapter reviews basic techniques and methods related to online transaction systems, including formal methods, such as automata, Petri nets, and so on. The transaction system can be completely modeled and verified based on the formalization method. Markov process can also be used to model and analyze the transition process of the transaction state. This chapter also briefly introduces commonly used authentication techniques in the industry.

References

[1] Eilenberg, S. and Tilson, B. *Automata, Languages, and Machines*, New York: Academic Press, (1974).

[2] Wolfram, S. *Theory and Applications of Cellular Automata*, Singapore: World scientific, (1986).

[3] Minsky, M. L. *Computation: Finite and Infinite Machines*, Prentice-Hall, Inc., Engelwood Cliffs, NJ, (1967).

[4] Chen, W. Z., Ou, Q., and Cheng, L. *Formal Language and Automata*, Beijing: Posts and Telecommunications Press, (2005).

[5] Antimirov, V. Partial Derivatives of Regular Expressions and Finite Automaton Constructions. *Theoretical Computer Science*, 155(2): 291–319 (1996).

[6] Wu, Z. H. *Introduction to Petri Net*, Beijing: Machinery Industry Press, (2006).

[7] Wu, Z. H. Analysis and Implementation of Liveness and Fairness of Bounded Petri Nets. *Chinese Journal of Computer*, 12(4): 267–278 (1989).

[8] Jiang, C. J. *Petri Net Theory of Discrete Event Dynamic System*, Beijing: Science Press, (2000).

[9] Jiang, C. J. Dynamic Invariance of Petri nets. *Science China (Series E)*, 27(5): 567–573 (1997).

[10] Jiang, C. J. Research Review on Theory and Method of Petri Nets. *Control and Decision*, 12(6): 631–636 (1997).

[11] Yuan, C. Y. *Principle and Application of Petri Nets*, Beijing: Electronic Industry Press, (2005).

[12] Gu, C. H. SOA Process Project: Business Flow or Workflow. http://www.ibm.com/developerworks/cn/webservices/1011_guch_soaprocess/1011_guch_soaprocess.html.

[13] Business Process Management (BPM) at http://wiki.mbalib.com/wiki/.

[14] What is BPM. https://bpm.com/what-is-bpm.

[15] Business Process Management. https://en.wikipedia.org/wiki/Business_process_management.

[16] The BPM Profession. http://www.abpmp.org/?page=BPM_Profession.

[17] Meyn, S. and Tweedie, R. L. *Markov Chains and Stochastic Stability*, New York, USA: CUP, 2nd edition, (2009).

[18] Su, C. *Modeling and Simulation of Manufacturing System*, Beijing: Machinery Industry Press, (2014).

[19] Li, Y. Q. and Liu, C. *Random Process*, Beijing: National Defence Industry Press, (2014).

[20] Rabiner, L. R. A Tutorial on Hidden Markov Models and Selected Applications in Speech Recognition. In *Proceedings of the IEEE*, NY, USA, Vol. 77, No. 2, pp. 257–286 (Feb. 1989).

[21] Florencio, D. and Herley, C. A Large-Scale Study of Web Password Habits. In *Proceedings of the 16th International Conference on World Wide Web*, International World Wide Web Conference Committee (IW3C2), NY, USA, pp. 657–666 (2007).

[22] Lu, K. C. *Computer Cryptography*, Beijing: Tsinghua University Press, (1990).

[23] Zhang, X. and Parhi, K. K. Implementation Approaches for the Advanced Encryption Standard Algorithm. *IEEE Circuits and Systems Magazine*, 2(4): 24–46 (2002).

[24] Lauer, R. F. *Computer Simulation of Classical Substitution Cryptographic Systems*, Laguna Hills, Calif.: Aegean Park Press, (1981).

[25] Reeds III, J. A. Method and Apparatus for Autokey Rotor Encryption: U.S. Patent 5,724,427, 3 March 1998.

[26] ElGamal, T. A Public Key Cryptosystem and a Signature Scheme Based on Discrete Logarithms. In *Workshop on the Theory and Application of Cryptographic Techniques*, Berlin Heidelberg: Springer, pp. 10–18 (1984).

[27] Kim, J. J. and Hong, S. P. A Method of Risk Assessment for Multifactor Authentication. *Journal of Information Processing Systems*, 7(1): 187–198 (2011).

[28] Ishai, Y., Kushilevitz, E., Ostrovsky, R. *et al.* Batch Codes and Their Applications. In *Proceedings of the Thirtysixth Annual ACM Symposium on Theory of Computing*, ACM, NY, USA, pp. 262–271 (2004).

[29] Haller, N., Metz, C., Nesser, P. *et al.* A One-Time Password System, Network Working Group Request for Comments 2289 (1998).

[30] Jain, A., Bolle, R., Pankanti, S. *et al.* *Biometrics: Personal Identification in Networked Society*, Springer Science & Business Media, NY, Vol. 479 (2006).

[31] Tycksen Jr., F. A. and Jennings, C. W. Digital Certificate: U.S. Patent 6,189,097. 2001-2-13.

[32] Merkle, R. C. A Certified Digital Signature. In *Conference on the Theory and Application of Cryptology*, New York: Springer, pp. 218–238 (1989).

[33] Shimizu, A. A Dynamic Password Authentication Method Using a Oneway Function [J]. *Systems and Computers in Japan*, 22(7): 32–40 (1991).

[34] Petsas, T., Voyatzis, G., Athanasopoulos, E. *et al.* Rage Against the Virtual Machine: Hindering Dynamic Analysis of Android Malware. In *Proceedings of the Seventh European Workshop on System Security*, ACM, NY, USA, pp. 1–6 (2014).

[35] RFC4226-HOTP: An HMAC-Based One-Time Password Algorithm. https://tools.ietf.org/html/rfc4226.

[36] RFC6238-TOTP: Time-Based One-Time Password Algorithm. https://tools.ietf.org/html/rfc6238.

Chapter 3

Modeling of Transaction Systems

3.1 Introduction

Building a behavioral model for a business process is the basis of effective analysis of its related properties. A formal analysis of the online transaction system is possible only if the appropriate basic model is available. In the online transaction system, a transaction activity requires the relevant entities to cooperate to perform the established business process. The functional and performance requirements of the online transaction system's transaction process are ultimately achieved through the interactive operation of the business processes on behalf of each entity. The online transaction business process has the characteristics of multi-agent, multi-session, distributed, complex interaction, and data-oriented operations. Data errors, non-deterministic data states, multi-session patterns, and complex malicious behavior must be accurately characterized by the model. Therefore, a formal model that correctly demonstrates process logic and behavioral dependencies needs to combine data flow, control flow, capital flow, and multi-session mode in an online transaction process, to characterize software which is involved by multiple parties in online environment behavior and semantics, to ensure that the execution of business software is consistent with the functional requirements of business processes. This chapter will introduce the online transaction system briefly and introduce two formal models based on Petri nets for the new characteristics of online transactions.

3.2   The Architecture of the Transaction System

In the past ten years, online transactions and online shopping have been developing rapidly. The important factors that promote the emergence and development of online transaction are mainly derived from the following aspects: (1) with the speeding up of computer processing, the enhancement in processing capacity, and the price decrease, computer applications are getting extensive and popular, therefore providing a solid foundation for the application of online transactions; (2) due to the intermediation effect of the Internet being the media of global communication and transactions, global Internet users are growing in series. Internet technology is getting popular and mature, and the online transaction has the traits of being fast, safe, and low in cost, which provides the application conditions for the development of online transaction; (3) with the global trends of emerging online payment platforms and online banking, the online payment and settlement system is constantly improving. It has the advantages of convenience, rapidity, security, and so on. It provides an important instrument for the consumption payment of online transactions.

The online transaction system lies generally in an open, dynamic, online, Internet environment, which relies on B/S architecture (browser/server) to implement the application system. Regarding different application modes, the online transaction platform is divided into B2B, B2C, C2C, and O2O, and so on. No matter what kind of application mode, the online transaction system is a complex distributed system that is composed of the business platform, third-party payment platform, banking system, logistics system, user client, and so on. It has the characteristics of parallelism, distribution, interaction, real-time, and so on. Figure 3.1 is the basic architecture of the mainstream online transaction system. Different participants are responsible for different functions in the whole transaction process. With the development of online transactions, the scale of users and the volume of transactions continue to climb, and the pursuit of transaction functions and experiences also urges the online transaction platform to continue to develop new business, resulting in the increasing complexity of business processes. In addition to the payment platform and self-business platform, more and more enterprises began to integrate third-party services to expand their

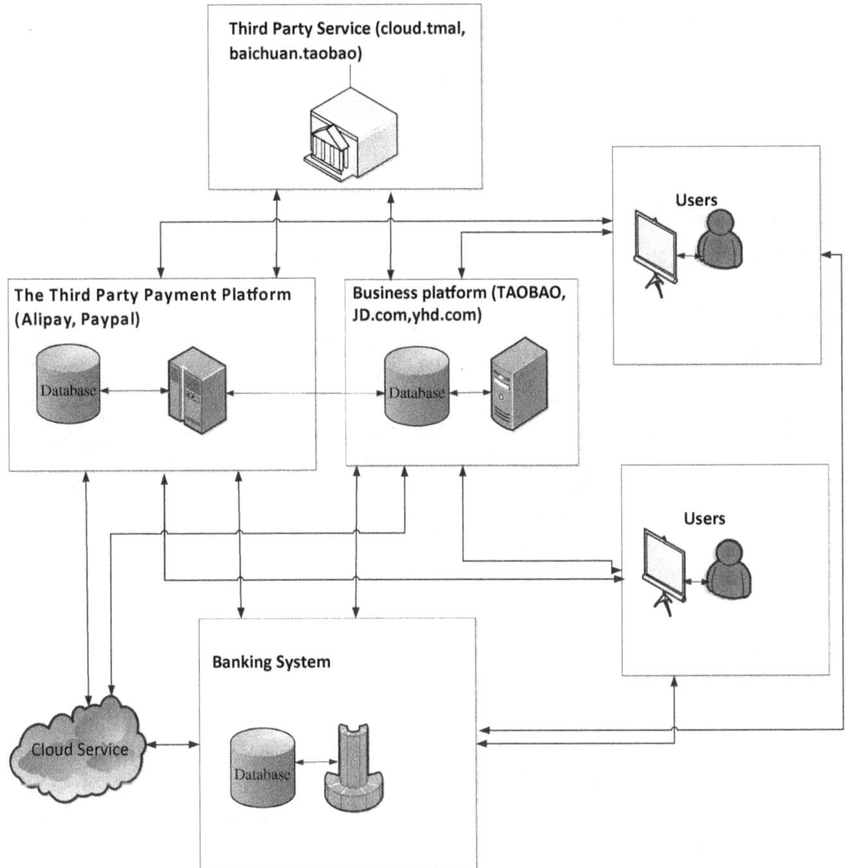

Figure 3.1   Online transaction system architecture.

business functions, such as Tmall Stone Tower and Ali Bai Chuan Project [1].

The business process of each transaction subject party constitutes complete, loose coupling, and complex online transaction business processes. Each participant has its own relatively independent business architecture and process. Figure 3.2 shows the system architecture of a third-party payment platform and Figure 3.3 shows the basic processing model of the platform. The online transaction system should deal with the challenges of flexible situations, asynchronous processing, data distribution, data cache, etc., to ensure the absolute security of funds under massive access, low probability

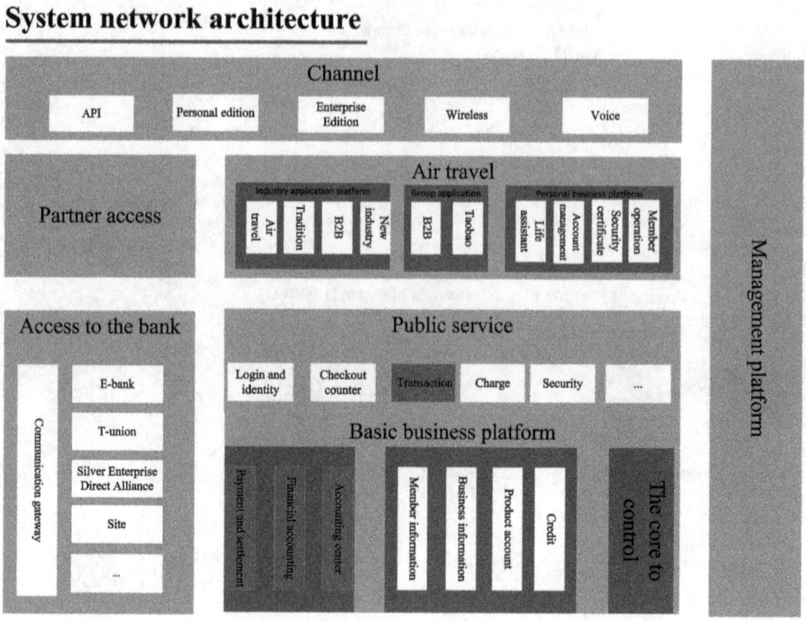

System network architecture

Figure 3.2   System architecture of a third-party payment platform [2].

of delay, and low delay. In general, a complete business activity consists of a master business service and many slave business services. The master business service is responsible for initiating and completing the whole business activity, providing some specific business operations from the business service [2].

The complex business integration among the participants in the online transaction system also brings new security challenges. The participants in the transaction have their internal state, and the data state between different participants is difficult to coordinate and unify, which can easily lead to the emergence of business defects. It may result in the violation of transaction attributes and the loss to enterprises and users. Besides, the online transaction system is in a dynamic and open online environment, and the malicious behavior of users will also lead to the disorder of the data state, which makes the system unreliable. Therefore, to ensure the credibility of the online transaction system, it is necessary to grasp the overall situation, take into account the transaction status and process structure within each subject, so that the whole transaction process is consistent and the system is credible.

Typical Processing mode

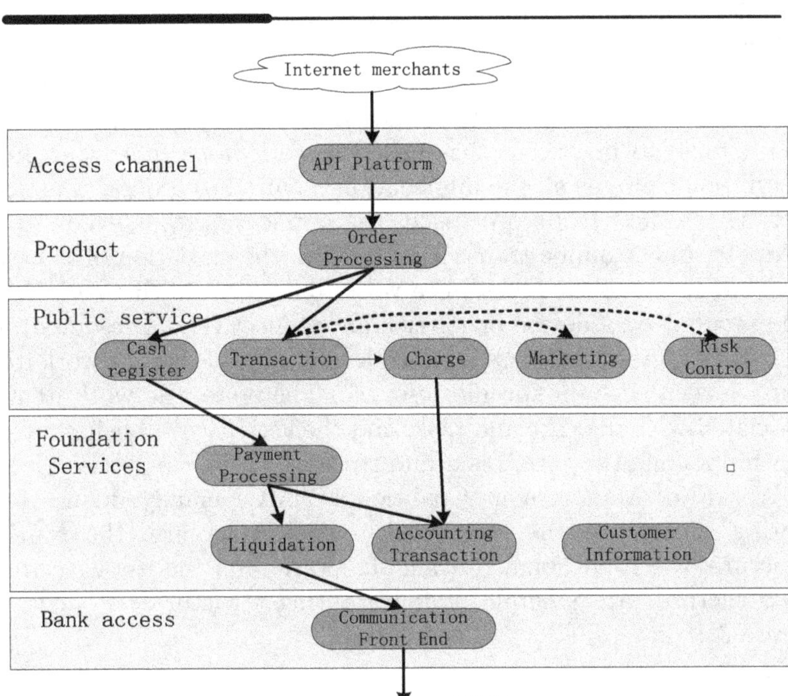

Figure 3.3   Basic processing flow of a third-party payment platform [2].

3.3   Transaction and Process

A transaction, in other words, generally refers to something to do or pay for. The term is widely used in database operations and business processing. In database theory, a transaction is a program execution unit that accesses and may update various data items in a database that has the basic attributes of atomicity, consistency, isolation, and persistence. In a business process, the transaction typically refers to an operation or task, which is a basic component of a complete business process.

In a Workflow Management System (WfMS), the workflow design is based on a case study, i.e., for a specific case, each task in the workflow is executed or called a transaction. A workflow process can handle many similar cases by performing tasks in a particular order. Therefore, in the workflow process definition, the execution of each task has a prerequisite and an execution result. Once the prerequisites for the task are satisfied, the task can be executed and produce a determined execution result. Once the WfMS performs a specific case, a task to be executed is called a work item. The work item description contains all the information required to process this task, such as the data to be processed, the application that needs to be used, etc. In the online transaction system, the execution of the task "Send an order to the Seller" is a work item. Most of the work items are executed by a device or participant (collectively, a resource) for processing. A resource class is called a role. An activity is a work item that is executed by a specific resource. Therefore, the work item is associated with the case and task, and the activity establishes a relationship among the case, task, and resource [3–7].

WorkFlow Management Coalition (WfMC) mainly defines four routing structures: the sequential routing structure, the routing structure, the conditional routing structure, and the iterative routing structure. An example of four routing structures is shown in Figure 3.4.

(1) Sequence routing structure:

In a sequential routing structure, the execution of the tasks is performed in sequence, i.e., the latter task can be executed once the previous task has been executed. In Figure 3.4(a), once task A is executed, and task B is performed, then the execution of task C must be completed after the completion of task B.

(2) Parallel routing structure:

In that structure, several tasks may be performed at the same time or in any order. In Figure 3.4(b), once task A is executed, tasks B and C are executed in parallel, or B is first executed after C; or C is executed first. However, task D can only be performed when both tasks B and C are executed. In an e-commerce system, to simulate this parallel structure, two components are introduced: AND-split and AND-join. In Figure 3.4(b), for the component AND-split, once task A is executed, tasks B and C meet the prerequisites for execution at the same time. The component AND-join results in the last synchronization of all the parallel tasks, i.e., after both the tasks B and C have been performed, task D is performed.

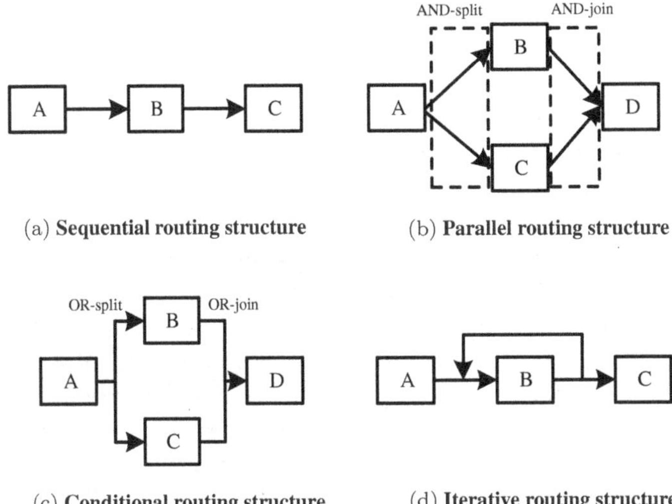

(a) **Sequential routing structure**   (b) **Parallel routing structure**

(c) **Conditional routing structure**   (d) **Iterative routing structure**

Figure 3.4   Examples of four routing structures.

(3) Conditional routing structure:

In a conditional routing structure, one of the tasks is conditionally selected from several tasks. As shown in Figure 3.4(c), after
task A is executed, the execution task B or C is selected following
the condition requirements. After the selected task is executed,
task D can be performed. In an e-commerce system, two components are also introduced to simulate a conditional routing
structure: OR-split and OR-join. In Figure 3.4(c), the function
of the component OR-split is to select the next executed task
in tasks B and C after task A is executed. The function of the
component OR-join is that after task B or C is executed, task D
can be executed.

(4) Iterative routing structure:

In an iterative routing structure, one or a set of tasks may be
repeated multiple times. In Figure 3.4(d), task B may be repeat-
edly executed multiple times before task A and C are executed.

The structure mentioned above basically describes the routing
structure that needs to be used in a business process. For some
complex applications, several structures may need to be used in
a staggered mode, or the loop is nested to lay the foundation for
the analysis and verification of the later system. Meantime, to

facilitate the analysis, it is necessary to avoid the appearance of a complex circular structure.

In a practical application process that is user-oriented, the business process model is described by a diagram, text, symbol, and so on. First of all, business modeling provides a consistent form of business representation, i.e., an instrument of communication, so that business personnel can describe the business and express requirements. It is easier for software developers to understand the business, which lays the foundation for a better description of the existing business processes and clear requirements. Secondly, business modeling technology can help business personnel and software developers to establish a detailed business process model, realize the visualization of business process analysis and design, and provide basic material for standardizing and improving business processes. The workflow model is an abstract representation of the workflow, i.e., an abstract representation of the business process. The formal description of the business flow model is the theoretical basis for accurately defining the business flow process model and model verification and simulation. The Petri net model, as a formal model, is an ideal model to describe the business process of the system. The separation of static syntax and dynamic semantics of the transaction process is the reason why the behavior of the business system is so difficult to describe and understand. It also explains why the Petri net can take into account the grammatical and semantic problems and realize the unity of the two. In the Petri net method, the transition is generally regarded as an event or task, and the physical structure of the Petri net can effectively describe the static structure and attributes of the process. The operation of the net provides a method to describe the dynamic semantics of the process [8–17].

3.4   Business Flow System

Under the dynamic and open Internet environment, the business process of an e-commerce system has the traits of distributed, multi-agent, multi-session, interactive behaviors, and so on. Different agents have their own relatively complete business processes, which are called through application program interface, message delivery, and related interaction mechanisms to form a complete loose coupling transaction process. For example, the third-party payment platform has the background payment process and security process when a user is shopping. Meanwhile, the bank is responsible for the clearance and liquidation business process. The integration of these processes leads to the complexity of interaction behavior, the diversity of data transmission, and the difficulty of unifying control flow and data flow. Due to the complexity of coordination between applications, if the business process is not designed properly, the complex linkage between control flow and data flow may lead to inconsistency between fund processing and business processing.

The construction of the business process behavior model is the basis of effective analysis of its related properties. Only with the appropriate basic model can the formal analysis of the security and trust problem be carried out. In the e-commerce system, a transaction activity needs the cooperation of the relevant subjects, and then the implementation of the established business process can be completed. The functional and performance requirements of the e-commerce system's transaction process are finally realized by the interactive operation of the business processes on behalf of each agent. Petri net is a formal model describing concurrent and distributed systems and can describe true concurrency. To describe the e-commerce system more accurately, it is necessary for it to be extended. This section will introduce two kinds of business flow model systems based on Petri net: Labeled Petri net (LaPN) [18–22] and E-commerce Business Process Net (EBPN) [23–25].

3.4.1 *LaPN*

In an open network, one cannot have complete control of the behavior of other remote partners. The obligation-conforming local realization of e-commerce systems and the proper handling of proofs can ensure that a common goal is achieved for real cooperation even without having to require globally the correctness of implementation on the other side. The obligations and proofs of participants have to play together, forcing a common goal achieved. Besides, it can be susceptible to disputes among participants if cooperation in an e-commerce system cannot assure accountability. Without the adequate accountability assurances of cooperative actions, there would be no means to reliably enforce punitive measures against fraudulent participants. To analyze the obligations and accountability, the LaPN is introduced in this section [26]. It is mainly motivated by the formal language and process language method. LaPNs integrate formal notation with commonly used graphical notations and formal proof with commonly used verification techniques. Cooperative procedures are graphically represented by LaPNs, while the obligations of participants and the accountability of their actions are analyzed based on LaPN languages.

In an LaPN, places only include control tokens, and they control the progress of the LaPN together with the exchanged messages from or to other LaPNs via the network. All the exchanged messages among LaPNs are recorded from cooperation in an e-commerce system. Transitions are classified into three mutually exclusive types: *In, Out,* and *Inner* transitions. *In* transitions denote the actions of receiving a message from a partner via the network; *Out* ones denote the actions of sending a message to a partner via the network and the message will be included in an exchanged message set; and *Inner* ones contain all inner actions, i.e., non-cooperative actions, in the LaPN. Notations $t^{\bullet}$ and $^{\bullet}t$ denote the post and pre-sets of transition t, respectively.

Definition 3.1 A LaPN is a 7-tuple LaPN $= (P, T, F, M_0, \Psi, \Sigma, l)$ where

(1) (P, T, F) is a Petri net, where $T = T_{in} \cup T_{out} \cup T_{inn}$, and T_{in}, T_{out}, and T_{inn} are mutually exclusive subsets of *In, Out,* and *Inner* transitions, respectively;

(2) $M\colon P \to \{0, 1\}$ is a marking function, and M_0 denotes the initial marking;

(3) Ψ is a set of the messages exchanged between LaPNs via the network, and each message in Ψ is of the form $[(msg, S, R)]$, where msg is the name, S is the sender, and R is the receiver of the message; (M, Ψ) denotes a state of LaPN, and (M_0, Ψ_0) is an initial state where $\Psi_0 = \varnothing$;

(4) Σ is a finite set of action labels, i.e., an alphabet;

(5) $l\colon T \to \Sigma$ is a label function;

(6) $\forall t \in T$, t is enabled at (M, Ψ) if $t \in T_{out} \cup T_{inn}$, $\forall p \in {}^{\bullet}t$: $M(p) = 1$; or $t \in T_{in}$: $l(t) = In(msg, S, R)$, $\forall p \in {}^{\bullet}t$: $M(p) = 1$ and $\exists[(msg, S, R)] \in \Psi$; and

(7) $\forall t \in T$, if t is enabled at (M, Ψ), it may fire and firing it generates a new state (M', Ψ'), i.e., $(M, \Psi)[t > (M', \Psi')$, where if $p \in t^\bullet - {}^\bullet t$, $M'(p) = M(p) + 1$; if $p \in {}^\bullet t - t^\bullet$, $M'(p) = M(p) - 1$, and otherwise $M'(p) = M(p)$; and if $l(t) = Out(msg, S, R)$, $\Psi' = \Psi \cup \{[(msg, S, R)]\}$, and otherwise $\Psi' = \Psi$.

Note that Ψ is emptied once a new case starts, and all recorded messages are always available within the life cycle of a case. $R(M_0)$ represents a set of all markings reachable from (M_0, Ψ_0). Since an e-commerce system includes a communication network system, firing an *In* transition copies a message sent by a partner from Ψ, while firing an *Out* transition adds a message to Ψ. Transition labeling is used to map either several transitions involving in a single task to a label or internal actions to silent actions denoted with a label τ. Label τ is sufficient, since all internal actions of cooperative partners are equal in the sense that the internal actions of one partner are not known by the others, i.e., $\forall t \in T_{inn}$, $l(t) = \tau$. For the transitions in $T_{in} \cup T_{out}$, assume that their transition labels are identical to their transition identifiers unless specifically explained otherwise. Each message *msg* in Ψ, denoted as $[msg]$, on the communication system must be a message sent by some partner. Therefore, Ψ realizes the dependencies among participants, while the dependencies among the internal actions in one party are realized via control conditions. In an asymmetric cryptographic key system, two counterpart keys (a private key and a public key) are used for encryption and decryption. The public key of a principal can be used to authenticate the signature of this principle or to associate the principal unambiguously with any statement encrypted with her/his private key. Each message in Ψ should include its name, receiver, and sender, as it has been encrypted with the receiver's public key and signed with the sender's private key. Therefore, the accountability of cooperative actions can be verified based on the messages in Ψ and their public/ private keys.

In the graphical representation of LaPNs, control places are represented by circles, *Inner* transitions by bars, *In* and *Out* transitions by the rectangles with built-in identifiers $In(msg, S, R)$ and $Out(msg, S, R)$, respectively. Attached to each place is its identifier, while attached to each *Inner* transition is a label τ and its identifier (see Figure 3.5).

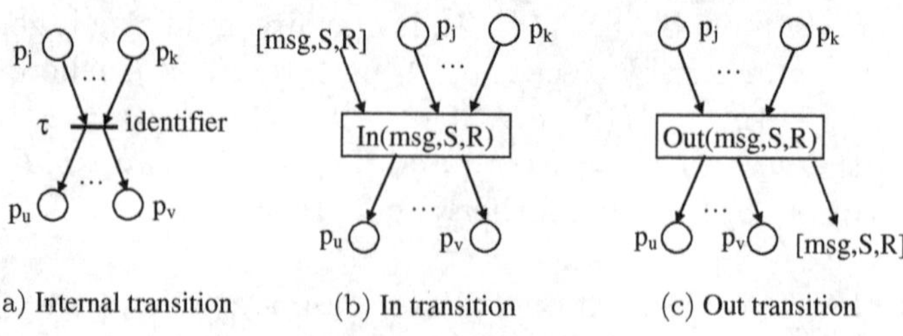

Figure 3.5 Building blocks of three types of transitions [20].

The building blocks of three types of transitions in LaPN models are shown in Figure 3.5, where p_j, p_k, p_u, and p_v are places, and (msg, S, R) is a message in Ψ. The occurrence of each action results in the process control evolving in an LaPN. An *Inner* action is involved only in places. For an *In/Out* transition, however, firing it not only causes the progress of control processes but also relates to Ψ. A message in Ψ is connected graphically to an *In* or *Out* transition through a dotted arc.

An e-commerce system must be described understandably before executing it. However, it is composed of several autonomous workflows containing private control flows communicating with each other asynchronously or synchronously. Therefore, a workflow can describe the business processes on a partner's side, and there exist external dependencies between some tasks belonging to different workflows.

We define a Labeled Workflow net — LaWN in the following. Notations $\mathbb{K}$ and $\mathbb{N}$ are used to denote two sets $\{1, 2, \ldots, k\}$ and $\{1, 2, \ldots, n\}$, respectively.

Definition 3.2 A LaPN $= (P, T, F, M_0, \Psi, \Sigma, l)$ is a LaWN *iff*

(1) P includes a source place i: $^\bullet i = \varnothing$;

(2) P includes sink places $o_1, o_2, \ldots, o_k$, and for $\forall j \in \mathbb{K}$, $o_j^\bullet = \varnothing$;

(3) If transitions $t_1^\#, t_2^\#, \ldots, t_k^\#$ are added to LaPN which connect places $o_1, o_2, \ldots, o_k$ with i, respectively, i.e., $^\bullet t_j^\# = \{o_j\}$ and $t_j^{\#\bullet} = \{i\}$, $j \in \mathbb{K}$, then LaPN$^\# = (P, T \cup \{t_1^\#, t_2^\#, \ldots, t_k^\#\}, F \cup \{\cup_{j \in \mathbf{K}} (o_j, t_j^\#), \cup_{j \in \mathbf{K}} (t_j^\#, i)\}, M_0, \Psi, \Sigma, l)$ is strongly connected.

Note that LaWN$^\#$ is strongly connected if and only if $\forall x, y \in P \cup T \cup \{t_1^\#, t_2^\#, \ldots, t_k^\#\}$, there is a path leading from x to y. $t_j^\#$

is an *Inner* transition, i.e., $l(t_j^{\#}) = \tau$, $j \in \mathbb{K}$. The dotted arcs are not considered in Definition 3.2, since the messages in Ψ are not put graphically in a state (M, Ψ) of LaWN. Place i corresponds to the starting state, while the sink places $o_1, o_2, \ldots, o_k$ correspond to k ending states. For the sake of simplicity, we assume that $M_0(i) = 1$ implies $M_0(i) = 1$ and $\forall p \in P - \{i\}$: $M_0(p) = 0$ unless specially stated otherwise. A complete run of workflow means that a terminating state $(M(o_j) = 1, \Psi)$ $(1 \leq j \leq k)$ is obtained from the initial state $(M_0(i) = 1, \Psi_0)$, i.e., an individual goal of a cooperative partner in e-commerce systems.

Since an e-commerce system refers usually to multiple cooperative partners, the workflow process of each partner is modeled by an LaWN, called an LaWN subnet. As a result, an overall LaWN model of an e-commerce system is composed of several LaWN subnets. The communication among LaWN subnets is carried out through the messages in Ψ.

Definition 3.3 Let LaPN $= (P, T, F, M_0, \Psi, \Sigma, l)$ be an LaWN, then LLaPN $= (P, T, F, M_0, \Sigma, l)$ is called a Local Labeled Workflow net-LLaPN of LaPN, in which $M_0 = (M_{p0}, M_{net0})$.

All transitions in an LLaPN depend only on control tokens. Thus, the enabling conditions and firing rules of the transitions are the same as those of Petri nets. Similarly, LLaPN$^{\#}$ represents the local net of LaPN$^{\#}$.

Definition 3.4 Let LaPN$_i$ $= (P_i, T_i; F_i, M_0^{(i)}, \Sigma_i, l_i)$ be an LaWN, $i = 1, 2, \ldots, n$. ILaPN $= (P, T; F, M_0, \Sigma, l)$ is an Interorganizational Labeled Workflow net-ILaWN composed of LaPN$_1$, LaPN$_2$, ..., LaPN$_n$, *iff*

(1) $P = \cup_{1 \leq i \leq n} P_i$, $T = \cup_{1 \leq i \leq n} T_i$, $F = \cup_{1 \leq i \leq n} F_i$; $\Sigma = \cup_{1 \leq i \leq n} \Sigma_i$;

(2) $M_0 = (M_{p0}, M_{net0})$, in which $M_{p0} = (M_{p0}^{(1)}, M_{p0}^{(2)}, \ldots, M_{p0}^{(n)})$, $M_{net0} = M_{net0}^{(1)} = M_{net0}^{(2)} = \ldots = M_{net0}^{(n)}$, $M_{0(i)} = (M_{p0}^{(i)}, M_{net0}^{(i)})$, $i = 1, 2, \ldots, n$;

(3) for $\forall t \in T$, if $t \in T_i$ $(1 \leq i \leq n)$, then $l(t) = l_i(t)$.

Since the ILaPN is used to simulate a complete e-commerce system, we require that the network conditions of all its partners are the same, that is, the network conditions are visible to each partner in the system. In the ILaPN, the data exchange or transmission among

LaPNs is realized by firing the transition of input and output with the network conditions.

Definition 3.5 $L(\langle \text{LWN}, G_f \rangle)$ is an LWN language iff

(1) $G_f \subseteq R(M_0)$ is a finite set of terminal markings on P;
(2) $L(\langle \text{LWN}, G_f \rangle) = \{l(\sigma) \in \Sigma^* | (\sigma \in T^*) \wedge ((M_0, \Psi_0)[\sigma > (M, \Psi) \wedge (M \in G_f)\}$.

Note that $M \in R(M_0)$ means that there is a set Ψ of exchanged messages such that $(M, \Psi) \in R((M_0, \Psi_0))$. $L(\langle \text{LLWN}, G_f \rangle)$ represents a set of all firing sequences from M_0 to $M \in G_f$.

3.4.2   EBPN

Online shopping systems have their security properties such as Atomicity and Payment Completion Invariant. Hybrid web applications that combine the Application Programming Interfaces (APIs) of multiple web services into integrated services like online shopping websites have been rapidly developing and bringing in new security concerns. The web programming paradigm is already under threat from malicious web clients who exploit logic flaws caused by improper distribution of the application functionality between a client and server. Even if the security requirements of enterprise business processes are met, the online shopping business process may not be flawless, and malicious users can obtain additional benefits through a series of actions. Many accidents of existing online shopping systems are caused by data errors and state inconsistency as exploited by malicious users. Thus, both the data properties and data state non-determinacy must be depicted. Additionally, a formal model is needed which can accurately depict the mainstream online shopping business consisting of data flow, control flow, and three parties: Shopper, Merchant, and Third Payment Platform (TPP). Thus, this section introduces the EBPN [27–31].

Definition 3.6 An EBPN is a 7-tuple $EN = (P, T; F, D, W, S, G)$ where:

(1) P is a finite set of places;
(2) T is a finite set of transitions T such that $P \cap T = \varnothing$ and $P \cup T \neq \varnothing$;
(3) $F \subseteq (P \times T) \cup (T \times P)$ is a set of directed arcs;

(4) D is a finite, non-empty set of symbol strings denoting the types of tokens;

(5) $W\colon F \to \langle a_1 d_1,\, a_2 d_2,\, a_3 d_3,\, \ldots,\, a_l d_l \rangle$, $a_l \in \{0,1\}$, $d_l \in D$, and $l > 0$ is the number of elements in D;

(6) $S \subset D$ denotes a set of key token types; and

(7) $G\colon T \to II$ is a predicate function that assigns a predicate to each transition $t \in T$ where II is the set of Boolean expressions on D.

An EBPN is a formal model used to portray an online shopping business process. T is used to depict APIs and operation events of a transaction process, and P is used to describe data channels and states. D is the set of types of tokens that depict the data elements used in the transaction process. There are some key data elements in an online shopping business process. Correspondingly, an EBPN has some key token types denoted by S, and tokens belonging to such types have two fixed values, i.e., $\mathbf{T}$ (true) and $\mathbf{F}$ (false). In this chapter, we also use $d_l \in D$ as a token with the type of d_l to facilitate the expression. The weight function W assigns an l-dimensional vector to each arc, and the l-dimensional vector is an order of D. Predicates are assigned to some transitions that are used to judge whether a validation result is true or false in a trading process.

For example, Figure 3.7 is a schematic example of EBPN depicting the paying operation of TPP, and the phrase in the transition is used to signal its function. It has five data types, i.e., token types in D. They are *TListen*, *orderID*, *gross*, *transactionID*, and *TPaid*, in which $S = \{orderID, gross, transactionID\}$, and their order is $\langle TListen,\ orderID,\ gross,\ transactionID,\ TPaid \rangle$ for five-dimensional vector. The operation needs two inputs, one of which is the current state of TPP, i.e., *TListen*, and the other one is the trading parameters including *orderID* and *gross*. After the paying operation is finished, two data items are generated, one of which is *TPaid* representing that the money has been paid, and the other one is a transaction number, i.e., *transactionID*. Note that a predicate $[orderID = \mathbf{T} \wedge gross = \mathbf{T}]$ is assigned to t_1.

Definition 3.7 A marking of an EBPN $EN = (P, T; F, D, W, S, G)$ is $M\colon P \to \langle n_1 d_1, n_2 d_2, n_3 d_3, \ldots, n_l d_l \rangle$, $n_l \in \mathbb{N} = \{0, 1, 2, \ldots\}$; $d_l \in D$, and $l > 0$ is the number of data elements in D.

A marking M of an EBPN assigns k-dimensional vectors to places. The vector's component $n_k d_k$ means that a place has n_k tokens belonging to type d_k. Here, a token is a trading parameter that belongs to some type in an EBPN. For example, the marking of Figure 3.7(a) is $M = [\langle TListen, 0, 0, 0, 0\rangle, \langle 0, 2orderID, gross, 0, 0\rangle, \langle 0, 0, 0, 0, 0\rangle, \langle 0, 0, 0, 0, 0\rangle]$. This means that p_1 has a token whose type is $TListen$ representing a state of TPP, and p_2 has three tokens representing the trading parameters, two of which are the type of $orderID$, and the other one is $gross$.

Definition 3.8 If $p \in P$, then the multiset [32, 33] of k-dimensional vector $M(p)$ is represented by $M(p)$, and the data element set of $M(p)$ is represented by $M(p)$. The number of times that element $d \in D$ appears in $M(p)$ is denoted by $\#(d, M(p))$.

In this work, for simplicity, the expression of a marking $M = [p_i(\lambda)|p_i$ is the place that has tokens, and $\lambda = M(p_i)]$. For example, the marking of Figure 3.7(a) is $M = [p_1(TListen), p_2(2orderID, gross)]$. $M(p_2) = \{orderID, orderID, gross\}$, $\widetilde{M}(p_2) = \{orderID, gross\}$, and $\#(orderID, \widetilde{M}(p_2)) = 2$.

Definition 3.9 If $p \in P$, $t \in T$, then the weight of an arc (p, t) or (t, p) is represented by $W(p, t)$ or $W(t, p)$, and the data element set of k-dimensional vector $W(p, t)$ or $W(t, p)$ is represented by $W(p, t)$ or $W(t, p)$.

Satisfying $W(p, t)$ is a requirement for enabling and firing t at the current marking. $W(t, p)$ indicates what the output data is in p after firing t. In Figure 3.7(a), $W(p_1, t_1) = \langle TListen, 0, 0, 0, 0\rangle$ means that firing t_1 requires that p_1 must have at least one token whose type is $TListen$; $W(p_2, t_1) = \langle 0, orderID, gross, 0, 0\rangle$ means that firing t_1 requires that p_2 must have at least two tokens whose types are respectively $orderID$ and $gross$, and the tokens in p_1 and p_2 satisfy these conditions; $W(t_1, p_3) = \langle 0, 0, 0, TPaid, 0\rangle$ means that firing t_1 deposits a token with the type of $TPaid$ to p_3; and $W(t_1, p_4) = \langle 0, 0, 0, 0, transactionID\rangle$ means that firing t_1 deposits a token with the type of $transactionID$ to p_4. $W(p_1, t_1) = \{TListen\}$, $W(p_2, t_1) = \{orderID, gross\}$, $W(t_1, p_3) = \{TPaid\}$, and $W(t_1, p_4) = \{transactionID\}$.

To facilitate graphic expression, the vector $\langle a_1 d_1, a_2 d_2, a_3 d_3, \ldots, a_k d_k\rangle$ would be simplified as a set on the arc. For example, Figures 3.7(a) and (b) represent the same transition of a paying operation in TPP. This is purely for graphical clarity, as an EBPN may have dozens of trading parameters, and the k-dimensional vector would be so long that it is impossible to represent it in a graph. In an EBPN, solid arcs represent the control flow depicting control structures and state transition relations, and dashed arcs represent the data flow among APIs. Two flows may overlap.

Definition 3.10 δ_G is a Boolean function that assigns a Boolean value $\mathbf{T}$ (true) or $\mathbf{F}$ (false) to each $G(t)$ such that $\delta_G: G(t) \rightarrow \{\mathbf{T}, \mathbf{F}\}$, $t \in T$.

In this work, ${}^\bullet t = \{p \in P | (p, t) \in F\}$ is called the pre-set of t, i.e., a set of its input places. Its post set is $t^\bullet = \{p \in P | (t, p) \in F\}$.

Definition 3.11 A pair $\Lambda(M, \delta_D)$ is a data state of *EN*, if M is a marking of *EN*, and δ_D is called a data allocation which assigns a value $\mathbf{T}$ (true), or $\mathbf{F}$ (false) to each $d \in \{M(p) | p \in P\}$ such that $d \in (D - S) \rightarrow \delta_D(d) = \mathbf{T}$, and $\delta_D: S \rightarrow \{\mathbf{T}, \mathbf{F}\}$.

In this work, if $d \in \{M(p) | p \in P\} \cap S$ at a data state (M, δ_D), and $\delta_D(d) = \mathbf{F}$, then we use notation "$d\mathbf{F}$" to express its value. Otherwise, if $d \in D$, and $\delta_D(d) = \mathbf{T}$, then its value would not be displayed for clarity. In Figures 3.7(a) and 3.7(b), the data state is $(M, \delta_D) = [p_1(\textit{TListen}), p_2(\textit{orderID}, \textit{orderIDF}, \textit{gross})])$.

Definition 3.12 A transition $t \in T$ is enabled at a data state $\Lambda = (M, \delta_D)$ if

(1) $\forall p \in {}^\bullet t, M(p) \geq W(p, t)$; and
(2) $\exists G(t) \rightarrow \delta_G(G(t)) = \mathbf{T}$.

Here, $M(p) \geq W(p, t)$ means that $\{n_1, n_2, n_3, \ldots, n_k\}^k \geq \{a_1, a_2, a_3, \ldots, a_k\}^k$, and the arithmetic of $M(p)$ and $W(p, t)$ is based on $\{n_1, n_2, n_3, \ldots, n_k\}^k$ and $\{a_1, a_2, a_3, \ldots, a_k\}^k$. For example, given $M(p) = (n_1 d_1, n_2 d_2, n_3 d_3, \ldots, n_k d_k)$, and $W(p, t) = (a_1 d_1, a_2 d_2, a_3 d_3, \ldots, a_k d_k)$, $M(p) - W(p, t) = ((n_1 - a_1)d_1, (n_2 - a_2)d_2, (n_3 - a_3)d_3, \ldots, (n_k - a_k)d_k)$.

We use $M \xrightarrow{t}$ to denote that t is enabled at M, and a new marking M' can be produced through notation $M \xrightarrow{t} M'$. $\neg M \xrightarrow{t}$ means that t is not enabled at M. In the following sections, the notation $\xrightarrow{t}$ is also used in a data state $\Lambda = \langle M, \alpha \rangle$, i.e., $\langle M, \alpha \rangle \xrightarrow{t}$

means that t is enabled at a data state $\langle M, \alpha \rangle$, and $\langle M, \alpha \rangle \xrightarrow{t} \langle M', \alpha' \rangle$ describes that $\langle M', \alpha' \rangle$ is produced by firing t at $\langle M, \alpha \rangle$.

Likewise, $\neg \langle M, \alpha \rangle \xrightarrow{t}$ means that t is not enabled at $\langle M, \alpha \rangle$. If there exists a transition sequence $\sigma = t_1, t_2, \ldots, t_{k-1}$ and data state sequence $\langle M_1, \alpha_1 \rangle$, $\langle M_2, \alpha_2 \rangle, \ldots, \langle M_k, \alpha_k \rangle$ making that $\langle M_1, \alpha_1 \rangle \xrightarrow{t_1} \langle M_2, \alpha_2 \rangle, \ldots, \langle M_{k-1}, \alpha_{k-1} \rangle \xrightarrow{t_{k-1}} \langle M_k, \alpha_k \rangle$, then $\langle M_k, \alpha_k \rangle$ is reachable from $\langle M_1, \alpha_1 \rangle$, and this can be denoted by $\langle M, \alpha \rangle \xrightarrow{\sigma} \langle M_k, \alpha_k \rangle$. All the reachable data states from $\langle M, \alpha \rangle$ are denoted by $R\langle M, \alpha \rangle$.

The web programming paradigm of an e-commerce system is already under threat from malicious web clients that exploit logic flaws caused by improper distribution of the application functionality between a client and server. The program logic of a hybrid web application is further complicated by the need to securely coordinate different web services that it integrates: failing to do so leaves the door open for attackers to violate security invariants by inducing inconsistencies among these services. Endless varieties of methods of attacks are emerging all the time, and clients (browsers) are controlled by users, otherwise, the data handled by them are not safe. There may be some wrong and tampered data flowing in the system resulting in the violation of transaction property and logic errors [34–38]. Thus, we define key data elements in Definition 3.6 and key transitions next. Key transitions exist only in clients of an e-commerce business process, i.e., handled by the users, and the key data elements output by them have two values.

Definition 3.13 Given $t \in T$, $^{\bullet}t = P'$, and $t^{\bullet} = P''$, t is called a key transition if

(1) $S \cap \{W(t, p) | p \in P''\} \neq \varnothing$; and
(2) The token $s \in S \cap \{\widetilde{W}(t, p) | p \in P''\}$ is produced by $t \to \delta_D(s) \in \{\mathbf{T}, \mathbf{F}\}$.
   If $t \in T$ is a key transition, then the token with the type of key data element produced by firing it has non-determinacy Boolean values, either true or false, and this is expressed by the data state. The changing rules of data states are illustrated next.

Definition 3.14 Let $EN = (P, T; F, D, W, S, G)$ be an EBPN, and $\Lambda = (M, \delta_D)$ be a data state of EN. A transition $t \in T$, which is enabled at (M, δ_D), can fire under $M(M \xrightarrow{t})$, and a new marking $M'(M \xrightarrow{t} M')$ is

$$M'(p) = \begin{cases} M(p) - W(p,t), & \text{if } p \in {}^\bullet t - t^\bullet \\ M(p) + W(t,p), & \text{if } p \in t^\bullet - {}^\bullet t \\ M(p) - W(p,t) + W(t,p), & \text{if } p \in {}^\bullet t \cap t^\bullet \\ M(p), & \text{otherwise.} \end{cases}$$

If t is not a key transition, a new data state Λ' is

$$\Lambda' = (M', \delta'_D)$$
$$= (M', \forall d \in \{M(p) | p \in P\} \to \delta'_D(d) = \delta_D(d)$$
$$\wedge \forall d \in \{W(t,p) | p \in t^\bullet\} - \{M(p) | p \in P\} \to \delta'_D(d) = \mathbf{T}).$$

Else if t is a key transition, a new state set Γ is

$$\Gamma = \{(M', \delta'_D) | M \xrightarrow{t} M',$$
$$\forall s \in \{W(t,p) | p \in t^\bullet\} \cap S \to \delta'_D(s) \in \mathbf{T}, \mathbf{F}\},$$
$$\forall d \in \{M(p) - \{W(t,p) | p \in t^\bullet\} \cap S\} \to \delta'_D(d) = \delta_D(d)\}.$$

We have two changes when firing t: marking and data allocation. There is only one marking that is newly produced, but data allocation is divided into two situations, i.e., whether t is a key transition or not. If not, only one data state is produced after firing t, because any token produced by firing t is assigned with a fixed value. Otherwise, any token with the type of a key data element is assigned with $\mathbf{T}$ or $\mathbf{F}$, and each situation results in the generation of a data state. Thus, a new data state set is produced, which reflects the non-determinacy of EBPN. In Figures 3.7(a) and 3.7(b), as the current data state $(M, \delta_D) = ([p_1(\textit{TListen}), p_2(\textit{orderID}, \textit{orderID}\mathbf{F}, \textit{gross})])$ satisfies the firing conditions, t_1 can fire, and three tokens in p_1 and p_2 are consumed. Note that one token with the type of $\textit{orderID}$ whose value is $\mathbf{F}$ is not consumed because it cannot satisfy the predicate.

After firing t_1, p_3 and p_4 have one token with a type of $\textit{TPaid}$ and $\textit{transactionID}$ in Figures 3.7(c), respectively. $\textit{TPaid}$ means that TPP is at the state of finished payment, and $\textit{transactionID}$ is the data produced by the operation $\textit{Paying}$. The marking in Figure 3.7(c) is $M' = ([p_2(\textit{orderID}), p_3(\textit{TPaid}), p_4(\textit{transactionID})])$.

If t_1 is not a key transition, the current data state is $(M', \delta'_D) = ([p_2(orderID\mathbf{F}), p_3(TPaid), p_4(transactionID)])$. Otherwise, if t_1 is a key transition, $\delta'_D(transactionID) \in \{\mathbf{T}, \mathbf{F}\}$, $\Gamma = \{([p_2(orderID\mathbf{F}), p_3(TPaid), p_4(transactionID)]), ([p_2(orderID\mathbf{F}), p_3(TPaid), p_4(transactionID\mathbf{F})])\}$, i.e., two data states are produced by firing t_1. Non-determinacy of EBPN is expressed by producing all possible follower states related to a transition occurrence instead of only one single follower state.

Definition 3.15 Let (M_0, δ_{D0}) be the initial data state of $EN = (P, T; F, D, W, S, G)$. EN is a data-bounded EBPN if $\forall p \in P$, $M \in R(M_0)$, $d \in M(p) \to \#(d, M(p)) \leq 1$.

Definition 3.16 Let $EN = (P, T; F, D, W, S, G)$ be an EBPN, (M_0, δ_{D0}) be its initial data state, and $t \in T$. If $\forall (M, \delta_D) \in R(M_0, \delta_{D0})$, $\exists (M', \delta_{D'}) \in R(M, \delta_D)$, such that $(M', \delta_{D'}) \xrightarrow{t}$, then t is data-live. If $\forall t \in T$ is data-live, then EN is data-live.

3.5 Analysis and Verification

3.5.1 *Analysis and verification of LaPN*

In the e-commerce system, an LaWN can simulate the workflow process of a participant. Since the workflow process of one participant is closely related to the workflow processes of other participants, it cannot independently describe the workflow of the entire process. However, without considering the network conditions, we can discuss some properties of the LLaPN, and analyze these local properties to lay a foundation for studying the overall properties of the entire system. In this subsection, we analyze the behavior properties of LLaPN, such as soundness and non-blocking properties.

Definition 3.17 LLaPN $= (P, T, F, M_0, \Sigma, l)$ is sound iff for $M_0(i) = 1$:

(1) LLaPN$^{\#}$ is safe;
(2) $\forall M \in R(M_0)$, $\exists 1 \leq j \leq k : M(o_j) = 1$;
(3) $\forall M \in R(M_0)$, $\exists \sigma \in T^*$, and $1 \leq j \leq k: M[\sigma > M_1(o_j) = 1$;
(4) In LLaPN$^{\#}$, $\forall t \in T \cup \{t_1^{\#}, t_2^{\#}, \ldots, t_k^{\#}\}$, $\exists M \in R(M_0)$, $M[t >$.

The soundness property describes the dynamic behavior of an LLaPN.

Theorem 3.1 *An LLaPN is sound iff for $M_0(i) = 1$, $LLaPN^\#$ is live and safe.*

For convenience, if σ_1 and σ_2 are two transition sequences in LaPNs, $\sigma_1 \circ \sigma_2$ is used to denote their concatenation, where $\circ$ is a concatenation operator. For $\sigma \in T^*$, if $\sigma = \sigma_1 \circ \sigma_2$, σ_1 is the prefix of σ, while σ_2 is the postfix of σ.

Definition 3.18 Let LLaPN $= (P, T, F, M_0, \Sigma, l)$ and $M_0(i) = 1$. $\langle \text{LLaPN}, G_f \rangle$ is not blocked iff $\forall \sigma \in L(\langle \text{LLaPN}, R(M_0) \rangle)$, $\sigma \notin L(\langle \text{LLaPN}, G_f \rangle)$, then $\exists \sigma' \in T^*$: $\sigma \circ \sigma' \in L(\langle \text{LLaPN}, G_f \rangle)$.

By Definition 3.18, $\langle \text{LLaPN}, G_f \rangle$ possesses the non-blocking property if and only if each path in its run can continue and arrive at a terminal state $M \in G_f$. In an e-commerce system, the business processes of each participant can be modeled by an LaWN. G_f is usually used to denote the set of goal markings of a partner. Therefore, the non-blocking property of $\langle \text{LLaPN}, G_f \rangle$ declares explicitly that for any firing sequence σ in LLaPN, there is a continuation σ' such that one goal marking of G_f is achieved through firing sequence $\sigma \circ \sigma'$. This property is very important for the analysis of the accountability and obligations of cooperative actions to arrive at a common goal in e-commerce systems. If $G_f = \{M_j(o_j) = 1, j \in \mathbb{K}\}$, the non-blocking property of $\langle \text{LLaPN}, G_f \rangle$ relates to the soundness of LLaPN. Note that the non-blocking property focuses on the analysis of the transition sequences approaching terminal markings (goals).

Theorem 3.2 *Let $G_f = \{M_j(o_j) = 1,\ j \in \mathbb{K}\}$, if an LLaPN is sound, then $\langle LLaPN, G_f \rangle$ is not blocked.*

From Theorem 3.1 and Definition 3.17, for $M_0(i) = 1$, $LLaPN^\#$ is live and safe. For $\forall \sigma \in L(\langle \text{LLaPN}, R(M_0) \rangle)$, $\sigma \notin L(\langle \text{LLaPN}, G_f \rangle)$, if $\forall j \in \mathbb{K}$, $\forall \sigma' \in T^*$, $(M_0, \Psi_0)[\sigma \circ \sigma' > (M, \Psi)$ and $M(o_j) = 0$, then $\forall l \in \mathbb{K}$, there is no marking M reachable from M_0 such that $t_l^\#$ is enabled at M. This is in contrast with the liveness of $LLaPN^\#$. Thus, $\exists j \in \mathbb{K}$, $(M_0, \Psi_0)[\sigma \circ \sigma' > (M, \Psi)$, $M(o_j) = 1$. However, if

$\exists p \in P - \{o_j\}$: $M(p) \geq 1$, this contradicts the safeness of LLaPN$^\#$ or Definition 3.17.

Definition 3.19 Let ILaPN be an ILaWN composed of LaPN$_1$–LaPN$_n$ which are LaWNs. For $\forall i \in \mathbb{N}$, $G_{fi} \subseteq R(M_0^{(i)})$ is a set of all terminal markings of LaPN$_i$, G_{fi} is a cooperative marking set iff $\forall \sigma^{(i)} \in \mathrm{L}(\langle \mathrm{LLaPN}_i,\ G_{fi}\rangle)$, there is at least an *In/Out* transition in $\sigma^{(i)}$.

Assume that $\forall i \in \mathbb{N}$, G_{fi} is a cooperative marking set in LaPN$_i$. Since each of *In/Out* transitions in LaPN$_i(1 \leq i \leq n)$ is very important for performing the communication between cooperative partners, we give a type of well-behaved LaPNs in which some conditional routing constructs of workflows are restricted appropriately to analyze the non-blocking property of an ILaPN.

Definition 3.20 Let ILaPN be an ILaWN composed of LaPN$_1$–LaPN$_n$ which are LaWNs, $i, j \in \mathbb{N}$, and $i \neq j$. $In(msg1, A, B)$ in T_i depends on $Out(msg2, C, D)$ in T_j iff $msg1 = msg2$, $A = C$ and $B = D$, notation $In\ (msg1, A, B) \leftarrow Out(msg2, C, D)$. If $\exists t_1 \in T_i$, $t_2 \in T_j$, and $t_1 \leftarrow t_2$, then there is the dependency between LaPN$_i$ and LaPN$_j$.

It is obvious that if $t_1 \leftarrow t_2$, firing t_1 means that t_1 receives the message sent by t_2. In this work, notation $\neg(t_1 \leftarrow t_2)$ denotes that t_1 does not depend on t_2.

Figure 3.8 presents the LaWN model of a buyer workflow process. It has two terminal states: $M_{p1}(o_{b1}) = 1$ and $M_{p2}(o_{b2}) = 1$. The initial control marking is $M_{p0}(i_b) = 1$. LaPN$_s$ and LaPN$_b$ represent the LaWNs in Figures 3.6 and 3.8, respectively, and ILaPN$_{sb}$ represents the ILaWN composed of LaPN$_s$ and LaPN$_b$. According to the model structure of LaPN$_s$ and LaPN$_b$, the *Int* transition In(goods, S, B) of LaPN$_b$ depends on the *Out* transition Out(goods, S, B) of LaPN$_s$, for In(goods, S, B) $\leftarrow$ Out(goods, S, B). From Definition 3.20, there is a dependency between LaPN$_s$ and LaPN$_b$.

Definition 3.21 Let ILaPN be composed of LaPN$_1$–LaPN$_n$. ILaPN is *sound* iff

(1) $\forall i \in \mathbb{N}$, LLaPN$_i$ is sound;
(2) ILaPN$^\#$ is live, where ILaPN$^\#$ is composed of LaPN$_1^\#$–LaPN$_n^\#$.

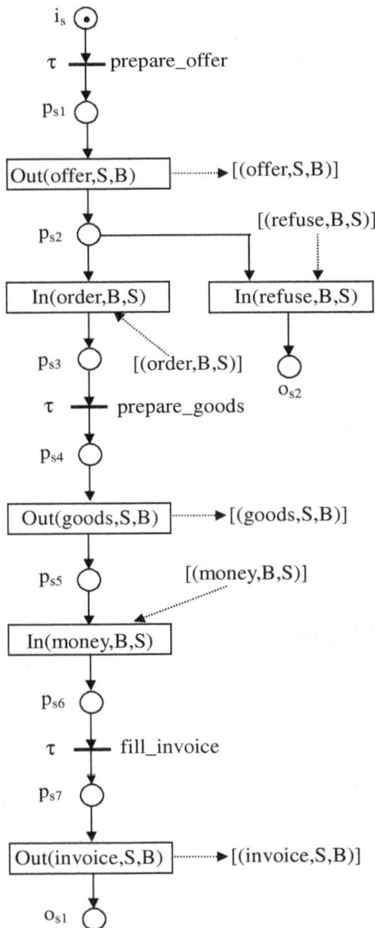

Figure 3.6   LaPN model of seller workflow process [20].

In Figure 3.9, LLaPN$_1$ and LLaPN$_2$ are sound, but their ILaPN$^{\#}$ is non-live. Two *In* transitions are dead, as firing $In(msg1, N_2, N_1)$ (or $In(msg2, N_1, N_2)$) needs an exchanged message $[(msg1,N_2, N_1)]$ (or $[(msg2, N_1, N_2)]$) in Ψ obtained by firing a subsequent transition $Out(msg1, N_2, N_1)$ (or $Out(msg2, N_1, N_2)$).

Definition 3.22 Let $G_f \subseteq R(M_0)$ be a terminal marking set of an LaPN that is an LaWN. LaPN is well-behaved iff $\forall M \in G_f$, $\forall \sigma_1$, $\sigma_2 \in L(\langle \text{LLaPN}, M \rangle)$, $\&(\sigma_1) \cap (T_{in} \cup T_{out}) = \&(\sigma_2) \cap (T_{in} \cup T_{out})$.

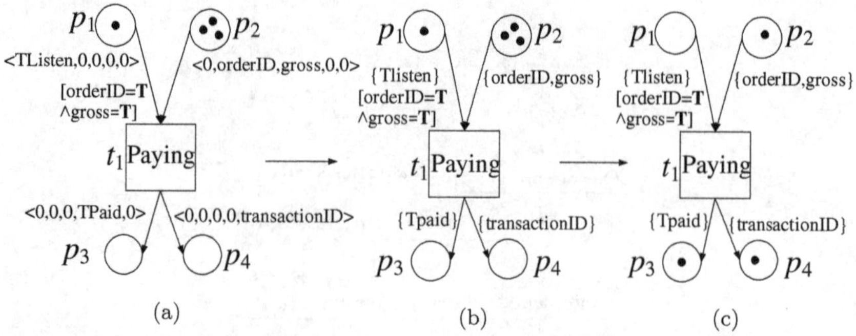

Figure 3.7   A transition of EBPN and its firing [23].

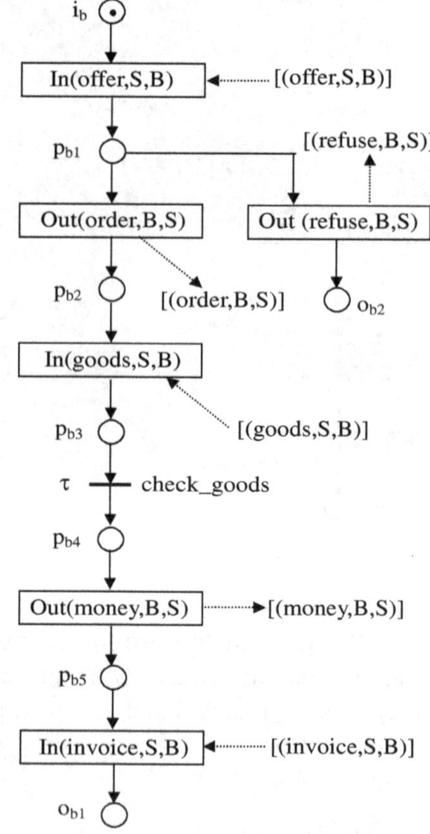

Figure 3.8   LaPN model of buyer workflow process [20].

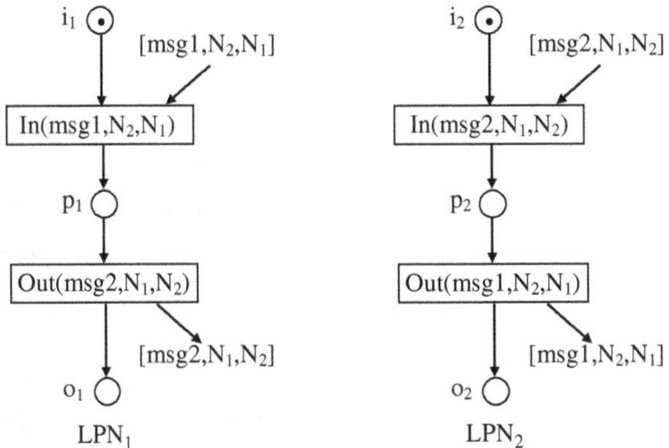

Figure 3.9 An illustration that ILaPN composed of LaPN$_1$ and LaPN$_2$ is non-live [20].

This definition implies that $\forall M \in G_f$, any firing path from (M_0, Ψ_0) to (M, Ψ) contains the same *In/Out* transitions. The requirement can be used to impel a partner in performing his tasks for achieving a common goal. Notation $t_i \prec_\sigma t_j$ denotes that t_i precedes t_j in σ.

By Definitions 3.21 and 3.22, we give the following inheritance conditions of the non-blocking property of ILaPNs. For convenience, we use notations $T_{in}^{(i)}$ and $T_{out}^{(i)}$ to denote the sets of the *In* and *Out* transitions of LaPN$_i$, respectively, i.e., $T_i = T_{in}^{(i)} \cup T_{out}^{(i)} \cup T_{int}^{(i)}$.

Theorem 3.3 *Let ILaPN be composed of LaPN$_1$–LaPN$_n$ which are LaWNs. $\forall i \in \mathbb{N}$, G_{fi} is the cooperative marking set of LaPN$_i$, LaPN$_i$ is well-behaved, G_f is a set of terminal markings of ILaPN, and $\Gamma_{P \to Pi}(G_f) = G_{fi}$. $\langle ILaPN, G_f \rangle$ is not blocked iff $\forall i \in \mathbb{N}$*

(1) *$\langle LLaPN_i, G_{fi} \rangle$ is not blocked; and*
(2) *For $\forall M = (M^{(1)}, M^{(2)}, \ldots, M^{(n)}) \in G_f$, $\sigma^{(i)} \in L(\langle LLaPN_i, M^{(i)} \rangle)$, and $t_1^{(i)} \in \&(\sigma^{(i)}) \cap T_{in}^{(i)}$, $\exists j \in \mathbb{N} - \{i\}$, $\forall \sigma^{(j)} \in L(\langle LLaPN_j, M^{(j)} \rangle)$, $\exists t_{1(j)} \in \&(\sigma^{(j)})$, then $t_1^{(i)} \leftarrow t_1^{(j)}$, and $\forall t_2^{(i)} \in \&(\sigma^{(i)})$, $t_2^{(j)} \in \&(\sigma^{(j)}) : (t_1^{(i)} \prec_{\sigma^{(i)}} t_2^{(i)}) \wedge (t_2^{(j)} \prec_{\sigma^{(j)}} t_1^{(j)})$, then $\neg(t_2^{(j)} \leftarrow t_1^{(i)})$.*

Theorem 3.3 gives the sufficient and necessary conditions of non-blocking $\langle \text{ILaPN}, G_f \rangle$, i.e., achieving a common goal. That is, a common goal G_f can be achieved if and only if ILaPN satisfies the conditions of Theorem 3.3. The presented theorems will be used to analyze the obligations of participants. If $\langle \text{ILaPN}, G_f \rangle$ is not blocked and a common goal cannot be achieved within a life cycle of a case, a partner must take the responsibility of doing some follow-up actions for achieving a common goal.

The common goals defined in G_f can ensure that the profit of each cooperative partner is not jeopardized. However, it is by no means to exclude that the partners get out of the cooperation prematurely once they obtain themselves private goals prior to any of the common goals having been achieved. To avoid this from happening, $\forall \sigma \in$ L($\langle \text{ILaPN}, M_0 \rangle$), if $\sigma \notin$ L($\langle \text{ILaPN}, G_f \rangle$), some partner is obliged to take specific follow-up actions such that the cooperation approaches a common goal in G_f.

A partner under an obligation means that "if so-and-so actions have been taken by this partner, she/he must continue with so-and-so actions". In LaPNs, however, taking any action changes control conditions. The change specifies explicitly that the specific continuation actions have to be carried out by the partners under the obligation. The common goal set G_f of all cooperative parties includes all success linkage goals and regular abort goals. One of the common goals should be achieved once starting to run a process. Therefore, at least one of the parties is responsible for taking an enabled In/Out action if a common goal cannot be obtained. This concept can be formalized as follows.

Definition 3.23 Let ILaPN be composed of LaPN_1–LaPN_n which are LaWNs, $G_{fi} \subseteq R(M_0^{(i)})$, $i \in \mathbb{N}$, and $G_f \subseteq R(M_0)$. $\sigma \in$ L($\langle \text{ILaPN}, M_0 \rangle$), $(M_0, \Psi_0)[\sigma > (M, \Psi)$ and $M \notin G_f$. For any $i \in \mathbb{N}$, $\forall t \in T_i$, partner LaPN_i is under the obligation of firing t iff

(1) For $t \in T_{inn}^{(i)} \cup T_{out}^{(i)}$, t is enabled at $\Gamma_{P \rightarrow Pi}(M) \notin G_{fi}$ in Z_i; or
(2) For $t \in T_{in(i)}$, t is enabled at $\Gamma_{P \rightarrow Pi}(M) \notin G_{fi}$ in Z_i and there is a message in Ψ that matches with one in t.

Partner LaPN_i is under an obligation iff $\exists t \in T_i$, LaPN_i is responsible for firing t.

For the sake of convenience, we adopt the identifier of a partner with the name of a correspondent LaPN. According to Definition 3.23, $\forall t \in T_i$, partner LaPN_i is responsible for firing t in the ILaPN, if t is enabled at current state (M, Ψ) where $\Gamma_{P \to Pi}(M) \notin G_{fi}$. In LaPN_i, if some transitions are enabled simultaneously at (M, Ψ), LaPN_i is under the obligation of firing at least one of them conditionally, selectively, or firing them concurrently. For instance, in Figure 3.8, after firing In(offer, S, B), the buyer is responsible for firing selectively action Out(order, B, S) or Out(refuse, B, S). However, in Figure 3.6, after the seller had fired Out(offer, S, B), the seller is responsible for firing conditionally action In(order, B, S) or In(refuse, B, S). $\forall i \in \mathbb{N}$, if LaPN_i is under no obligation, a common goal is achieved. Thus, the following conclusion is obtained.

Theorem 3.4 *Let ILaPN be composed of $LaPN_1$–$LaPN_n$ which are LaWNs, $\langle ILaPN, G_f \rangle$ be not blocked, $i \in \mathbb{N}$, $G_{fi} \subseteq R(M_{0(i)})$, $G_f \subseteq R(M_0)$ and $\Gamma_{P \to Pi}(G_f) = G_{fi}$. For $\sigma \in T^*$, $(M_0, \Psi_0)[\sigma > (M, \Psi)$, $M \in G_f$ iff any $LaPN_i$ $(1 \le i \le n)$ is under no obligation.*

Through Theorem 3.4, $\forall i \in \mathbb{N}$, if LaPN_i is under no obligation, a common goal in G_f is achieved. Therefore, if an ILaPN is not blocked and each $\text{LaPN}_i(1 \le i \le n)$ can implement its obligations, there is an action sequence $\sigma \in T^*$ such that $(M_0, \Psi_0)[\sigma > (M, \Psi)$ and $M \in G_f$.

Theorem 3.5 *Let ILaPN be composed of $LaPN_1$–$LaPN_n$ which are LaWNs, and $\langle ILaPN, G_f \rangle$ be not blocked. $i \in \mathbb{N}$, $G_{fi} \subseteq R(M_0^{(i)})$, $G_f \subseteq R(M_0)$, and $\Gamma_{P \to Pi}(G_f) = G_{fi}$. For $\forall M \in G_f$, M can be achieved iff $\forall i \in \mathbb{N}$, $LaPN_i$ is under the obligation of firing a sequence $\sigma_i \in L\left(\langle LLaPN_i, \Gamma_{P \to Pi}(M) \rangle\right)$.*

Through Theorems 3.4 and 3.5, therefore, if all partners perform their obligations, they can arrive at a common goal, i.e., either regular abort or success linkage of cooperation.

Accountability usually refers to a party denying the receipt of a document, a commitment, or receipt of payment. Accountability is evidently against such denials. Moreover, in this section, we assume that the communication system is safe, i.e., (a) the message sent is bound to result in its receipt on the other side and (b) receiving a message is bound to be a result of sending it by the other side. Therefore, we consider no cases that a message sent by a partner is lost and received by a wrong partner on the network. Since some partners may not continue a follow-up action in $\sigma \in L(\langle \text{ILaPN}, G_f \rangle)$, each cooperation party has to provide evidence to verify accountability. According to the evidence, any third-party (the arbitrator) can prove that some *Out* actions have been carried out on a partner's side or some *In* actions cannot be performed as some required messages from the other sides are not sent to the network. For this purpose, therefore, each partner and the communication system must collect proof.

In fact, since the network conditions of an ILaPN contain all messages sent by each partner and they are preserved throughout the life cycle of a case, the origins are provable using the digital signatures [39–43] of the corresponding senders. Consequently, an *Out* action is provable based on the messages in Ψ. Concerning the *In* actions, however, participants must depend on the network conditions and the controlling progress sequence appearing on their side for reasoning the non-repeatable proofs of their partners. Moreover, under the assumption that the communication system is safe, each message sent by partners can be received by a correspondent receiver once being sent by a partner.

3.5.2   *Analysis and verification of EBPN*

The EBPN integrates both data and control flows based on Petri nets. Defects and errors in business processes can, therefore, be revealed. Through the proposed methodology, designers can identify errors early in a design process and correct them before the system actualization. More reliable systems can be generated faster and at lower costs. Designing an e-commerce business process model is a complicated and error-prone task even for experienced process designers. To avoid errors as much as possible at the modeling phase, we model an e-commerce business process step by step and present control flow and data flow models locally. Firstly, the control flow of the e-commerce business process is modeled. It consists of a set of coordinated events describing the behavior of three parties. Later, the data flow is constructed, and at last, a completed model for integrating control and data flows from a global viewpoint is obtained. The benefit of such models is to provide different views of a composite business process, which helps designers or users understand and analyze the e-commerce business process.

Definition 3.24 Suppose that $EN_1 = (P_1, T_1; F_1, D_1, W_1, S_1, G_1)$ and $EN_2 = (P_2, T_2; F_2, D_2, W_2, S_2, G_2)$ are two nets satisfying Definition 3.6, $P_1 \cap P_2 = \emptyset$, $T_1 \cap T_2 \neq \emptyset$, $F_1 \cap F_2 = \emptyset$, $D_1 \cap D_2 = \emptyset$, $W_1 \cap W_2 = \emptyset$, $S_1 \cap S_2 = \emptyset$, $G_1 \cap G_2 \neq \emptyset$. Their composition is $EN = EN_1 \odot EN_2 = (P_1 \cup P_2, T_1 \cup T_2, F_1 \cup F_2, D_1 \cup D_2, W_1 \cup W_2, S_1 \cup S_2, G_1 \cup G_2)$.

Definition 3.24 specifies a synthesis method of EBPN. In this work, we use it to synthesize control and data flows. The following steps illustrate how to construct an EBPN.

(1) Constructing the control flow models $EN_i = (P_i, T_i; F_i, D_i, W_i, S_i, G_i)$, $i = 1, 2$, and 3, which correspond to Shopper, Merchant, and TPP, respectively;
(2) Constructing the data flow model of the e-commerce system $EN_4 = (P_4, T_4; F_4, D_4, W_4, S_4, G_4)$;
(3) Composing the four nets to obtain $EN = EN_1 \odot EN_2 \odot EN_3 \odot EN_4 = (P, T; F, D, W, S, G)$;
(4) Obtaining the initial marking $M_0 - p_i(\lambda_i), p_j(\lambda_j), p_k(\lambda_k)]$, where $p_i \in P_1$, $p_j \in P_2$, $p_k \in P_3$, $\lambda_i \in D_1$, $\lambda_j \in D_2$, $\lambda_k \in D_3$, and $p_i(\lambda_i)$, $p_j(\lambda_j)$, $p_k(\lambda_k)$ represent that Shopper, Merchant, and TPP are ready for a deal.

These steps describe the process of constructing an EBPN model. First, constructing the control flow models of three parties in an e-commerce system: Shopper, Merchant, and TPP. Second, constructing a data flow model according to data exchange among the three parties. At last, composing these nets to obtain the final net with its initial marking.

In this section, Rationality and Transaction Consistency are defined and validated to guarantee the transaction properties of an e-commerce business process. Therefore, the fuzzy structures and transaction properties in the actual e-commerce system design can be converted into formal EBPN language. These properties can then be validated with clarity and determinedly through a formal approach. First, we give the following definitions.

Definition 3.25 A pair $\Lambda = \langle M, \alpha \rangle$ is an extended data state of *EN*, if M is a marking of *EN*, and $\alpha = (\beta, \delta_D)$ is an extended data allocation, where $\beta \subseteq D$ and δ_D assigns a Boolean value $\mathbf{T}$ (true) or $\mathbf{F}$ (false) to each $d \in \beta \cup \{\widehat{M}(p) | p \in P\}$.

In an e-commerce system, some trading parameters are not transmitted continuously but stored in the database of the session to be used for subsequent operations. Thus, to validate the properties of the e-commerce business process itself, the data state is extended and the concept of extended data state is proposed, and β is used to depict this situation. Here, M, β, and α_D together constitute an extended data state. In Figures 3.7(a) and (b), the data state is $\langle M, \alpha \rangle = \langle [p_1(TListen), p_2(2orderID, gross)], (\varnothing, \delta_D) \rangle$. For simplicity, it can also be shown as $\langle M, \alpha \rangle = \langle [p_1(TListen), p_2(orderID, orderID\mathbf{F}, gross)], \varnothing \rangle$.

The extended data state is just a simple extension of the data state. Their operation rules are basically the same but slightly different in the state generation. Its generation rules are given in what follows.

Definition 3.26 Let $EN = (P, T; F, D, W, S, G)$ be an EBPN, and $\Lambda = \langle M, \alpha \rangle = \langle M, (\beta, \alpha_D) \rangle$ be an extended data state of *EN*. A transition $t \in T$, which is enabled at $\langle M, \alpha \rangle$, can fire under $M(M \xrightarrow{t}$), and a new marking $M'(M \xrightarrow{t} M')$is

$$M'(p) = \begin{cases} M(p) - W(p, t), & \text{if } p \in {}^\bullet t - t^\bullet \\ M(p) + W(p, t), & \text{if } p \in t^\bullet - {}^\bullet t \\ M(p) - W(p, t) + W(t, p), & \text{if } p \in {}^\bullet t \cap t^\bullet \\ M(p), & \text{otherwise} \end{cases}$$

Meanwhile, if t is not a key transition, a new extended data state $\Lambda' = \langle M', \alpha' \rangle$ is

$$\Lambda' = \langle M', \alpha' \rangle$$
$$= \langle M', (\beta', \delta'_D) \rangle$$

$$= \langle M', (\beta' = \{M(p)|p \in P\} \cup \beta \cup \{W(t,p)|p \in t^\bullet\}$$
$$- \{M'(p)|p \in P\}, \forall d \in (\beta \cup \{M(p)|p \in P\}) \rightarrow \delta'_D(d) = \delta_D(d)$$
$$\wedge \forall d \in \{W(t,p)|p \in t^\bullet\} - (\beta \cup \{M(p)|p \in P\})$$
$$\rightarrow \delta'_D(d) = \mathbf{T})\rangle$$

Else, if t is not a key transition, a new extended data state set Γ is

$$\Gamma = \{\langle M', \alpha' \rangle = \langle M', (\beta', \delta'_D)\rangle | M \xrightarrow{t} M',$$
$$\beta' = \{M(p)|p \in P\} \cup \beta \cup \{W(t,p)|p \in t^\bullet\} - \{M'(p)|p \in P\},$$
$$\forall s \in \{W(t,p)|p \in t^\bullet\} \cap S \rightarrow \delta'_D(s) \in \{\mathbf{T}, \mathbf{F}\},$$
$$\forall d \in (\beta' \cup M'(p)) - \{W(t,p)|p \in t^\bullet\} \cap S \rightarrow \delta'_D(d) = \delta_D(d)\}$$

Definition 3.27 An EBPN $EN = (P, T; F, D, W, S, G)$ is terminable under an initial extended data state $\langle M_0, \alpha_0 \rangle$ if

(1) $\exists \Delta = \{\langle M', \alpha' \rangle | \langle M', \alpha' \rangle \in R\langle M_0, \alpha_0 \rangle, \forall t \in T \rightarrow \neg \langle M', \alpha' \rangle \xrightarrow{t}\}$; and
(2) $\forall \langle M, \alpha \langle \in R \rangle M_0, \alpha_0 \rangle$, there exists a transition sequence $\sigma = t_1, t_2, \ldots, t_k$ making that $\langle M, \alpha \rangle \xrightarrow{\sigma} \langle M', \alpha' \rangle$, $\langle M', \alpha' \rangle \in \Delta$.

Definition 3.28 An EBPN $EN = (P, T; F, D, W, S, G)$ is rational under an initial extended data state $\langle M_0, \alpha_0 \rangle$ if

(1) EN is data-bounded;
(2) EN is terminable; and
(3) $\forall t \in T$, there exists a data state $\langle M, \alpha \rangle \in R\langle M_0, \alpha_0 \rangle$ making that $\langle M, \alpha \rangle \xrightarrow{t}$.

When an EBPN is being constructed, its structural rational should be guaranteed. First, if an EBPN is rational, data-boundedness must be satisfied because it is used to ensure the consistency of the same variable. Second, an EBPN cannot run indefinitely. Instead, it must reach some terminated states representing that an e-commerce system has completed the transaction successfully or terminated the present transaction for some reason. In another word, it does not allow such a situation as a transaction being stuck in a loop without any exit. At last, every transition of EBPN must have one chance to be fired, i.e., an EBPN must not have dead transitions.

If the rationality is guaranteed, the next validation work is to guarantee the transaction properties of the EBPN. The main security goal of an e-commerce business process is to guarantee the following transaction conditions: (1) Merchant and TPP change the state of a transaction made by Shopper to "paid" if the fund has been transferred from the account of Shopper to that of Merchant in TPP; (2) If Shopper has paid, then TPP is at the state of "paid" and Merchant can ship the goods to Shopper; (3) The amount of this payment conforms to the price of goods and should not be tampered; and (4) The electronic fund cannot be lost or destructed while it is being transferred.

To facilitate the analysis of e-commerce business processes, we define transaction consistency as the secure property concerned in an EBPN.

Definition 3.29 If an EBPN $EN = (P, T; F, D, W, S, G)$ is rational under an initial extended data state $\langle M_0, \alpha_0 \rangle$, then EN satisfies the transaction consistency if every $\langle M, \alpha \rangle = \langle M, (\beta, \delta_D) \rangle \in \Delta$ satisfies the following conditions:

(1) If $\exists M(p_t)$, $M(p_m)$, $M(p_s)$ such that TTP is at the paid state, and the finished-transaction state of Merchant is reached, and the finished-order state of Shopper is reached, then there does not exist data element d such that $d \in \beta \cup \{M(p)|p \in P\} \cap S \rightarrow \delta_D(d) = \mathbf{F}$.
(2) $\exists M(p_t)$ such that TTP is at the paid state $\leftrightarrow \exists M(p_m)$ such that the finished-transaction state of Merchant is reached.
(3) $\exists M(p_t)$ such that TTP is not at the paid state $\leftrightarrow \exists M(p_m)$ such that the finished-transaction state of Merchant is not reached.

Condition 1 means that if there exists invalid data in an EBPN, it would not allow the transaction to reach the completed state. Condition 2 means that if Shopper has paid and TPP is at the paid state, then Merchant has to reach the state of a finished-transaction. On the other side, if Merchant cannot reach the state of a finished-transaction forever, then TPP cannot reach the paid state forever. Condition 3 means that if Shopper has not paid and TPP is not at the paid state, then Merchant cannot be at the shipping state of a to-be-finished transaction. The above conditions protect the interests of both parties and guarantee that both Shoppers and Merchants are in a fair state, i.e., there is no possibility of paying without receiving goods and vice versa. In other words, one party does not damage the interests of another.

To enrich the EBPN analysis theory, we propose a method of the Three-dimensional Incidence Matrix based on the structural features of EBPN. By this method, we determine whether a specific data state is reachable from the initial one [25].

Unlike original Petri nets, the weight function W assigns a k-dimensional vector to each arc in EBPN. Thus, we can define the incidence matrix as follows.

Definition 3.30 Let $EN = (P, T; F, D, W, S, G)$ be an EBPN, $P = \{p_1, p_2, \ldots, p_m\}$, $T = \{t_1, t_2, \ldots, t_n\}$, $D = \{d_1, d_2, \ldots, d_l\}$, m, n, $l \in \mathbb{N}^+ = \{1, 2, \ldots\}$; then the static structure of EN can be expressed by a three-dimensional incidence matrix $\Psi = [\psi_{ijk}]_{n \times m \times l}$, where $\psi_{ijk} = \psi_{ijk}^+ - \psi_{ijk}^-$

$$
\psi_{ijk}^+ = \begin{cases} W(t_i, p_j)_k, & \text{if } (t_i, p_j) \in F, i \in \{1, 2, \ldots, n\}, \\ \quad j \in \{1, 2, \ldots, m\}, k \in \{1, 2, \ldots, l\} \\ \text{an } l - \text{dimensional } \mathbf{0}\,\text{vector } \langle 0, 0, \ldots, 0 \rangle, & \text{otherwise} \end{cases}
$$

$$
\psi_{ijk}^- = \begin{cases} W(p_j, t_i)_k, & \text{if } (p_j, t_i) \in F, i \in \{1, 2, \ldots, n\}, \\ \quad j \in \{1, 2, \ldots, m\}, k \in \{1, 2, \ldots, l\} \\ \text{an } l - \text{dimensional } \mathbf{0}\,\text{vector } \langle 0, 0, \ldots, 0 \rangle, & \text{otherwise} \end{cases}
$$

The above two equations can also be expressed as

$$
\psi_{ij}^+ = \begin{cases} W(t_i, p_j), & \text{if } (t_i, p_j) \in F, i \in \{1, 2, \ldots, n\}, \\ \quad j \in \{1, 2, \ldots, m\} \\ \text{an } l - \text{dimensional } \mathbf{0}\,\text{vector } \langle 0, 0, \ldots, 0 \rangle, & \text{otherwise} \end{cases}
$$

$$
\psi_{ij}^- = \begin{cases} W(p_j, t_i), & \text{if } (p_j, t_i) \in F, i \in \{1, 2, \ldots, n\}, \\ \quad j \in \{1, 2, \ldots, m\} \\ \text{an } l - \text{dimensional } \mathbf{0}\,\text{vector } \langle 0, 0, \ldots, 0 \rangle, & \text{otherwise} \end{cases}
$$

$$
\psi_{ij} = \psi_{ij}^+ - \psi_{ij}^-
$$

In original Petri nets, the two-dimensional incident matrix is defined by the relations of places and transitions, i.e., the arcs. There are two dimensions, i.e., places and transitions. In EBPN, the three-dimensional matrix is defined by the relations of places, transitions, and W. Thus, it has three dimensions, i.e., places, transitions, and W. In Definition 3.30, $W(p_j, t_i)$ is an l-dimensional vector, and $W(p_j, t_i)_k$ is the k-th scalar in $W(p_j, t_i)$. ψ is a notation of the element in Ψ. ψ_{ijk}^+ and ψ_{ijk}^- are scalars. ψ_{ij}^+ and ψ_{ij}^- are l-dimensional vectors. If we see Ψ as a three-dimensional matrix, every element in it is a scalar ($\psi_{ijk} = \psi_{ijk}^+ - \psi_{ijk}^-$); If we see Ψ as a two-dimensional matrix, every element in it is an l-dimensional vector ($\psi_{ij} = \psi_{ij}^+ - \psi_{ij}^-$).

Then, $\Psi = \Psi^+ - \Psi^-$, where $\Psi^+ = [\psi_{ijk}^+]_{n \times m \times l}$, and $\Psi^- = [\psi_{ijk}^-]_{n \times m \times l}$. In the following, we use bold zero ($\mathbf{0}$) to represent the l-dimensional 0 vector. According to Definition 3.12 and 3.30, we have the following result.

Lemma 3.1 *Let $EN = (P, T; F, D, W, S, G)$ be an EBPN, (M_0, δ_{D0}) be the initial data state, Ψ be the three-dimensional incidence matrix of EN, and $(M, \delta_D) \in R(M_0, \delta_{D0})$. Transition $t_i \in T$ is enabled at M if $\forall p_j \in {}^\bullet t$ and $\forall k \in \mathbb{N}_l = \{1, 2, \ldots, l\} \rightarrow M(p_j)_k \geq \psi_{ijk}^-$, i.e., $M(p_j) \geq \psi_{ij}^-$.*

In Lemma 3.1, $M(p_j)_k$ means the k-th component of $M(p_j)$. In traditional two-dimensional matrix $\mathbf{A}$ in linear algebra, $\mathbf{A}_{i*}$ means i-th row, and $\mathbf{A}_{*j}$ means j-th column, $i, j \in \mathbb{N}^+$. Let $EN = (P, T; F, D, W, S, G)$ be an EBPN, $\Psi = [\psi_{ijk}]_{n \times m \times l}$ is a three-dimensional incidence matrix. Here, we see Ψ as a two-dimensional matrix, Ψ_{i*} means the i-th row of Ψ, and every element in the i-th row is an l-dimensional vector.

Definition 3.31 Let $EN = (P, T; F, D, W, S, G)$ be an EBPN, $\Psi = [\psi_{ijk}]_{n \times m \times l}$ is the three-dimensional incidence matrix. $\Sigma = \Psi^T$ is the transpose of Ψ, i.e., $\varepsilon_{ij} = \psi_{ji}$, where ε is an element in Σ.

Here, Ψ^T can be seen as the transpose of a two-dimensional matrix, and Ψ_{i*}^T can be seen as the transpose of a row-vector. The difference from the transpose of a traditional two-dimensional matrix is that every element in the three-dimensional matrix is an l-dimensional vector, which doesn't participate in the transpose.

Lemma 3.2 *Let $EN = (P, T; F, D, W, S, G)$ be an EBPN, (M_0, δ_{D0}) be the initial data state, $(M, \delta_D) \in R(M_0, \delta_{D0})$, and Ψ be the three-dimensional incidence matrix of EN. If $t_i \in T$, $M \xrightarrow{t_i} M'$, then $M' = M + (\Psi_{i*})^T$.*

If V is an n-dimensional non-negative integer vector, then

$$
\Psi^T V = \begin{bmatrix} \psi_{11}, \psi_{21}, \ldots, \psi_{n1} \\ \psi_{12}, \psi_{22}, \ldots, \psi_{n2} \\ \cdots\cdots\cdots\cdots\cdots\cdots \\ \cdots\cdots\cdots\cdots\cdots\cdots \\ \cdots\cdots\cdots\cdots\cdots\cdots \\ \psi_{1m}, \psi_{2m}, \ldots, \psi_{nm} \end{bmatrix} \times \begin{bmatrix} V[1] \\ V[2] \\ \cdot \\ \cdot \\ \cdot \\ V[n] \end{bmatrix}
$$

$$
= \begin{bmatrix} \psi_{11} \times V[1] + \psi_{21} \times V[2] + \cdots + \psi_{n1} \times V[n] \\ \psi_{12} \times V[1] + \psi_{22} \times V[2] + \cdots + \psi_{n2} \times V[n] \\ \cdots\cdots\cdots\cdots\cdots\cdots\cdots\cdots\cdots\cdots\cdots \\ \cdots\cdots\cdots\cdots\cdots\cdots\cdots\cdots\cdots\cdots\cdots \\ \cdots\cdots\cdots\cdots\cdots\cdots\cdots\cdots\cdots\cdots\cdots \\ \psi_{1m} \times V[1] + \psi_{2m} \times V[2] + \cdots + \psi_{nm} \times V[n] \end{bmatrix}
$$

In the above definition, ψ_{nm} is an l-dimensional vector, and $V[n]$ is a non-negative integer. $\psi_{nm} \times V[n]$ follows the vector multiplication. As every l-dimensional vector in Ψ can be seen as a separate element, they do not change after transposing Ψ.

Theorem 3.6 *Let $EN = (P, T; F, D, W, S, G)$ be an EBPN, (M_0, δ_{D0}) be the initial data state, and Ψ be the three-dimensional incidence matrix of EN. If $(M, \delta_D) \in R(M_0, \delta_{D0})$, then there exists an n-dimensional non-negative integer vector V, such that $M = M_0 + \Psi^T V$.*

Here, M_0 can be seen as an n-dimensional column vector in which an element is an l-dimensional non-negative integer vector.

Corollary 3.1 *Let* $EN = (P, T; F, D, W, S, G)$ *be an EBPN,* (M_0, δ_{D0}) *be the initial data state, and* Ψ *be the three-dimensional incidence matrix of EN. There exist* $(M_0, \delta_{D0}) \xrightarrow{\sigma} (M, \delta_D)$ *and a* n-*dimensional non-negative integer vector* V, *such that* $M = M_0 + \Psi^T V$. *Then* $\#(t_i, \sigma) = V[i]$, *where* $i \in \mathbb{N}_n = \{1, 2, \ldots, n\}$, $n = |T|$, *and* $\#(t_i, \sigma)$ *means the number of occurrences of* t_i *in* σ.

Theorem 3.6 is a necessary condition for judging the reachability of a specific data state in an EBPN. Then, we give the steps of determining the reachability of a data state (M, δ_D) in an EBPN $EN = (P, T; F, D, W, S, G)$ under the initial data state (M_0, δ_0).

Step 1: Construct Ψ;

Step 2: According to Theorem 3.1, compute whether the non-negative integer n-dimensional vector V exists;

Step 3: If not so, conclude that (M, δ_D) is not reachable in EN under the initial data state (M_0, δ_{D0}).

The existence of non-negative integer n-dimensional vector V is a necessary condition, not a necessary and sufficient condition. However, it is also useful in EBPN. Usually, in e-commerce business processes, we need to confirm that the wrong data state is not reachable. If V exists and the transition sequences σ such that $M_0 \xrightarrow{\sigma} M$ can be found, executing σ in EN, and the reachability of (M, δ_D) can be determined.

3.6   Chapter Summary

Many incidents of existing e-commerce systems are caused by data errors and state inconsistency. Since e-commerce sites require the unity of data flow, control flow, and fund flow, the model must be able to reflect them and help one verify the transaction properties. In addition to potential system crashes and accompanying message failures, one has to deal with the security flaws of an e-commerce business process. As a distributed application on the web, e-commerce business processes are complex and loosely coupled. The integration introduces new security challenges due to the complexity of an application in coordinating its internal states with those of the component services and web clients across the Internet. The complex linkage of control and data flows in e-commerce systems may produce very serious problems, e.g., the violation of the transaction properties and losses of user funds.

Thus, we need means for proving the expected transaction guarantee of e-commerce systems and studying the protection mechanisms against potential flaws in business processes at the design phase and application levels. In this chapter, in view of the properties of existing online transaction business processes, LaPN and EBPN have been proposed, with structural and dynamic properties specified and corresponding analysis methods given.

References

[1] iResearch. Research Report on Chinese E-Commerce Software Industry, (2015).

[2] Alipay. Communication with Ali Finance — Alipay Structure and Technology, (2010).

[3] Adam, N. R., Atluri, V., and Huang, W. K. Modeling and Analysis of Workflows Using Petri Nets. *Journal of Intelligent Information Systems*, 10(2): 131–158 (1998).

[4] Shi, M. L., Xiang, Y., Yang, G. X. *et al. Collaborative Work Theory and Application of Computer Support*, Beijing: Electronic Industry Press, (2000).

[5] WFMC. Workflow Management Coalition Terminology and Glossary (WFMC-TC-1011). Technical Report. Workflow Management Coalition, Brussels, (1996).

[6] Van der Aalst, W. M. P. The Application of Petri Nets to Workflow Management. *The Journal of Circuits, Systems and Computers*, 8(1): 21–66 (1998).

[7] Van der Aalst, W. M. P., Lohmann, N., and La Rosa, M. Ensuring Correctness during Process Configuration via Partner Synthesis. *Information Systems*, 37(6): 574–592 (2012).

[8] Yuan, C. Y. *Petri Net Principle and Application*, Beijing: Electronic Industry Press, (2005).

[9] Wu, Z. H. *Petri Net Introduction*, Beijing: Machinery Industry Press, (2006).

[10] Jiang, C. J. *Theory of PN Machine for Discrete Event Dynamic System*, Beijing: Beijing Science Press, (2000).

[11] Jiang, C. J. *Behavior Theory of Petri Nets and Its Application*, Beijing: Higher Education Press, (2003).

[12] Jiang, C. J. A Polynomial Time Algorithm for the Determination of Transition Sequence for a Class of Synchronous Synthetic Petri Net, *Science China*, 32(1): 116–124 (2002).

[13] Zhao, W., Yuan, C. Y., Liu, G. *et al.* Workflow Process Model Verification Based on P/T Systematic Approach. *Chinese Journal of Software*, 15(10): 1423–1430 (2004).

[14] Tan, W. and Zhou, M. C. *Business and Scientific Workflows: A Service-Oriented Approach*, Hoboken, NJ, USA: IEEE Press/Wiley, (2013).

[15] Tan, W., Fan, Y., and Zhou, M. C. A Petri Net-Based Method for Compatibility Analysis and Composition of Web Services in Business Process Execution Language. *IEEE Transactions on Automation Science and Engineering*, 6(1): 94–106 (2009).

[16] Xiong, P. C., Fan, Y., and Zhou, M. C. A Petri Net Approach to Analysis and Composition of Web Services. IEEE Transactions on Systems, Man, and Cybernetics Part A, 40(2): 376–387 (2010).

[17] Zeng, Q. T., Lu, F. M., Liu, C. *et al.* Modeling and Verification for Cross-Department Collaborative Business Processes Using Extended Petri Nets. *IEEE Transactions on Systems, Man, and Cybernetics: Systems*, 45(2): 349–362 (2015).

[18] Du, Y. Y. and Jiang, C. J. Verifying Functions in Online Stock Trading Systems. *Journal of Computer Science Technology*, 19(2): 203–212 (2004).

[19] Du, Y. Y., Jiang, C. J., and Zhou, M. C. A Petri Net-Based Model for Verification of Obligations and Accountability in Cooperative Systems. *IEEE Transactions on Systems, Man, and Cybernetics Part A: Systems and Humans*, 39(2): 299–308 (2009).

[20] Du, Y. Y., Jiang, C. J., Zhou, M. C. *et al.* Modeling and Monitoring of E-Commerce Workflows. *Information Sciences*, 179(7): 995–1006 (2009).

[21] Du, Y. Y., Jiang, C. J., and Zhou, M. C. A Petri Net Based Correctness Analysis of Internet Stock Trading Systems. *IEEE Transactions on Systems, Man, and Cybernetics Part C*, 38(1): 93–99 (2008).

[22] Du, Y. Y., Jiang, C. J., and Zhou, M. C. Modeling and Analysis of Real-Time Cooperative Systems Using Petri Nets. *IEEE Transactions on Systems, Man, and Cybernetics Part A*, 37(5): 643–654 (2007).

[23] Yu, W. Y., Yan, C. G., Ding, Z. J. *et al.* Modeling and Validating E-commerce Business Process Based on Petri Nets. *IEEE Transactions on Systems, Man, and Cybernetics: Systems*, 44(3): 327–341 (2014).

[24] Yu, W. Y., Yan, C. G., Ding, Z. J. *et al.* Modeling and Verification of Online Shopping Business Processes by Considering Malicious Behavior Patterns. *IEEE Transactions on Automation Science and Engineering*, 13(2): 647–662 (2016).

[25] Yu, W. Y., Yan, C. G., Ding, Z. J. *et al.* Analyzing E-commerce Business Process Nets via Incidence Matrix and Reduction. *IEEE Transactions on Systems, Man, and Cybernetics: Systems*, 48(1): 130–141 (2018).

[26] Du, Y. Y. *Research on Petri Net Modeling Theory and Analysis Technology of E-Commerce System*, Tongji University, (2003).

[27] Wang, R., Chen, S., Wang, X. F. *et al.* How to Shop for Free Online–Security Analysis of Cashier-as-a-Service Based Web Stores. In *32th IEEE Symposium on Security and Privacy (S&P)*, Oakland, USA, pp. 465–480 (2011).

[28] Chen, E., Chen, S., Qadeer, S. *et al.* Securing Multiparty Online Services via Certification of Symbolic Transactions. In *36th IEEE Symposium on Security and Privacy (S&P)*, San Jose, USA, pp. 833–849 (2015).

[29] Chen, E., Chen, S., Qadeer, S. *et al.* A Practical Approach to Protocol-Agnostic Security for Multiparty Online Services. Technical Report(MSR-TR-2014-72), Microsoft Research, Redmond, WA, USA, (2014).

[30] Sun, F. Q., Xu, L., and Su, Z. D. Detecting Logic Vulnerabilities in E-Commerce Applications. In *21st Network and Distributed System Security Symposium (NDSS)*, San Diego, USA, pp. 1–16 (2014).

[31] Katsaros, P., Odontidis, V., and Gousidou-Koutita, M. Colored Petri Net Based Model Checking and Failure Analysis for E-Commerce Protocols. In *Proceedings of the 6th Workshop and Tutorial on Practical Use of Coloured Petri Nets and the CPN Tools*, pp. 267–283, (2005).

[32] Jensen, K. and Kristensen, L. M. *Coloured Petri Nets: Modeling and Validation of Concurrent Systems*, New York, NY, USA: Springer-Verlag, (2009).

[33] Jensen, K. Coloured Petri Nets-Basic Concepts, Analysis Methods and Practical Use. In *EATCS Monographs on Theoretical Computer Science*, Springer, Vol. 1–3, (1997).

[34] Accorsi, R., Lehmann, A., and Lohmann, N. Information Leak Detection in Business Process Models: Theory, Application, and Tool Support. *Information Systems*, 47: 244–257 (2015).

[35] Ben, O. L., Angin, P., Weffers, H. *et al.* Extending the Agile Development Process to Develop Acceptably Secure Software. *IEEE Transactions on Dependable and Secure Computing*, 11(6): 497–509 (2014).

[36] Li, X. and Xue, Y. A Survey on Server-Side Approaches to Securing Web Applications. *ACM Computing Surveys (CSUR)*, 46(4): Article No. 54(1–29) (2014).

[37] Hoglund, G. and McGraw, G. *Exploiting Software: How to Break Code*, Addison-Wesley Professional, (2004).

[38] Katsaros, P. A Roadmap to Electronic Payment Transaction Guarantees and a Colored Petri Net Model Checking Approach. *Information and Software Technology*, 51(2): 235–257 (2009).

[39] Tycksen, Jr. F. A. and Jennings, C. W. Digital Certificate: U.S. Patent 6,189,097. 2001-2-13.

[40] Barikisu, A. Implementation of Cryptographic Algorithm (A Case Study of 4-rows Rail Fence Cipher). Unpublished B.Sc. Project Under the Supervision of Abikoye OC (Mrs), (2005).

[41] Reeds, III J. A. Method and Apparatus for Autokey Rotor Encryption: U.S. Patent 5,724,427. 199-8-3-3.

[42] Merkle, R. C. *A Certified Digital Signature//Conference on the Theory and Application of Cryptology*, New York: Springer, pp. 218–238 (1989).

[43] Hoon, W. L., Kerschbaum, F., and Wang, H. X. Workflow Signatures for Business Process Compliance. *IEEE Transactions on Dependable and Secure Computing*, 9(5): 756–769 (2012).

Chapter 4

Risk Prevention and Control
of Software Systems

4.1 Introduction

In the recent past, the world has witnessed the emergence of online transactions and payment platforms, albeit with the security system of online transactions still not being perfect. The risk and credibility of behaviors in the online transaction process have also become increasingly prominent. They have gradually become the bottleneck in the development of online transactions. There are currently two main ideas on how to build a trustworthy transaction component system. The first is to consider the credible indicators of the software, analyze the various credibility attributes of the software, propose a comprehensive evaluation index, and then analyze the combined software system to determine whether it is credible. The second is to consider identity credibility. It is mainly through access control and identity trust management, to ensure the credibility of the software system, such as digital certificate technology. In any regard, it is based on the risk prevention and control of the online transaction software systems. Nowadays, the widely used and studied software risk prevention and control technologies in the industry and academia mainly include software testing technology, quantitative evaluation technology, formal methods, and system behavior certificate methods independently developed by our research group. This chapter will provide an overview of these techniques and methods.

4.2   Software Testing

Computer software is the core of computer science and application. Quality control is related to the success of computer application systems. Software test technology is an important part of the software development process. It is an activation process that verifies and confirms software products throughout the software development life cycle. The purpose of software testing is to ensure the final quality of software products and achieve the quality control of software products. Generally speaking, software testing should be carried out by an independent product evaluation center that strictly follows the software testing process, makes testing plans, testing programs, and testing specifications, implements testing, analyzes testing records, and writes testing reports based on conditions. The testing is to prove that the programs are wrong, but there is no guarantee that the programs have no errors [1–5].

Software testing is accompanied by the generation of software. In the early software development process, the software scale was small and the complexity was low. The software development process was chaotic and random, and the meaning of the testing was relatively narrow. Developers equate software testing with "debugging" to correct faults already known in the software, often introduced by developers themselves. In the early 1980s, the software and IT industry entered a great development phase, software became larger and more complex, and the quality of software became more and more important. At that time, some basic theories and practical techniques of software testing began to be formed. Designers began to design various processes and management methods for software development. The way of developing software gradually shifted from a chaotic development process to a structured development process, which was characterized by structured analysis and design, structured programming, and structured tests [2–6].

In principle, software testing methods can be divided into two categories: static testing and dynamic testing. Static testing is a general term for the method of characterizing the software under testing. The main feature is that the software to be tested is not run by the computer, but the manual and static analysis performed on the documents and source programs. For example, the requirement description and the design file to ensure the software quality.

Dynamic testing is the test that runs the software on the computer. It judges whether the software being tested is correct, reliable, and effective by selecting the appropriate test case and determining whether the execution result meets the requirements. These two main methods of dynamic testing are white-box testing and black-box testing. White-box testing is a detailed examination of the internal working process of the software. It allows testers to design or select test cases and test all logical paths of the program by using the internal logic structure and related information. Black-box testing focuses on the external structure of the software, regardless of the logical structure and internal characteristics of the program. It checks whether the function of the program meets the requirements of the software interface. Therefore, black-box testing is also called function testing or data drive testing. White-box testing and black-box testing cannot replace each other and should complement each other, and be flexible in the different stages of software testing to find errors of different types.

The software testing process is generally carried out in four steps: unit testing, assembly testing, validation testing, and system testing. First, unit testing focuses on testing each program unit implemented with source code and checking that each program module correctly implements the specified functions. Second, assembly or integration testing assembles tested modules primarily to test the construction of the software architecture associated with the design. Third, validation testing is to check that the implemented software meets the various requirements identified in the requirements specification and whether the software configuration is complete and correct. Last, system testing incorporates the confirmed software into the actual operating environment and combines it with other system components for testing [2–4]. Figure 4.1 shows a testing model.

The emergence of object-oriented software design ideas has had a major impact on software testing techniques, especially on dynamic testing. The object-oriented technology introduces the concept of a class based on process-oriented programming, therefore data and processing are relatively independent. Different from the control flow of "top to bottom", "branch" and "loop" in traditional programs, the classes deal with a kind of "outside to inside" penetration order when defining and citing data. There has also been a "flow from inside to outside" level, resulting in new control flows

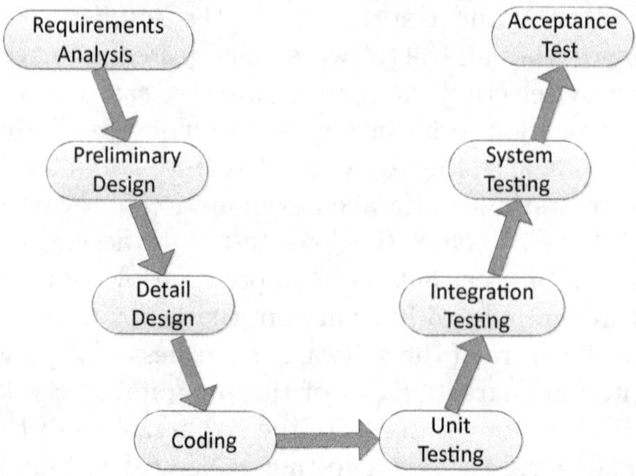

Figure 4.1   Software testing V model.

and data flows, and correspondingly, software testing has to add new content.

The software model is an abstract description of the software structure and software behavior. Based on the full understanding of the tested software, a software model that can be used for testing is constructed according to the requirements of the software under testing to confirm that "the program correctly fulfills its requirements". The model-based test applies to test phases, such as unit testing, integration testing, and system testing. Model-based testing can discover features that are not implemented by the program and is specifically programming language-independent, therefore model-based test also provides the possibility to reuse testing cases.

As a new technology, software reuse has been receiving attention in the industry and from researchers in recent years [7–9]. Software reuse refers to the technology that uses the original software knowledge, results, and experience to develop new software. The object of software reuse refers to all labor outcomes in the production process of software products, including project plan, feasibility report, system requirements analysis, software design, testing, and other related documents. Test reuse is to reuse all valuable resources accumulated in the previous test process, such as test ideas, test theory, test techniques, test tools, test plans, test procedures, test specifications, test cases, test strategies, test reports, and so on.

Due to the complexity of the original problems, every aspect of development processes can cause errors. For example, the complex and abstracted software, the diversified work in all stages of software development, and the coordination of work among people at all levels. In that regard, software testing is not only an independent stage of software development, but a process that should be carried out in various stages of software development, and adhere to the technical review of each stage, to detect and prevent errors as early as possible.

4.3　Software System Assessment

With the rapid development of network technology, the security of software systems is also threatened in many aspects. In recent years, people have paid more attention to the risk prevention and control of online transaction systems, such as e-commerce, e-banking, and electronic voting systems. These application services consist of network devices and computer hosts. It is very important to protect these application services and network devices. To prevent malicious attacks, some commercial hardware and software have been designed, such as firewalls, intrusion detection systems, virus protection software, and vulnerability scanning software. These protections can help reduce security risks. However, before any protection measures are implemented, software developers should first understand clearly the security risks in their systems. A cybersecurity risk assessment helps accomplish this goal. Its main activities include identifying and classifying computer security risks and selecting appropriate strategies to reduce the impact of risk.

The online transaction systems are on a dynamic and open Internet. Due to the openness of the network, the fragility of the systems, and the intentional or unintentional improper operation of the user, online transaction systems are facing many risks. Based on cost and benefit, the risks need to be reduced to an acceptable level, thus ensuring the security of the system is improved. To achieve this goal, it is necessary to know the risks, distribution, and intensity of the system, and to identify the security risks of the information system according to the probability of occurrence of security events and the degree of negative impacts. It is the basic content of software system risk assessment. Risk assessment is an important technology in network security defense and an important part of information security engineering. The security of a software system, to some extent, is always related to security risk assessment.

Security risk assessment refers to the process of scientifically evaluating the security attributes such as the confidentiality, integrity, and availability of information systems and the information they process, and transmitting and storing following relevant information security technology standards. It assesses the vulnerability of information systems, the threats that information systems face, and the actual negative impacts while being exploited. The important result of risk assessment is to determine the security level of the computer information system of the organization, to identify key prevention sites such as security and confidentiality, to prevent the impact of possible threats, to identify and detect whether there are security incidents, and to propose the security protection management strategy. The overall plan provides a set of standardized design guidelines for the design of security precautions including contingency planning, so that the impacted computer information system can be restored to a normal state in a timely and effective manner. The ultimate goal of risk assessment is to ensure the integrity, confidentiality, availability, and controlability of computer information systems, to determine the risks and strengths of information systems, to select security measures, and reduce the risks to an acceptable level.

At present, the research of information security assessment is mainly the research on the theory and method of information security assessment, which mainly includes the two aspects of "standards" and "methods". Strictly speaking, these two have different connotations. The "standard" points out the objectives of the safety assessment, while the "method" clarifies how to achieve the various objectives of the safety assessment, which are interrelated and independent [10–14].

4.3.1 *Security risk assessment criteria*

In 1983, the US Department of Defense first released *the Trusted Computer System Evaluation Criteria* (TCSEC), which was mainly used to evaluate the operating systems, and was the first security evaluation standard in IT history [15]. The *Information Technology*

Security Evaluation Criteria (ITSEC) is a set of guidelines that was released in 1990. It is a unified security assessment standard developed by European countries, such as the United Kingdom, France, Germany, and the Netherlands. Its goal is to become the benchmark for the certification activities conducted by national certification bodies. And it can make the evaluation results mutually recognized [16]. In 1992, the *Canadian Trusted Computer Product Evaluation Criteria* (CTCPEC) was published [17]. BS7799 was first published by the British Standards Association in 1995 and is now an internationally recognized authority for safety management [18]. The first part of BS7799 has been accepted as an international standard in 2000. Japan Electronics Industry Development Association published *Japan Computer Security Assessment Guidelines — Functional Requirements* (JCSEC-FR) in 1992, [19]. The *Common Criteria for Information Technology Security Evaluation* (also called Common Criteria or CC) is a joint development between North America and the European Union. It is a unified international mutually recognized security standard becoming the international security assessment guidelines [20].

Chinese security assessment standards began to be established in the last decade. The current work is mainly focused on the establishment of organizational frameworks and business systems. The corresponding technical systems and standards systems are still in the research stage. The following standards have been published. In September 1999, the State Bureau of Quality and Technical Supervision issued the mandatory national security standard *Computer Information System Security Protection Level Division Rules* GB17859-1999, which is the basic standard for establishing a security level protection system and implementing security level management [21]. On March 8, 2001, the State Bureau of Quality and Technical Supervision officially announced the use of the CC standard GB/T18336-2001 *Information Technology, Security Technology, Information Technology Security Assessment Guidelines* [22].

4.3.2 *Information security risk assessment methods*

In general, the choice of security assessment methods is closely related to the size of the enterprise, the complexity of the information system, and the required level of security. Most scholars generally classify security assessment methods into four categories: quantitative assessment methods, qualitative assessment methods, comprehensive assessment methods, and model-based assessment methods.

The quantitative assessment method is to use quantitative indicators to assess risk. Typical quantitative analysis methods include factor analysis, cluster analysis, time series model, regression model, risk map method, and decision tree method. The advantage of a quantitative assessment method is that it uses intuitive data to express the results of the assessment, which is clear and objective.

The qualitative assessment method is based on the researcher's knowledge, experience, historical lessons, policy trends, and other non-quantitative data to judge the system risk status. It is mainly based on the case records of in-depth interviews with the respondents, then through a theoretical push of the analysis framework of the director, the data are compiled and collated, and the conclusions are made on this basis. Typical qualitative analysis methods are factor analysis, logic analysis, historical comparison, and Delphi [23].

Model-based security assessment techniques are also an effective method for assessing the entire computer network system. The prototype of the dynamic security model is the P2DR model. Under the control and guidance of the overall security policy, the P2DR model uses detection tools such as vulnerability assessment and intrusion detection while comprehensively using protection tools such as firewalls, operating system identity authentication, and encryption. It waits to understand and assess the security status of the system and adjust the system to the securest and least risky state with an appropriate response. From the perspective of the implementation and dynamics of the security system, the APPDDR model is designed with full consideration, such as risk assessment, security policy development, defense system, monitoring and detection, response, and recovery. And it considers the dynamic relationship and dependencies between various parts [24, 25].

Endless security vulnerabilities, automatically propagated network viruses, and attacking programs that can be downloaded anywhere on the network, especially distributed and collaborative attacks, pose a huge threat to network security. The traditional concept of static network security can no longer meet the needs of modern network security. It lacks sufficient description and countermeasures for dynamic security threats and system vulnerability. It cannot fully reflect distributed and dynamically changing Internet security issues. Therefore, the dynamic network security model came into being. The dynamic network security model emphasizes dynamic defense. The defense capability of the system is incremental with time and can be automatically adjusted according to the existing security conditions [10].

4.4 Formal Methods

In the field of computer science and software engineering, formal methods are mathematical model-based analysis techniques, suitable for the description, development, and verification of software–hardware systems, including the establishment of accurate mathematical models and analysis of models. Formal methods can find inconsistencies, ambiguities, or incompleteness of system specifications that are not easily discoverable by other methods, and help increase software developers' understanding of the system. Therefore, formal methods are an important means to improve the security of software systems, especially safety-critical systems. The development of formal methods is gradually integrated into all phases of the software development process, from requirements analysis, functional description, system design, programming, testing to maintenance [26, 27].

With the increasing number of online transaction users and the changing of online transaction service types, online transaction systems are becoming larger and more complex, which makes the design and analysis of online transaction systems more difficult. In general, the requirements specification of the online transaction system is described informally, and this description is ambiguous. However, applying the formal method to simulate and verify the online transaction system can provide the system designer a system architecture which is both clear and easy to understand and monitor, helping the designers find loopholes or defects in the system design, and verify the system's dynamic behavioral properties such as activity, safety, fairness, and correctness. Therefore, formal technology plays an important role in the design and analysis of online transaction systems. At present, the formal description and analysis methods for e-commerce systems can be divided into four categories: general formal methods, logic-based methods, Petri net-based methods, and workflow-based methods. However, there is no strict standard for the classification of formal methods. In fact, many formal methods do not use a single formalization technique, but a combination of two or more technologies.

At present, the general methods for formal description and verification of online transaction systems mainly include methods based on automata and formal language; methods based on custom information system description languages; methods based on graphical analysis tools, and process-based calculus and language Encryption protocol analysis method. Also, the formal analysis method of the encryption protocol focuses on analyzing the security nature of the system, such as the identification of the identity between the participants, random numbers, encryption, and decryption of information.

In the formal analysis of online transaction systems, common logical model checking methods are the methods based on modal logic, the methods based on computation tree logic (CTL), the methods based on Deontic Logic, the methods based on sequential logic, the methods based on Temporal Belief Logic, and so on. At present, there are many methods for applying the Petri network to online transaction systems from simulation and analysis. It mainly includes the methods based on time Petri net, the methods based on temporal Petri net, the methods based on document Petri net, general Petri net analysis methods, and advanced Petri net analysis methods. Besides, there are some cryptographic protocol analysis methods based on Petri nets and high-level Petri nets [28, 29].

The main problem in the design of the online transaction system is how to integrate the transaction process distributed among the participants as a whole, as well as to make it a public application system and use the network to realize communication along with processes. Workflow management is one of the main technologies that can accomplish the design of an e-commerce system. Workflow technology provides computer-supported simulation, execution, monitoring, and system reconfiguration for e-commerce system transaction processes. These computer-implemented processes can be viewed as workflows [30]. Therefore, workflow technology can be used to simulate and analyze the main parts of an e-commerce system. At present, many scholars are committed to the simulation verification of workflow management systems. Since the Petri net is suitable for describing the asynchronous and concurrent nature of systems and is a perfect tool for simulation and analysis processes, the Petri net has many advantages as an analytical tool for workflow management systems. On the one hand, Petri net can be used as a design language for complex workflow specifications; on the other hand, Petri net theory provides a powerful analytical technique for analyzing the correctness of workflow processes. Therefore, in the formal method of a workflow system, most developers use Petri net as the basic model tool [31–33].

4.4.1 *Vulnerability analysis of e-commerce systems*

Vulnerability analysis has a great impact on the trustworthiness of e-commerce systems, which is an issue stemming from data inconsistency problems. Data inconsistency problems affect the consistency of the EBPN transaction analysis. The underlying causes of inconsistent data are closely related to concurrent operations, such as control flow and data flow. In this section, a method based on the Dynamic Data Slice (DDS) that considers both transaction consistency and data state consistency is illustrated. The framework is shown in Figure 4.2.

First, by analyzing the control flow characteristics of EBPN, we obtain the dynamic slice. This dynamic slice is based on all paths of the EBPN reachability graph. Second, we construct a DDS to characterize behavioral logic and data dependence information. The DDS acquires the dynamic data firing sequence. Based on that sequence and a given data marking, we can construct the DDSs for several types of EBPNs. This method satisfies the EBPN need for transaction consistency by considering both the control and data states. Also, we can lock the vulnerable regions caused by abnormal trading. In the context of Petri nets, computing a net slice can be considered a graph reachability problem. Related concepts of slicing criteria and slices can be found in [34–36], and the following contents are from [36].

Definition 4.1 (*DDS*): Let $N = (P, T, F)$ be a Petri net and (M_0, Q) be a slicing criterion for N where $\sigma = t_1, t_2, \ldots, t_n$. Then, we compute a DDS N' of N with respect to (M_0, σ, Q) as follows.

(1) We have $N' = (P', T', F')$ where $M_0 \xrightarrow{t_1} M_1 \xrightarrow{t_2} \ldots \xrightarrow{t_n} M_n$, $P' \cup T' = \text{slice}(M_n, \alpha, Q)$, $P' \subseteq P, T' \subseteq T$, and $F' = F|_{(P', T')}$.

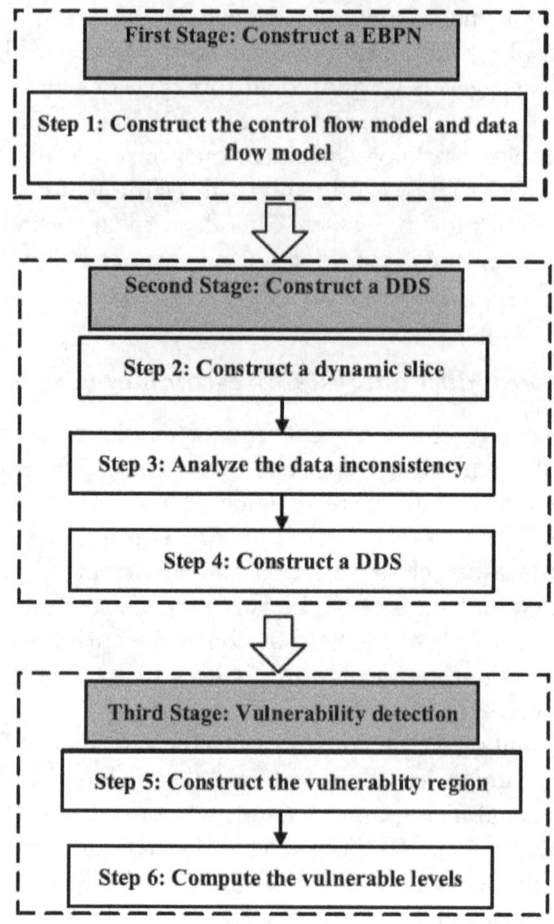

Figure 4.2   Framework of the proposed methods [36].

An auxiliary function slice is defined as follows:

$$
S_W = \begin{cases} W, & \text{if } i = 0 \\ \text{slice}(M_{i-1}, \alpha, W), & \text{if } M_{i-1}(p) \geq M_i(p) \\ \{t_i\} \cup \text{slice}(M_{i-1}, \alpha, W \cup {}^\bullet t_i, & \text{otherwise.} \end{cases}
$$

(2) The initial marking M_0' is the restriction of M_0 over P', i.e., $M_0' = M_0|_{P'}$.

(3) DDS is defined as follows:

$$\text{DDS} = \begin{cases} S_W, & \text{if } g_i = g_j \\ S_W \cup \text{slice}(M_i, \alpha, S_W), & \text{if } g_i \neq g_j \wedge g_i, g_j \notin S_W \\ S_W \cap \text{slice}(M_i, \alpha, S_W), & \text{otherwise.} \end{cases}$$

The difference between the slice and DDS is that DDS considers the data information. The slice does not consider the data information. Then, in this section, we propose an algorithm to construct a DDS and explain the methods to validate the EBPN [36]. Based on DDSs, we can then address the vulnerability detection problem. To better describe abnormal trading that tampers with or replaces behaviors in the electronic transaction process, we propose the concept of a vulnerable point based on the EBPN. Based on DDSs, we can then address the vulnerability detection problem. An attack is a sequence of actions $a_1 a_2 \ldots a_n \in T$ such that there exists an elementary path from some initial state induced by $a_1 \ldots a_n$ that reaches the set G. Let Attack (T) be the set of attacks in T. Attack (T) is finite. G represents the final states the attackers hope to achieve. To better describe abnormal trading that tampers with or replaces behaviors in the electronic transaction process, we propose the concept of a vulnerable point based on the EBPN.

Let EBPN $= (P, T, F, D, W, S, G)$ be an e-commerce transaction net. A *malicious place* p_Y is a place associated with malicious transitions, where p_Y in P.

For a reachability graph, more than one path to the malicious state may be possible, and the same points existing in different paths may not have the same vulnerabilities. From a computational viewpoint, we provide some related concepts. For the actual application needs, we give the following three types of vulnerable points sets.

Let EBPN $= (P, T, F, D, W, S, G)$ be an e-commerce transaction net where $\sigma_i = t_{i1} t_{i2} \ldots t_{im}$. Besides, for a state p_q, the *type-1 vulnerable points* set FVP satisfies the following conditions:

(1) FVP $\subseteq P$
(2) $\sigma_1 \cap \sigma_2 \cap \ldots \sigma n \neq \emptyset$
(3) FVP $= \{pi \in {}^\bullet t_i | t_i \in (\sigma_1 \cap \sigma_2 \cap \ldots \sigma_n)\}$

The path that leads to the type-1 vulnerable points set is the public path. Also, these points in FVP$\setminus\{M_0\}$ are considered to be a *minimal vulnerable region* as follows.

Let EBPN $= (P, T, F, D, W, S, G)$ be an e-commerce transaction net with $\sigma_i = t_{i1}t_{i2}\ldots t_{im}$. And for a state p_q, the *minimal vulnerable region M_i VR* satisfies the following conditions:

(1) $Mi\text{VR} \subseteq \text{FVP}$
(2) $M_0 \notin Mi\text{VR}$

Let EBPN $= (P, T, F, D, W, S, G)$ be an e-commerce transaction net where $\sigma_i = t_{i1}t_{i2}\ldots t_{im}$. For a state p_q, the *type-2 vulnerable points* set SVP satisfies the following conditions:

(1) $\text{SVP} \subseteq P$
(2) $\sigma_1 \cup \sigma_2 \cup \ldots \sigma_n \neq \emptyset$
(3) $\text{SVP} = \{p_i \in {}^{\bullet}t_i | t_i \in (\sigma_1 \cup \sigma_2 \cup \ldots \sigma_n)\}$

The path that leads to the type-2 vulnerable points set is the only path leading to a malicious state. Besides, these points in SVP $\setminus \{M_0\}$ are considered to be a dimly vulnerable region (DVR) as follows.

Let EBPN $= (P, T, F, D, W, S, G)$ be an e-commerce transaction net where $\sigma_i = t_{i1}t_{i2}\ldots t_{im}$. For a state p_q, the DVR also satisfies the following conditions:

(1) $\text{DVR} \subseteq \text{SVP}$
(2) $M_0 \in \text{DVR}$

Let EBPN $= (P, T, F, D, W, S, G)$ be an e-commerce transaction net where $\sigma_i = t_{i1}t_{i2}\ldots t_{im}$. For a state p_q, the *type-3 vulnerable points* set TVP also satisfies the following conditions:

(1) $\text{TVP} \subseteq P$
(2) No state can be reached by firing sequence σ except for state p_q
(3) $\text{TVP} = \{p_i \in {}^{\bullet}t_i | t_i \in \sigma\}$

The path that leads to the type-3 vulnerable points set consists of all the paths leading to the malicious state. In TVP $\setminus \{M_0\}$, these points are considered to be a maximally vulnerable region (MaVR) as follows.

Let EBPN $= (P, T, F, D, W, S, G)$ be an e-commerce transaction net where $\sigma_i = t_{i1}t_{i2}\ldots t_{im}$. For a state p_q, the $(M_\alpha\text{VR})$ satisfies the following conditions:

(1) $M\alpha\text{VR} \subseteq \text{TVP}$
(2) $M_0 \notin M\alpha\text{VR}$

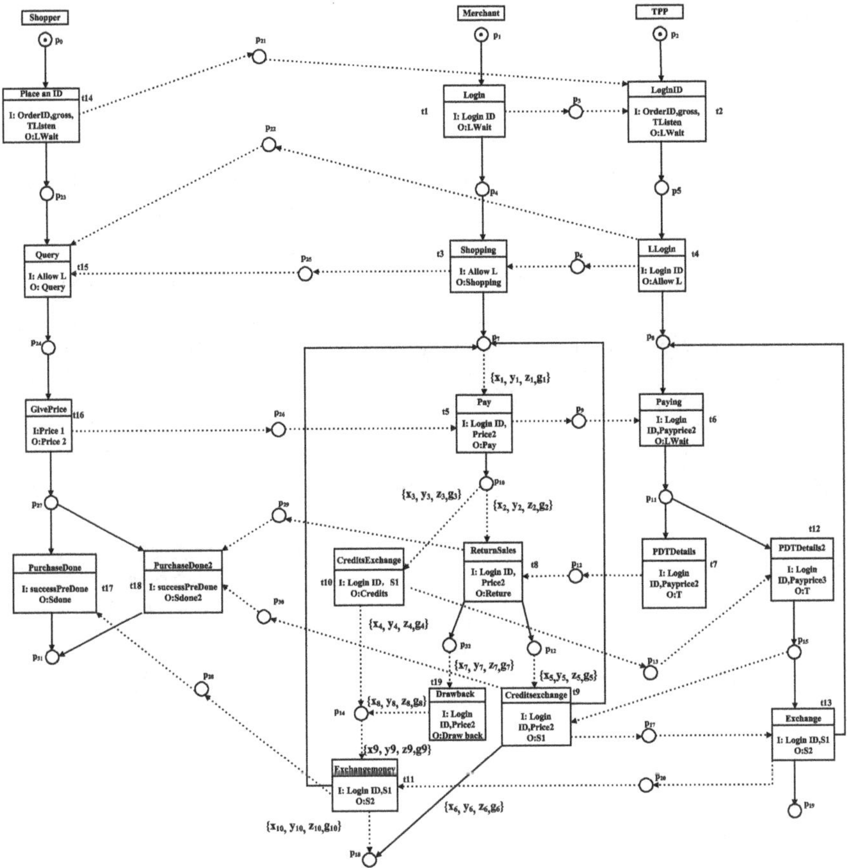

Figure 4.3   The credit-exchange process model [36].

Based on DDS, we can see that an EBPN vulnerability analysis can be translated into the computation of a DDS. According to the three vulnerable points set, we can see that the vulnerable levels are similar to the DDS. Therefore, we can learn from computing DDS. Figure 4.3 shows this simple credit-exchange process model. We trade trace behavior information to fire the transaction sequences. According to the transaction process, we construct the control flow model, which is also based on the data information in x, y, z, g. We present the data relation of Figure 4.3 as follows. Let x be original money, y be credits, and s be the price of each commodity.

Then, it holds that

$$z = f(x, y) = x + \frac{y}{n} \tag{4.1}$$

$$g = g(z, s) = z + \omega s \tag{4.2}$$

where n credits can be exchanged for one yuan, and ω is the weight. The data elements x, y, z, g, and the data relation functions (4.1) and (4.2) show the data information and data-change propagation process. Then, we can obtain all the paths π_i shown in Figure 4.4. There are four sequences ($\sigma_1 = t_1 t_2 t_4 t_7$, $\sigma_2 = t_1 t_2 t_3 t_6 t_5 t_7$, $\sigma_3 = t_1 t_2 t_3 t_5 t_6 t_7$, and $\sigma_4 = t_1 t_2 t_3 t_5 t_7 t_6$) to p_6. In addition, according to $z = f(x, y) = x + (y/100)$, the DDS of Figure 4.3 is shown in Figure 4.4. In Figure 4.4, we can see that the same state shown in the different colors means that the corresponding data functions are not equal (i.e., the same state allows different data to pass). This

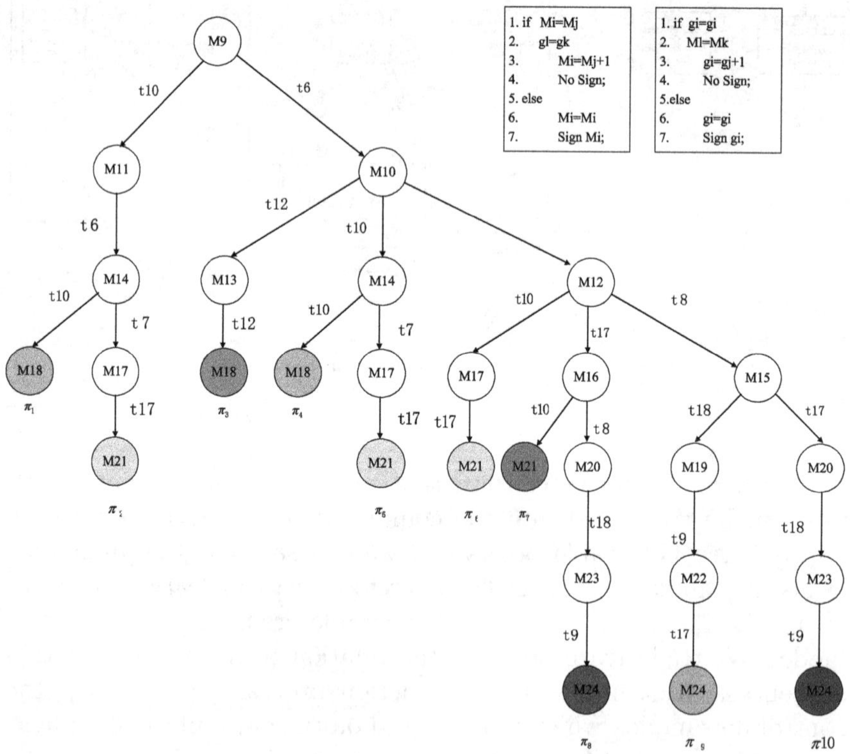

Figure 4.4   DDS of Figure 4.4 based on all paths [36].

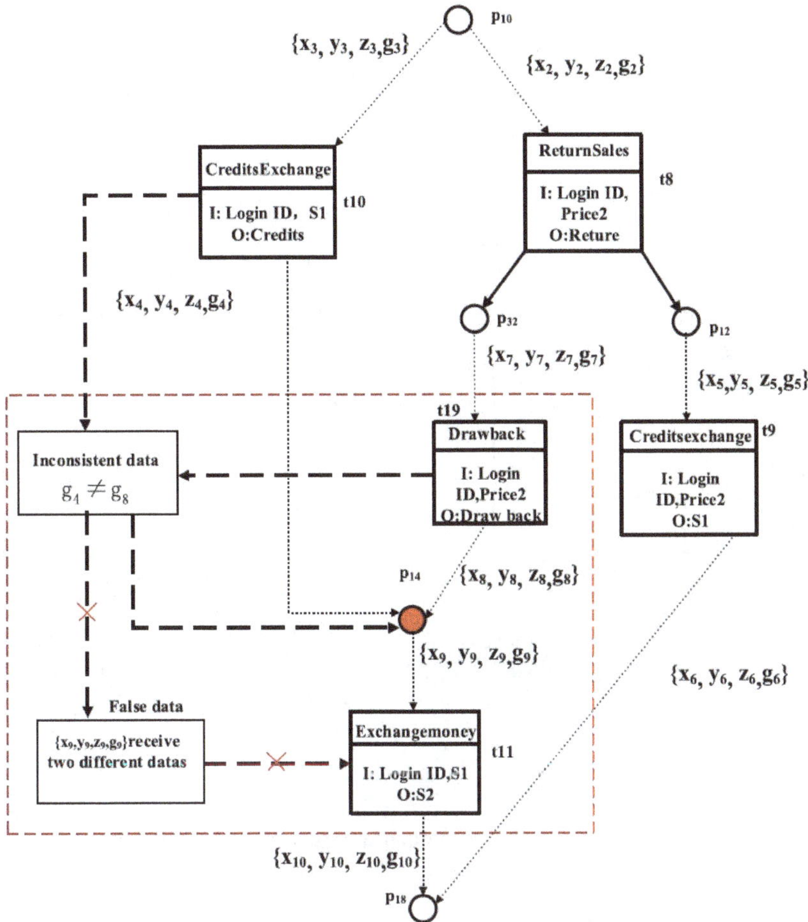

Figure 4.5   Data inconsistency of Figure 4.3 [36].

condition should not be permitted. This situation results in the data inconsistency shown in the red region of Figure 4.5. Then we can obtain the data and control the vulnerable region of Figure 4.3 as shown in Figure 4.6. We use yellow to express the control slice and blue to express the data inconsistency. Finally, the brown area shows the intersection of the yellow and blue parts. Because this intersecting area of the two parts leads to the dangerous state, the brown part represents the tiny vulnerable region.

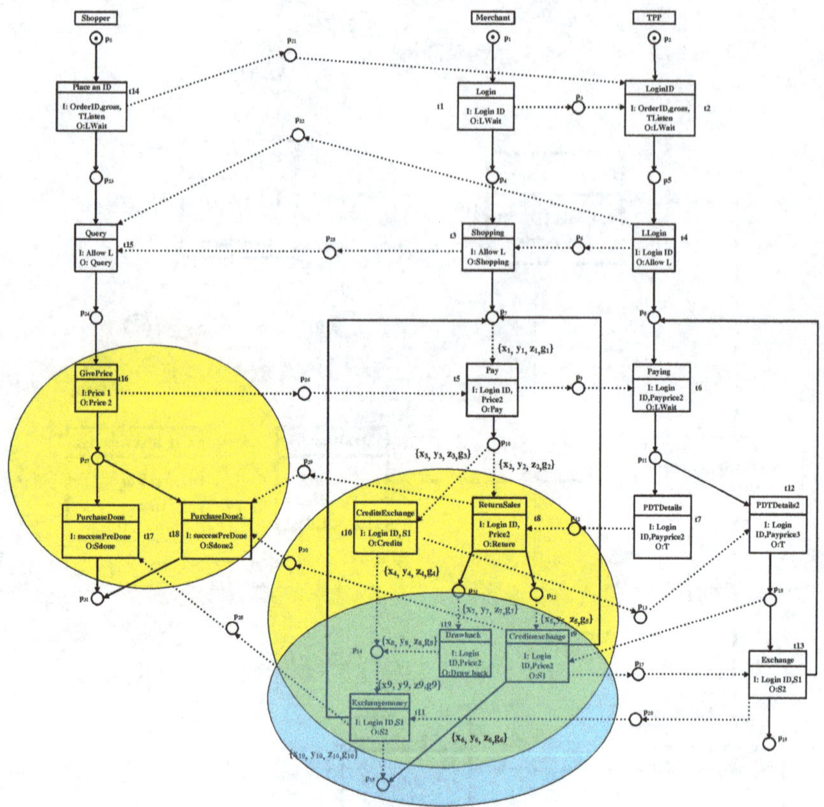

Figure 4.6   Data and control vulnerable regions of Figure 4.3 [36].

4.4.2   *Structural security in e-commerce business processes*

In this section, we study the structural security issues based on EBPN, and a framework for analyzing structural security in the e-commerce business process is proposed [37]. Given the specifications of e-commerce business processes, the proposed methods can help designers analyze structural security issues of an e-commerce business process.

Structural security issues are derived from the design of business structures. Hybrid web applications that combine multiple participants into integrated services like e-commerce websites have rapidly developed, and bring in new security concerns.

The structural integration of multiple participants introduces new security challenges due to the complexity of an application to coordinate its internal states with those of the component services and web clients across the Internet [38]. As the new security challenges of e-commerce business processes are at the application-level, structural security is beyond the capabilities of network-level and operating system-level security approaches. Even though the traditional security requirements are satisfied, there are still many structures and logic flaws at the design level of business processes [37,39,40].

Formal methods are mathematical techniques for specifying and verifying the correctness and trustworthiness of software systems. Consequently, we use the formal model EBPN to model e-commerce business processes and verify the structural security based on behavioral sequence and state analyzing methods. Figure 4.7 shows the framework. Given the specification of an e-commerce business process, including development documents, UML diagrams, and function specifications, we can model the business process by using EBPN. Then, verification methods are proposed based on the dynamic properties of EBPN. Two methods can be used to analyze the structural security issues of an e-commerce business process. One is the behavioral sequence method, and the other is the incidence matrix method.

The related definitions of structural security are as follows:

Proposition 1 *Let $\Re$ be a structural specification of an e-commerce business process, and $EN = (P, T; F, D, W, S, G)$ is an EBPN corresponding to $\Re$, (M_0, δ_{D0}) is the initial data state; γ is an illegal behavior sequence derived from $\Re$, and σ is a behavior sequence corresponding to γ. If $(M_0, \Re_{D0}) \xrightarrow{\sigma}$, then we say EN does not satisfy structural security.*

Proposition 2 *Let $\Re$ be a structural specification of an e-commerce business process, and $EN = (P, T; F, D, W, S, G)$ is an EBPN corresponding to $\Re$, (M_0, δ_{D0}) is the initial data state, (M, δ_D) is an illegal data state constructed according to $\Re$; If there is a behavioral sequence σ making that $(M_0, \delta_{D0}) \xrightarrow{\sigma} (M, \delta_D)$, then we say EN does not satisfy structural security.*

We analyze structural security in two ways according to Propositions 1 and 2. One is the behavioral sequence method, in which

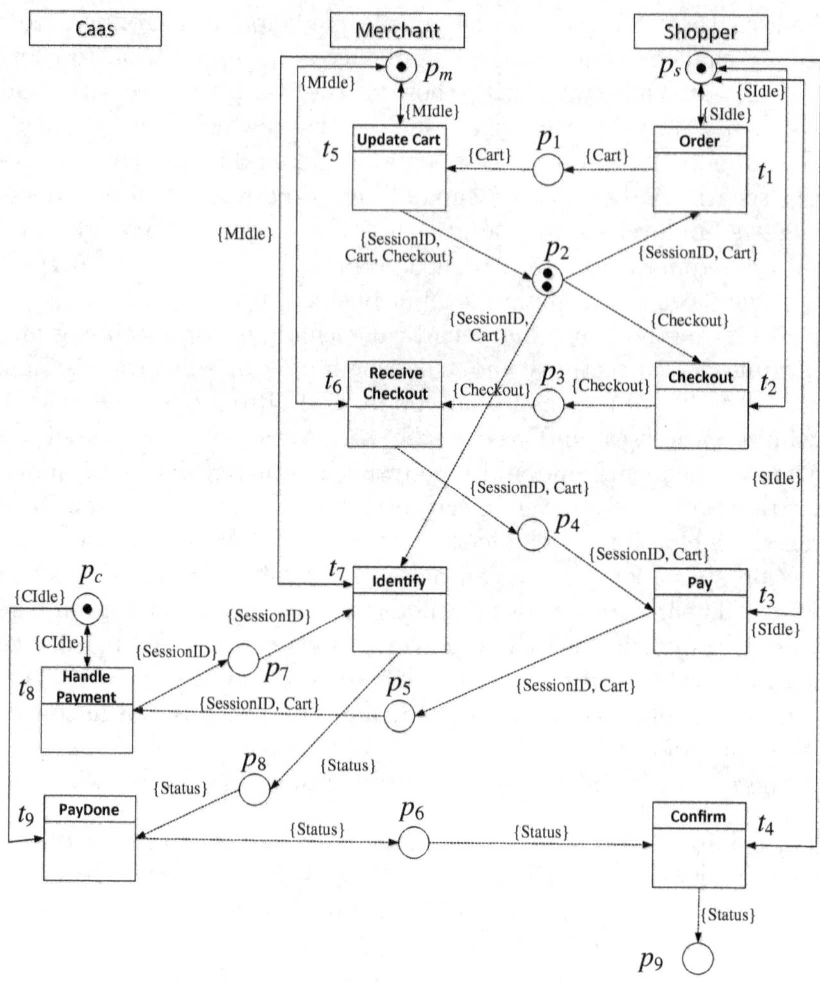

Figure 4.7   Business structure of an e-commerce system.

illegal behavior sequences are constructed and executed to verify the structural security of an e-commerce business process; the other one is the state analyzing method, in which an illegal state is constructed and analyzed by three-dimensional incidence matrix.

By analyzing the case of the e-commerce business process, we should construct illegal behaviors that result in security issues. Then, convert them to the behavioral sequence of EBPN model. At last, executing them and determining whether it can be executed successfully. If yes, the business structures have problems; if no, the business structures are immune to these illegal behaviors.

First, we should construct illegal behavior specifications from the cases. Illegal behavior specification is a description of illegal behaviors in the case. For example, in the case of motivation example, the illegal behavior specification is

(Order→Update Cart)* →Checkout→ ... →(Order→Update Cart)* → ... →Identity→ ...

The notation ()* means the loop executing of some events. The notation "..." means any executing events or transitions in the business process.

Definition 4.2 Suppose that $EN = (P, T; F, D, W, S, G)$ is an EBPN model, the illegal behavior sequence σ can be defined as follows:

(1) $t \in T$ can be an illegal behavior sequence;
(2) $t_1 t_2 \ldots t_n$ can be an illegal behavior sequence, $n \in \mathbb{N}^+$;
(3) $(t_1 t_2 \ldots t_n)^*$ can be an illegal behavior sequence;
(4) The composition of (1)–(3) can be an illegal behavior sequence.

Thus, the corresponding illegal behavior sequence of the above illegal behavior specifications is

$$(t_1 t_5)^* t_2 \ldots (t_1 t_5)^* \ldots t_7 \ldots$$

Then, we should conclude a specific behavior sequence according to the illegal behavior sequence. For example, according to the case of Figure 4.7 and the illegal behavior sequence, we can get a specific behavior sequence $t_1 t_5 t_2 t_1 t_5 t_6 t_3 t_8 t_7$. Using the dynamic properties of EBPN, execute the sequence, and the executing process is shown in Figure 4.8. The specific behavioral sequence can be executed successfully, and the business structures of motivation example do not satisfy structural security.

Also, we can use the state method to analyze structural security. First, we need to construct an illegal data state according to the structural security issue. Then, determine the reachability of the illegal data state using a three-dimensional incidence matrix. If yes, there is a structural security problem in the e-commerce business process; if no, the e-commerce business process is immune to the structural security issue.

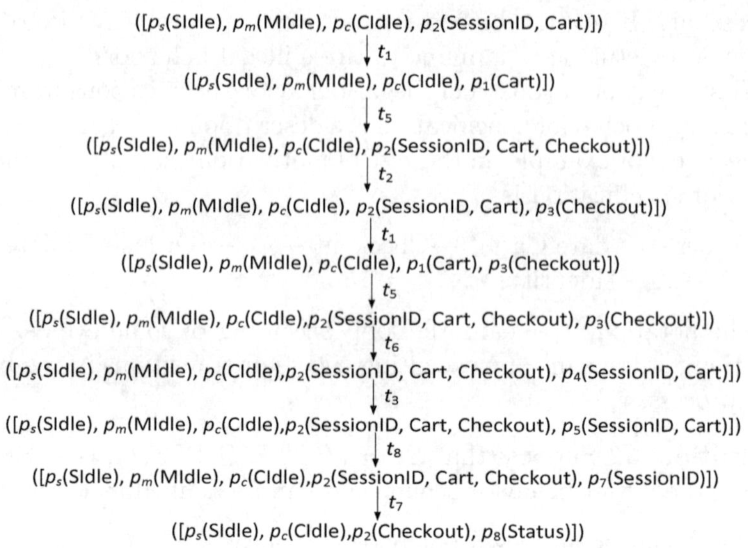

Figure 4.8   Executing process of the specific behavioral sequence.

Then, we give the steps of determining the reachability of a data state (M, δ_D) in an EBPN $EN = (P, T; F, D, W, S, G,)$ under the initial data state (M_0, δ_0).

(1) Construct Ψ;

(2) According to Theorem 3.6, compute whether the non-negative integer n-dimensional vector V exists;

(3) If not so, conclude that (M, δ_D) is not reachable in EN under the initial data state (M_0, δ_{D0}).

(4) If V exists and the transition sequences σ such that $M_0 \xrightarrow{\sigma} M$ can be found, execute σ in EN, and the reachability of (M, δ_D) can be determined.

In the case of Figure 4.7, we can obtain the illegal data state $(M, \delta_D) = ([p_s(SIdle), p_m(MIdle), p_c(CIdle), p_1(Cart), p_3(Checkout)])$, and it means that Shopper has sent the message of Checkout. However, he/she updated the cart again. This is not allowed in a security e-commerce business process. Then, we construct three-dimensional incidence matrix of the EBPN model according to Section 3.5.2. The non-simplified $M = [<1, 0, 0, 0, 0, 0, 0>, <0, 1, 0, 0, 0, 0, 0>, <0, 0, 1, 0, 0, 0, 0>, <0, 0, 0, 1, 0, 0, 0>, \mathbf{0}, <0, 0, 0, 0, 0, 1, 0>, \mathbf{0}, \mathbf{0}, \mathbf{0},$

0, **0**, **0**]. Therefore, for (M, δ_D), the matrix equation can be

$$
\begin{bmatrix}
<1,0,0,0,0,0,0> \\
<0,1,0,0,0,0,0> \\
<0,0,1,0,0,0,0> \\
<0,0,0,1,0,0,0> \\
\mathbf{0} \\
<0,0,0,0,0,1,0> \\
\mathbf{0} \\
\mathbf{0} \\
\mathbf{0} \\
\mathbf{0} \\
\mathbf{0} \\
\mathbf{0}
\end{bmatrix}
=
\begin{bmatrix}
<1,0,0,0,0,0,0> \\
<0,1,0,0,0,0,0> \\
<0,0,1,0,0,0,0> \\
\mathbf{0} \\
<0,0,0,1,1,0,0> \\
\mathbf{0} \\
\mathbf{0} \\
\mathbf{0} \\
\mathbf{0} \\
\mathbf{0} \\
\mathbf{0} \\
\mathbf{0}
\end{bmatrix}
+ \Psi^{\mathrm{T}}
\begin{bmatrix}
V[1] \\
V[2] \\
V[3] \\
V[4] \\
V[5] \\
V[6] \\
V[7] \\
V[8] \\
V[9]
\end{bmatrix}
$$

Solve the equation, and the following is one step of the process:

$$
\begin{bmatrix}
<1,0,0,0,0,0,0> \\
<0,1,0,0,0,0,0> \\
<0,0,1,0,0,0,0> \\
<0,0,0,1,0,0,0> \\
\mathbf{0} \\
<0,0,0,0,0,1,0> \\
\mathbf{0} \\
\mathbf{0} \\
\mathbf{0} \\
\mathbf{0} \\
\mathbf{0} \\
\mathbf{0}
\end{bmatrix}
$$

$$
= \begin{bmatrix}
<1 - V[4], 0, 0, 0, 0, 0, 0> \\
<0, 1 - V[7], 0, 0, 0, 0, 0> \\
<0, 0, 1 - V[9], 0, 0, 0, 0> \\
<0, 0, 0, V[1] - V[5], 0, 0, 0> \\
<0, 0, 0, 1 - V[1] + V[5] - V[7], 1 - V[1] + V[5] \\
\quad -V[7], 0 - V[2] + V[5], 0> \\
<0, 0, 0, 0, 0, V[2] - V[6], 0> \\
<0, 0, 0, V[6] - V[3], V[6] - V[3], 0, 0> \\
<0, 0, 0, V[3] - V[8], V[3] - V[8], 0, 0> \\
<0, 0, 0, 0, 0, 0, V[9] - V[4]> \\
<0, 0, 0, 0, V[8] - V[7], 0, 0> \\
<0, 0, 0, 0, 0, 0, V[7] - V[9]> \\
<0, 0, 0, 0, 0, 0, V[4]>
\end{bmatrix}
$$

Then, we obtain the unique solution $V = [V[1], V[2], V[3], V[4], V[5], V[6], V[7], V[8], V[9]]^{\mathrm{T}} = [2, 1, 0, 0, 1, 0, 0, 0, 0]^{\mathrm{T}}$. According to Corollary 3.1, it is easy to find a sequence $\sigma = t_1 t_5 t_2 t_1$ such that $M_0 \xrightarrow{\sigma} M$. Then, execute σ in Figure 4.7, and the executing process is shown in Figure 4.8. By analyzing Figure 4.8, we conclude that $(M, \delta_D) = ([p_s(SIdle), p_m(MIdle), p_c(CIdle), p_1(Cart), p_3(Checkout)])$ is reachable from initial data state. This means the business structure in Figure 4.7 has some problems, and we can find the problem and correct it. Figure 4.9 shows the correct structures and has no structure security issue in the motivation example.

4.5   Software System Behavior Certificate Method

The digital certificate is an effective identity authentication mechanism in the network environment. However, as a static authentication mechanism, it cannot deal with issues such as "theft of identity" and "use of legal identity to do illegal things". Once such a situation occurs, it can only be used for post-mortem analysis and offline detection, but not performing real-time authentication. So we propose the concept of a behavioral certificate and certify according to the behavior. The behavioral certificate and the digital certificate

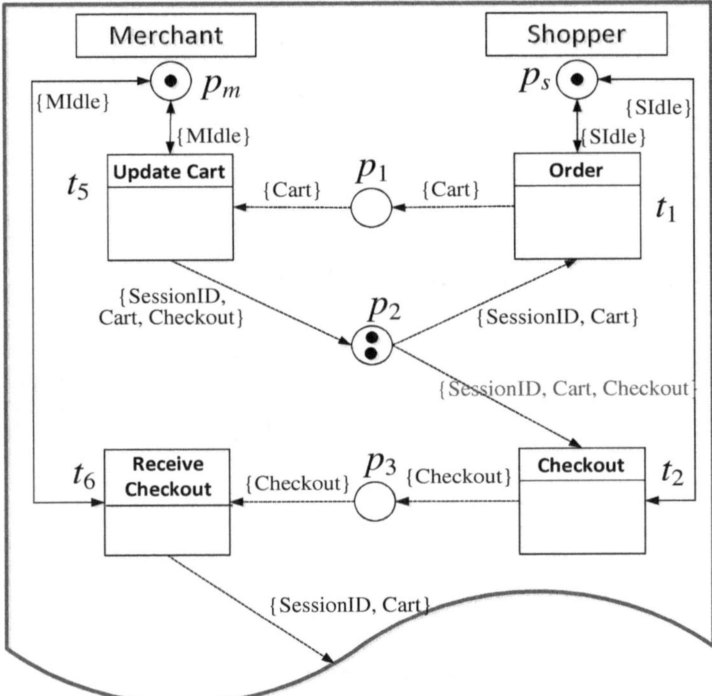

Figure 4.9   Correct business structure of the example.

complement each other and are used together in the online transaction authentication system. According to the different authentication objects, the behavior certificates are divided into user behavior
certificates and software behavior certificates. The software system
behavior certificate is firstly introduced in the following, and the user
behavior certificate will be introduced in Chapter 5.

The software behavior certificate is used to regulate the behavior
of the online transaction business process, and the actual execution
process of the transaction system will not exceed expectations. In
software behavior analysis and certificate construction, we designed
the software behavior certificate construction and authentication process, which is based on the above-mentioned Petri net model and
software behavior online analysis mechanism. The software behavior
certificate is based on the three-party communication data package of
the user, the e-commerce website, and the third-party payment platform under the correct transaction flow. The professional portrays

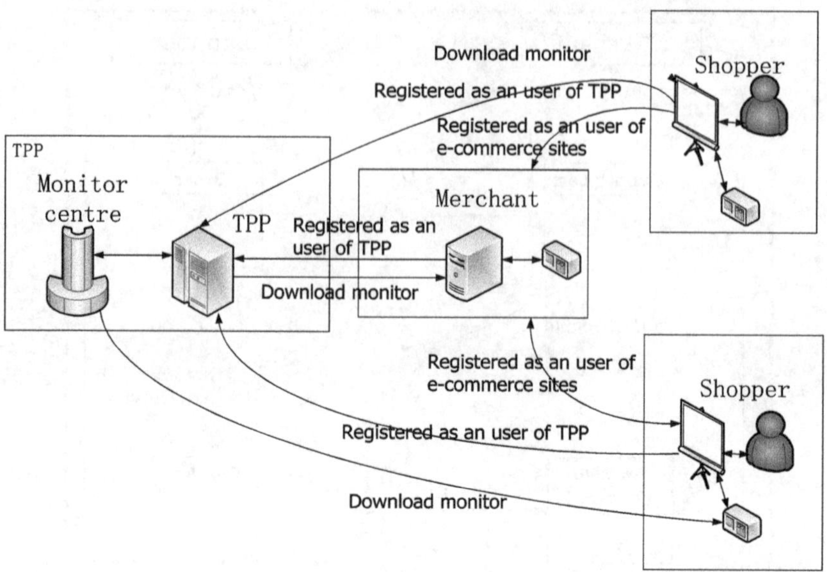

Figure 4.10   Software behavior analysis overall process.

the normal legal interaction behavior of the three parties to form a software behavior model, thereby constructing a software behavior certificate. The overall process of software behavior analysis is shown in Figure 4.10. It is assumed that the third-party payment platform is always trustworthy and will not use its legal identity to engage in illegal acts or impersonate other identities. Therefore, the behavior is certified and issued by the third-party payment platform CA, and the behavior certificate contains the entire multi-party transaction legal behavior pattern modeled and solidified by the Petri net. The monitor is also issued by Caas.CA. After the Merchant registers a third-party payment user, Caas.CA issues a behavior certificate and downloads the monitor. Since the e-commerce platform is not always trusted, its behavior is also necessary to monitor. After the Shopper registers e-commerce users and third-party payment users, Caas.CA issues a behavior certificate and downloads the monitor. Once the Shopper logs into the Merchant platform, the monitor automatically monitors and compares it to the behavioral certificate [41, 42].

The software behavior monitoring and verification system based on the Petri net is composed of an e-commerce simulation platform module, a tripartite behavior monitoring module, and a software

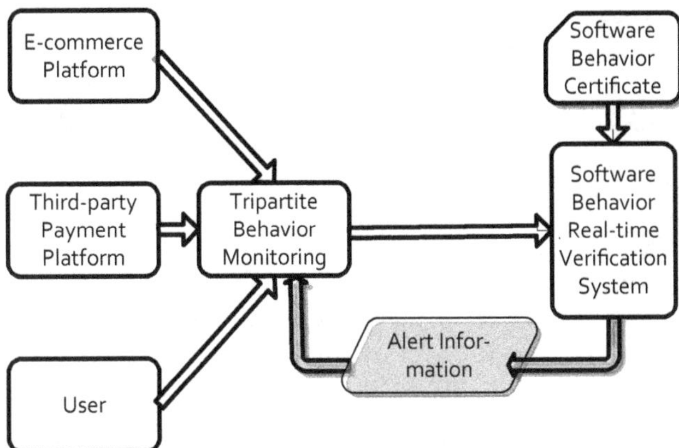

Figure 4.11 Software behavior monitoring verification overall architecture diagram.

behavior real-time verification module. The overall architecture of the system is shown in Figure 4.11. Among them, the behavior monitoring module and the software behavior real-time verification module are the core of the entire software behavior monitoring system. The three-party software behavior monitor mainly monitors the three-party transaction interaction data packet and extracts necessary information (URL address, parameters, etc.), and transmits the key information in the form of the data packet to the software behavior real-time verification system. The software behavior certificate abstracts the interaction process among the three parties into a Petri net, and takes each step of the three parties as a transition, such as modifying the database, modifying the order status, etc.; understanding the three-party specific behavior as a trigger condition and abstracting it into a library, such as order messages, status messages, etc., and clicking on the buy button behavior; meantime, specifying that each input library in a transition must have one and only one token, the transition is eligible to be triggered. After the software behavior certificate is constructed, the three-party identity is determined by the software behavior real-time verification system. The software behavior real-time verification system extracts and integrates the key sequence and information after receiving the transaction interaction information data packet submitted by the three-party monitor, and compares the user behavior interaction sequence

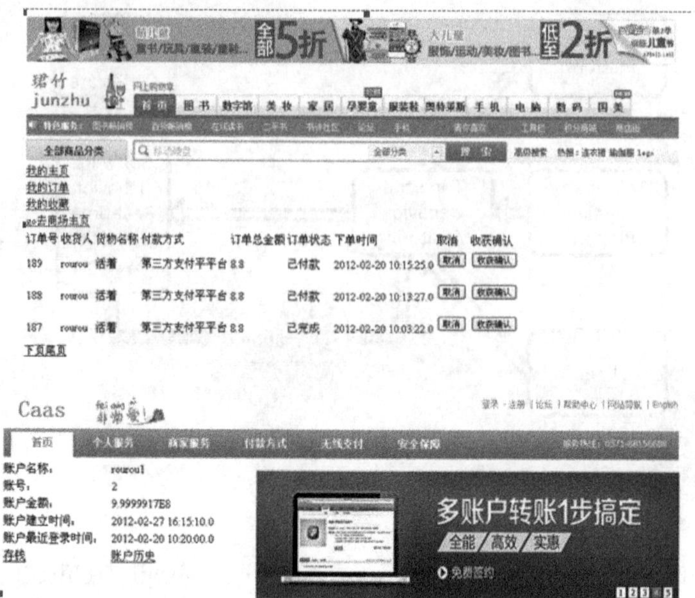

Figure 4.12   The online shopping simulation platform.

with the software behavior model in real-time according to the global unique order number. In the event of out-of-order, illegal behavior such as impersonation, an alert is issued and the transaction is closed.

We simulated an e-commerce website and a third-party payment platform and basically fulfilled the functions of an e-commerce website based on the discussion area, payment, and storage functions of the third-party payment platform. The e-commerce simulation platform is used to simulate the main functions of the commercial mall software Interspire and the third-party payment platform PayPal Standard as well as the communication between them. It mainly consists of two parts: an e-commerce website and a third-party payment platform. The screenshot of the program is shown in Figure 4.12.

Based on jpcap, the behavior monitoring module extracts necessary information, including URL address and parameter information, as well as the e-commerce number and third-party payment platform number of the transaction. It determines the three parties' real-time behavior by capturing and distinguishing the data packets generated

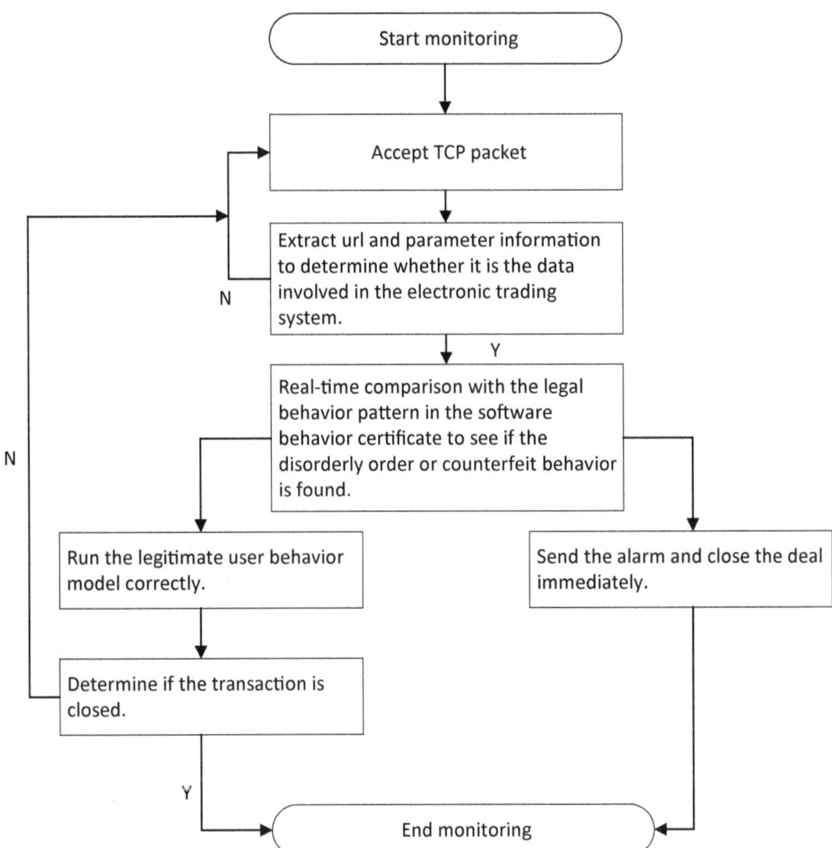

Figure 4.13   The software behavior real-time verification system flow chart.

during the three-party communication, then establishes a socket connection with the software behavior real-time verification system, and sends key information to the software behavior real-time verification system in the form of TCP data packets. The configuration file parsing module is mainly responsible for reading the configuration file and the Petri net in the behavior certificate. The behavior certificate is stored locally after being issued by Caas.CA, and the Petri net is stored in the XML file format. The configuration file parsing module is responsible for reading the storage address of the Petri net from the configuration file config.xml, and reading it into the memory in a specific data structure, so that the behavior monitor can compare in real-time. The three-party interaction behavior comparison module

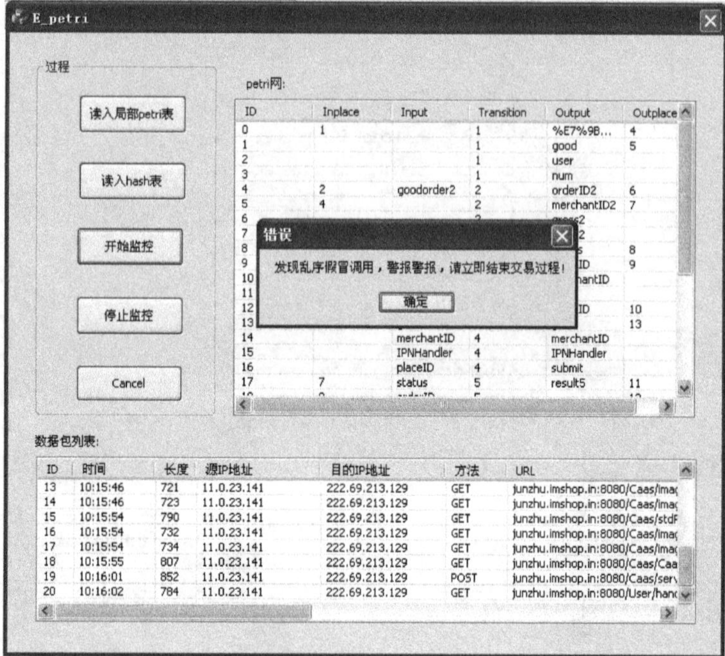

Figure 4.14   Event capture.

is mainly responsible for analyzing and real-time comparing of the data packet information submitted by the user behavior monitoring module to determine whether to include the token, input, output, etc. If the condition is met, the transition will be triggered, and the Petri net in the behavior certificate will run. The operation mechanism and event capture are shown in Figures 4.13–4.14.

4.6 Chapter Summary

With the continuous development of online transactions, the entities and methods of online transaction processes are constantly changing. The open and dynamic online environment also makes the environment faced by online transaction systems complex and diverse. Therefore, the credibility of the process design and construction of the online transaction software system can lead to unpredictable behavior of the online transaction system with the business process as the core. It is valuable to study and identify potential security risks in business processes and system implementation, as well as to design targeted prevention and control systems. Improper design of the online transaction system and its business processes will result in inconsistent fund processing and business processing, which cause losses to customers and third-party payment companies. For decades, global scholars have done a lot of valuable work in related fields, including early software testing techniques and current risk assessment methods. This chapter reviews the software risk prevention and control technologies widely used and studied in the industry and academia, including software testing techniques, risk assessment techniques, formal methods, and system behavior certificate methods independently developed by the research team. The behavior certificate formalizes the protocol and verification of the behavior of the online transaction system and dynamically reflects the behavior sequence and logic of the online transaction activity, to realize the real-time online monitoring of the behaviors of each transaction subject, and to meet the predictability of the online transaction system's behaviors.

References

[1] Yang, G. X. *Software Quality Assurance, Test and Evaluation*, Beijing: Tsinghua University Press, (2007).

[2] Xu, F. *Software Test Technology*, Beijing: Mechanical Industry Press, (2012).

[3] Xue, S. N. and Zhao, W. Software Test Technology — A New Field of Metrology and Test Technology. *Metrology Technology*, 5: 28–31 (2003).

[4] Zhou, W., Zhou, G. Q., and Yan, W. J. Software Test Technology Overview. *China Test Technology*, 31(3): 56–75 (2005).

[5] Mc Clure, C. *Software Reuse Techniques*. Prentice Hall PTR, (1997).

[6] Mayrhauser, A. V., Mraz, R. T., Walls, J. *et al.* Domain Based Testing: Increasing Test Case Reuse. In *Proceedings of ICCS '94: Proceedings of the1994 IEEE International Conference on Computer Design: VLSI in Computer & Processors*, Washington, DC, USA: IEEE Computer Society, pp. 484–491 (1994).

[7] Zhang, J. *Research on Test Case Reuse in Software Test*, Shanghai, China: Shanghai University, (2012).

[8] Xia, Q. M. *Research and Implementation of Reuse Strategy for Software Testing and Evaluation*, Wuhan, China: Wuhan University, (2010).

[9] Yang, F. Q., Mei, H., Xie, B. *et al. Software Asset and Process Management for Reuse*, Beijing: Tsinghua University Press, (2008).

[10] Liao, N. D. *Research on Dynamic Risk Assessment Model of Information Security*, Beijing: Jiaotong University, (2009).

[11] Hu, Y. *Research on Risk Assessment Method of Network Information System*, Chengdu, China: Sichuan University, (2007).

[12] Guo, H. F. and Zeng, X. Y. Research on Risk Analysis Methods. *Computer Engineering*, 27(3): 131–132 (2001).

[13] National Information Security Standardization Technical Committee, TC260 N0001, Evaluation framework for information systems security assurance Part 1: Introduction and General Model, (2004).

[14] Qu, C. Y. and Chen, X. H. Research on Information System Security Assessment Concept, Information Security and Communication Confidentiality, 9: 16–20 (2003).

[15] Trusted Computer System Evaluation Criteria, DoD 5200.28-STD, (1985). https://csrc.nist.gov/csrc/media/publications/conference-paper/1998/10/08/proceedings-of-the-21st-nissc-1998/documents/early-cs-papers/dod85.pdf.

[16] ITSEC (The Information Technology Security Evaluation Criteria version 1.2), (1991). http://www.iwar.org.uk/comsec/resources/standards/itsec.htm.

[17] Canadian Trusted Computer Product Evaluation Criteria. http://ieeexplore.ieee.org/document/143768/.

[18] BSI/DISC Committee BDD/2, BS7799 Code of Practice for Information Security Management, (1999).

[19] Japanese Computer Security Evaluation Criteria. https://www.acronymattic.com/Japanese-Computer-Security-Evaluation-Criteria-(JCSEC).html.

[20] The Common Criteria for Information Technology Security Evaluation. https://www.iso.org/obp/ui/fr/#iso:std:iso-iec:15408:-3:ed-3:v2:en.

[21] Standards of the People's Republic of China, Computer Information System Security Protection Level Classification Standard, State Bureau of Quality and Technical Supervision, Beijing, China, GB17859-1999.

[22] Standards of the People's Republic of China, Information Technology Security Technology Information Technology Security Evaluation Guidelines, State Bureau of Quality and Technical Supervision, 2001-03-08.

[23] Feng, D. G., Zhang, Y., and Zhang, Y. Q. Summary of Information Security Risk Assessment. *Journal of Communications*, 25(7): 10–18 (2004).

[24] P2DR. https://www.scientific.net/AMM.347-350.2773.pdf.

[25] Li, T. *Introduction to Network Security*, Beijing: Publishing House of Electronics Industry, (2004).

[26] Gu, T. L. *Formal Method of Software Development*, Beijing, China: Tsinghua University Press, (2008).

[27] Francez, N. *Program Verification*. New Jersey, USA: Addison-Wesley, (1992).

[28] Zhang, G. Q. On the Formalization of Software. *Journal of Chongqing Teachers College (Natural Science Edition)*, 19(2): 1–9 (2002).

[29] Du, Y. Y. Overview of Formal Analysis and Verification Techniques for E-Commerce Systems. *Journal of Liaocheng University (Natural Science Edition)*, 17(2): 15–27 (2004).

[30] Liu, G. J. and Jiang, C. J. Net-structure-based Conditions to Decide Compatibility and Weak Compatibility for a Class of Inter-Organizational Workflow Nets. *Science China Information Sciences*, 58(7): 1–16 (2015).

[31] Pan, L., Ding, Z. J., and Zhou, M. C. A Configurable State Class Method for Temporal Analysis of Time Petri Nets. *IEEE Transactions on Systems, Man and Cybernetics: Systems*, 44(4): 482–493 (2014).

[32] Yu, W. Y., Yan, C. G., Ding, Z. J. *et al.* Modeling and Verification of Online Shopping Business Processes by Verification of Online Shopping Business Processes by Considering Malicious Behavior Patterns. *IEEE Transactions on Automation Science and Engineering*, 13(2): 647–662 (2016).

[33] Wu, Y., Yan, C. G., Liu, G. J. *et al.* An Adaptive Multilevel Indexing Method for Disaster Service Discovery. *IEEE Transactions on Computers*, 64(9): 2447–2459 (2014).

[34] Llorens, M., Oliver, J., Silva, J. *et al.* Dynamic Slicing Techniques for Petri Nets. *Electronic Notes in Theoretical Computer Science*, 223: 153–165 (2008).

[35] Jiang, C. J., Ding, Z. J., and Fang, X. W. Dynamic Slicing of Petri Nets Based on Structural Dependency Graph and Its Application in System Analysis. *Asian Journal of Control*, 17(4): 1403–1414 (2015).

[36] Wang, M. M., Ding, Z. J., Zhao, P. H. *et al.* A Dynamic Data Slice Approach to the Vulnerability Analysis of E-Commerce Systems. *IEEE Transactions on Systems, Man and Cybernetics: Systems*, 50(10): 3598–3612 (2020).

[37] Yu, W. Y., Ding, Z. J., Liu, L. *et al.* Petri Net-Based Methods for Analyzing Structural Security in E-Commerce Business Processes. *Future Generation Computer Systems*, 109: 611–620 (2020).

[38] Wang, R., Chen, S., Wang, X. F. *et al.* How to Shop for Free Online-Security Analysis of Cashier-as-a-Service Based Web Stores. In *Proceedings of the 32nd IEEE Symposium on Security and Privacy (S&P)*, IEEE, Berkeley, CA, pp. 465–480 (2011).

[39] Yu, W. Y., Yan, C. G., Ding, Z. J. *et al.* Modeling and Validating E-Commerce Business Process Based on Petri Nets. *IEEE Transactions on Systems, Man, and Cybernetics: Systems*, 44: 327–341 (2014).

[40] Yu, W. Y., Yan, C. G., Ding, Z. J. *et al.* Analyzing E-Commerce Business Process Nets via Incidence Matrix and Reduction. *IEEE Transactions on Systems, Man, and Cybernetics: Systems*, 48: 130–141 (2018).

[41] Jiang, C. J., Chen, Y. Z., Yan, C. G. *et al.* Software Behavior Monitoring and Verification System. Invention Patent (CN201410014450.6), 2015.08.19.

[42] Zhong, J. Z., Yan, C. G., Yu, W. Y. *et al.* A Kind of Identity Authentication Method Based on Browsing Behaviors. In *2014 Seventh International Symposium on Computational Intelligence and Design (ISCID)*, IEEE, Hangzhou, China, pp. 279–284 (2014).

Chapter 5

Risk Prevention and Control of User Behaviors

5.1 Introduction

With the rapid development of e-commerce, online payment methods have gradually become the first choice for online shopping. However, online payment does not only bring people a convenient and fast experience but also the hidden dangers of network security, which becomes an opportunity for outlaws. Some user account leakage accidents are great challenges for the security of online transactions. User identity authentication is an essential part of risk prevention and control strategies. The purpose of identity authentication is to confirm the identity of the user as much as possible to ensure the successful access of the user and the privacy of the individual account. The existing authentication technologies mainly include three types: (1) memory information, such as password, PIN, etc.; (2) auxiliary devices, such as ID card, access token, PC card, smart card, wireless recognition agent, etc.; (3) biometric features, such as fingerprints, iris, palmprint, sound samples, etc., which are called biometric technology. These traditional identity authentication technologies have their own advantages and disadvantages: a user password and other information are difficult to remember but easy to leak; ID card needs to be carried and easy to be stolen or lost; biometric authentication requires additional hardware equipment, the cost is high, and it may intrude on the privacy of users. In this chapter, we briefly review the

109

existing identity authentication technology, including digital certificate technology, and introduce the related technologies and methods based on user behavior patterns developed by our research group. The user behavior certificate is constructed according to the user behavior characteristics excavated from the user electronic transaction log, and the generated behavior certificate is stored in the fourth-party authentication center for management.

5.2   Authentication Technologies

Accurate identification of user identity and verification of user legitimacy has always been the goal of various security organizations and enterprises, especially in the application fields such as fund transfer, private data acquisition, and so on. To authenticate user identity quickly and accurately without affecting the user experience is a problem that needs to be solved by identity authentication technology. With the development of hardware acquisition equipment and data analysis technology, identity authentication technology has been developed from single identity authentication with fixed mode to "integrated" identity authentication with the fusion of various identification technologies. The following will introduce several mainstream identity authentication methods that are widely used today.

The first and the most commonly used authentication method is account/password matching. Whether it is the six-digit password of online banking or other complex numbers, the combination of uppercase and lowercase letters, the password has always been the most direct and effective means to verify the identity of users. In recent years, with the popularity of smartphone users, dual authentication with password + mobile phone message verification code as content of verification has been the main method of authentication for network users. The basic idea of verification is to assume that the same user's multi-terminal information is less likely to be stolen at the same time, that is, if the user's PC account password information is stolen, it can be prevented by the mobile phone, and vice versa. However, this method cannot prevent the account from using false and other means of attack [1–4].

Second, the account/password is used to authenticate the identity information utilizing graphic verification code, problem verification, and so on [5, 6]. This verification method is mainly used to identify whether the user is a robot and because the graphics library can be marked by crowdsourcing, image recognition, and so on, the application cost is low. In recent years, verification methods have appeared one after another through supporting block sliding, mouse trajectory, and so on, which makes the means of man-machine recognition more diversified.

Third, physiological characteristics authentication, which includes fingerprint, facial, iris, vocal lines, veins, and other physiological characteristics, is used to authenticate user identity information. The physiological characteristics of users are unique and the recognition speed is fast so that the use of physiological features to identify users has been favored by various security organizations. However, due to the fact that information input needs additional hardware equipment to assist, it is difficult to popularize the application of physiological characteristic authentication on a large-scale. In recent years, intelligent terminals have gradually integrated various physiological feature input devices, that is, they want to identify users through physiological characteristics. However, with the improvement of information processing technology, physiological characteristic information becomes more and easier to be "imitated", thus crossing the verification system and posing a threat to the information security of users. For example, at the international conference ACM CCS'16, Mahmood Sharif *et al.* found that when the masquerade wears specific glasses designed according to the target user, the masquerade can easily pass through several of the mainstream face recognition systems, and then impersonate the target user [7]. Therefore, physiological characteristic certification cannot completely prevent the occurrence of malignant behavior.

The fourth, using the user's behavior to carry on identity authentication. The behavior of the user includes many aspects, such as the gait of the user, the stroke order of the signature can be regarded as the behavior of the user [8–11]. An intelligent terminal, terminal built-in gyroscope, gravity sensor, and other sensors can sense the user's grip posture and tilt angle for the terminal, which can be regarded as the user's behavior for the terminal. Through the modeling of these behaviors, we can depict the behavior model of each user for the intelligent terminal, and identify the user through the difference between the behavior model and the user data. For modeling and authentication of intelligent end-user behavior, the most representative should be Project Abacus by Google. Through gyroscopes, gravity sensors, front-facing cameras, and other sensors, the project strives to establish a user's facial image model, handheld model, and other end-use and physiological characteristic models, to replace the account/password authentication on the mobile [12]. On the PC side, the mouse sliding track, keyboard tapping sequence, and web browsing sequence of the user can all be characterized as the user's behavior, and then the personalized features of each user can be extracted and the identity authentication can be carried out [13, 14]. Different from the static one-time authentication method of account/password and biometric authentication, behavior authentication is a dynamic and continuous authentication process for user identity identification [15–17].

Behavior-based authentication has been a hot research topic of user identity authentication and network security in academic and industrial fields recently [18–20]. In China, Alipay, the largest third-party network payment platform, integrates the behavior characteristics of users in its risk control system to control the risk of network transactions and identify user identity and malicious cases. Therefore, the next section will discuss some of the techniques used in the process of behavior authentication.

5.3 Identity Authentication Technology Based on Behaviors

In this section, we discuss some identity authentication technology based on behavior collected from the user's smart terminal touch screen, keyboard typing, mouse movement track, and so on. Technology mainly uses some methods in machine learning to describe the user's behavior trajectory model, and give the confidence of the current user identity by comparing the matching degree between the current user's behavior sequence and the behavior model, thereby achieving the purpose of identity authentication and early warning.

5.3.1 *User mobile terminal behavior authentication technology*

The mobile terminal user behavior can be gathered from two aspects: touch screen behavior and handheld gesture; in terms of touch screen behavior, the user identity can be authenticated by constructing a user-to-screen pressure mode. At present, the model construction methods are mainly divided into statistical methods, neural network methods, fuzzy logic methods, and data mining methods. Considering the complex nonlinear relationships between the touch screen time feature data and pressure feature data of mobile terminal users, the neural network model which can map arbitrarily complex nonlinear relationships is used to model the mobile terminal touch screen behavior. Such as the radial basis function (RBF) neural network, which consists of three layers: the input layer, hidden layer, and output layer. The input layer node only passes the input signal to the hidden layer, the hidden layer node is composed of a radial action function like a Gaussian function, and the output layer node is usually a simple linear function. The basic function of the hidden layer node reacts locally to the signal transmitted by the input layer, that is, the closer the input signal is to the center of the basis function, the higher the output of the hidden layer. It indicates that the RBF neural network has local approximation ability. The basic training mode of the RBF neural network is that for each input vector in the training, we need to assign it to an expected output vector, which represents the expected classification of the input vector. For input vectors of the same class, you need to assign the same output vector to them as the basis for training. In the neural network, the number of nodes in the input layer is the same as the dimension of the input vector, the number of nodes in the output layer is the same as the expected output vector dimension, and the number of nodes in the hidden layer varies according to the specific training algorithm. The training algorithms of the RBF neural network include random algorithm, self-organizing learning algorithm, as well as the nearest neighbor cluster learning algorithm, which are used to select the base function center of the hidden layer nodes and the connection rights between hidden layer nodes and output layer nodes in the RBF neural network. The neural network is trained by using input–output pairs and training algorithms.

In terms of the feature selection, the mobile terminal user's touch screen behavior feature is the basis of the model construction. The user's touch screen operation can be divided into two events: button press and button bounce. We equip a touch screen mobile device, including a smartphone, etc., with a pressure sensor, which can be used to collect pressure and contact area information when the user clicks a button on the virtual soft keyboard as a pressure-related feature.

In the time feature selection, the virtual keyboard behavior of the mobile terminal user is similar to that of the traditional keyboard. Pressing refers to the user's finger touching the touch screen and causing the mobile system to generate touch feedback, and bounce refers to the user's finger leaving the touch screen and causing the tactile feedback of the mobile system to disappear. The button duration refers to the interval between the press of a button and the lift of the button, indicating the duration of a button event. The button interval time refers to the interval between one button and the next button in the sequence of characters continuously input, indicating the time interval between the end of one button event and the start of the next button event. Figure 5.1 depicts the time characteristic sequence of a user's touch screen behavior [21–23].

In the selection of pressure characteristics, since the user operates on the touch screen, the pressure and contact area of each key operation can be obtained through the sensor. It is an important point that the behavior of the mobile keyboard is different from the traditional keyboard. Under the Android platform, the pressure and contact area are relative values between 0 and 1, and the value is related to the hardware sensor range and sensitivity. The pressure and contact area can be combined into a pressure feature vector, which is a unique feature of the mobile terminal user's virtual keyboard behavior authentication. In addition to the characteristics defined above, the average duration of keystrokes touched by mobile users, that is, the average of the duration of keystrokes in the input string. The average pressure,

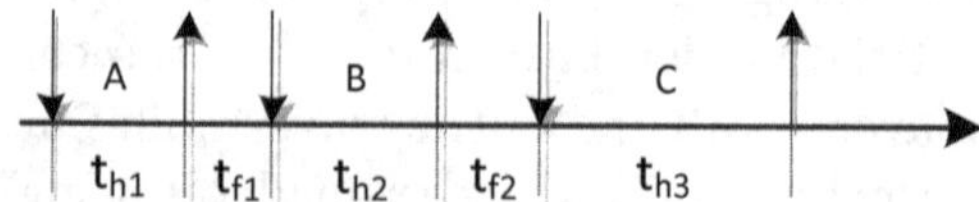

Figure 5.1   Time sequence of a user's touch screen behavior.

that is, the average pressure of all key operations in the input string, etc., can be used to model users as behavioral characteristics. In the process of constructing a model of the behavior characteristics of a mobile user's keyboard, a suitable feature may be selected for model construction according to the characteristics of the model.

In addition to the differences in touch screen behaviors of each user during the use of the smart terminal, there are also obvious personal differences in their holding gestures and postures. With the help of sensors such as the gyroscopes and magnetometers carried by smart terminals, this part of the behavior data can be collected to construct the behavior characteristics of the user's hand-held posture, and then identity authentication can be performed. The feature information extraction can describe the gesture behavior characteristics of the user input from two aspects, one is the gesture behavior of the user's finger on the mobile phone touch screen, the other is the gesture behavior of the user inputting the gesture password. To characterize the user's gesture behavior, the X, Y coordinates, pressure, and contact area of the center of the contact surface between the finger and the touch screen can be collected. To characterize the user's gesture behavior, we use the phone's orientation sensor to collect the X, Y, and Z coordinates of the phone's screen orientation, and the phone's acceleration sensor to collect the X, Y, and Z coordinates of the phone's acceleration. Among them, the X, Y, and Z coordinates of the mobile phone's screen orientation can adopt the following coordinates:

X-axis: Vector product of Y axis and Z axis (tangent to the location of the device and pointing approximately east).

Y-axis: Tangent to the ground at the location of the device and pointing to the magnetic north pole.

Z-axis: Pointing to the center of the earth and perpendicular to the ground where the device is located.

The schematic diagram is shown in Figure 5.2(a).

Therefore, from the definition of the above coordinate system, it can be known that the X coordinate of the screen orientation of the mobile phone represents the elevation angle, the Y coordinate represents the flip angle, and the Z coordinate represents the azimuth angle. Besides, the X, Y, and Z coordinates of the mobile phone

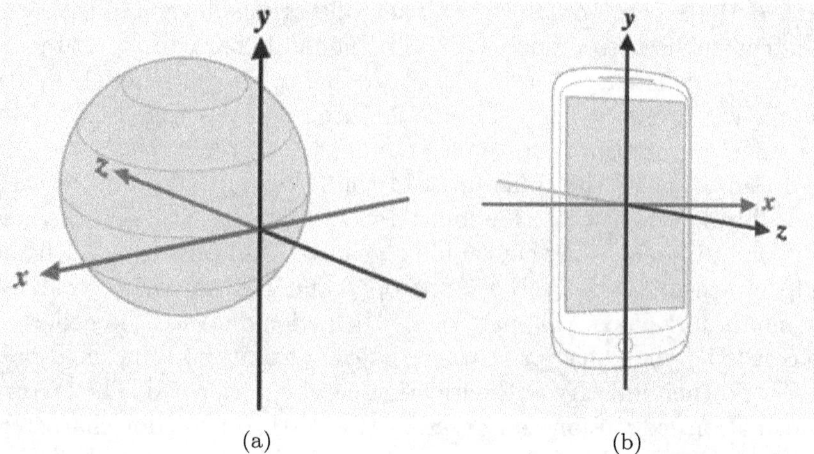

Figure 5.2   (a) Screen direction reference coordinate system. (b) Acceleration direction reference coordinate system.

acceleration use the following coordinate system, which is defined relative to the mobile phone screen:

X-axis: Horizontal and pointing to the right of the screen.
Y-axis: Vertical and pointing to the top of the screen.
Z-axis: Perpendicular to the screen and pointing outside the front screen of the phone.

Its schematic diagram is shown in Figure 5.2(b).

By extracting gesture and behavior data, user gesture data can be added to the user gesture authentication process. When a user inputs a gesture password, the user's gesture-related data and posture-related data can be used to construct a behavior authentication model. User's gesture-related data include finger coordinates, pressure, contact area, and so on, which are collected by a mobile phone touch screen. The user's posture-related data are collected by the phone's direction sensor and acceleration sensor. The user can log in normally only after inputting the correct gesture password and passing the authentication of the behavior model. In this way, even if the user's gesture password was stolen, the authentication model could still provide a certain security guarantee. Since the behavior characteristics include two aspects, the construction of the behavior authentication model can be divided into two steps: firstly, clustering several poses of the user based on the characteristics reflecting the pose of the user, and determining a threshold to determine whether the current pose belongs to the user; secondly, determining whether the gesture of the user is legal by using a classification algorithm to train a gesture authentication model for each gesture of the user. In this way, the gesture will firstly be examined whether it conforms to the habits of users and which current user the gesture belongs to, then the re-authentication using the gesture authentication model on the gesture will be performed.

5.3.2 *Users' keyboard tapping behavior recognition technology*

Aiming at the user's biological characteristics and behavior habits, such as the user's keystroke behavior, which are not easy to be imitated and obtained [24, 25], designing an authentication model based on the user's keyboard tapping behavior can better identify the user's identity. The user's keyboard behavior authentication collects the user's keyboard behavior data, analyzes and models the user's keyboard behavior data, and establishes a unique keyboard behavior mode for the user as a basis for identity authentication. The time characteristics of users when they type their passwords are related to age, gender, and computer familiarity. It is difficult for others to imitate and misappropriate keyboard behavior patterns of different users. By collecting user's keyboard behavior data, a user's unique keyboard behavior pattern is established, and the user's keyboard behavior pattern is used to authenticate and identify the user. According to the characteristics and functions of the Hidden Markov Model (HMM), the user's keyboard behavior pattern can construct a corresponding HMM. Using HMM to identify the user's tapping behavior belongs to the evaluation problem in hidden Markov models. By training the collected dataset D of the user's tapping keyboard, the corresponding HMM can be trained. When the user logs in to the system, by the act of user inputting the password, we will get a new set of observation sequences O. Therefore, $P(O|HMM)$ can be obtained, and according to the threshold TH, when $P(O|HMM) > TH)$, it can be determined that the user logging in is the same user.

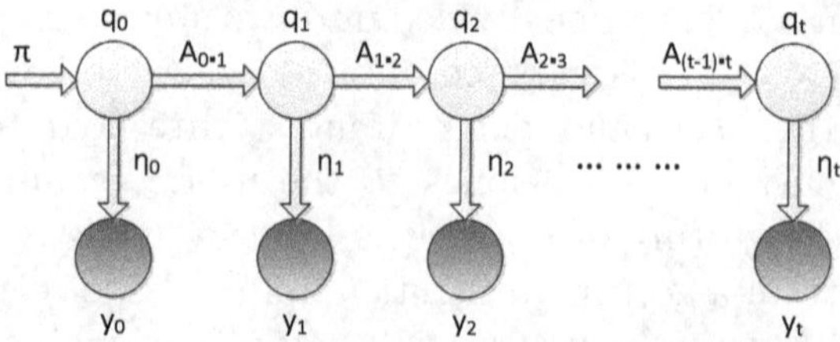

Figure 5.3   Hidden Markov model of keyboard behavior mode.

Figure 5.3 is the HMM of Keyboard Behavior Mode. In the figure, A is the state transition matrix, η_i is the emission vector, π is the initial vector, and $y_1 - y_n$ are the observed sequences, that is, the collected keyboard behavior data to be estimated. By calculating the probability of the observation sequence, it can be judged whether the observation sequence is legal data of a known keyboard behavior pattern. Among them, $P(q_{t+1}^j | q_\tau^i) = A_{ij}$, t represents a discrete-time point and q_i represents the ith state. η is the emission vector, $\eta_i = P(y_t | q_t^i)$, which represents the emission probability from the ith hidden state to the observed state.

The keyboard key behavior model and authentication is based on the historical key information of the user entering the password during account login for a period to perform data analysis and establish a corresponding user model, and perform model calculations on the new data to be tested to identify the user's identity. For multi-person shared accounts, each legal member has its own unique typing behavior pattern. Judging only by using the typing behavior will have a large false rate. So for multi-user accounts, the key to build a model is to distinguish the data sources. Cluster keyboard behavior data under the same account and the final result of the clustering requires the keyboard behavior data of the same user in the same cluster, different user's keyboard behavior data are in different clusters, and the clusters do not intersect with each other. Finally, the keyboard behavior pattern for each cluster can be modeled after clustering. After clustering, the keyboard behavior pattern is constructed, which improves the accuracy of the user's keyboard behavior pattern construction in such scenarios, and also provides a guarantee for the accuracy of later authentication.

To construct a user's keyboard behavior pattern, we must first select appropriate keyboard behavior characteristics as the basis for

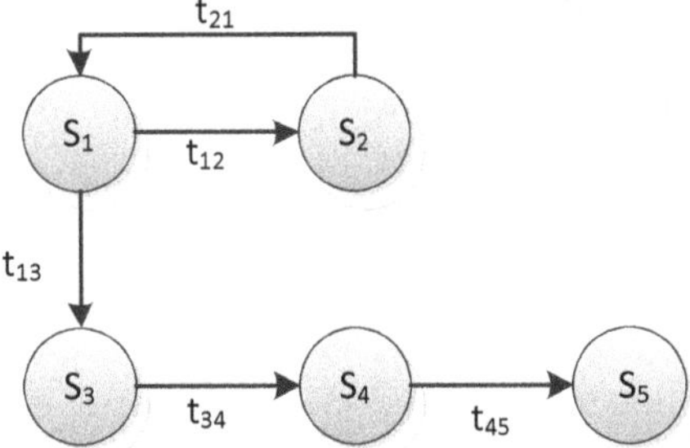

Figure 5.4   Example of a directed graph of key sequences.

pattern construction. A user's keyboard operation can be divided into two events: key press and key bounce. At present, the main characteristics of keyboard behavior research are generated based on the relevant quantities generated by the operation of these two events. The main keyboard behavior characteristics can be divided into two categories of temporal characteristics and non-temporal characteristics. The time characteristics are mainly the key duration, the key interval time, etc. The non-time characteristics are keystroke pressure, keystroke speed, etc. Based on basic features, there are other characteristics of the user's keyboard behavior, including keystroke pattern matrix, a directed graph of keyboard behavior pattern, keystroke pressure, the average number of keystrokes per second, and so on.

Figure 5.4 shows a directed graph of the keyboard behavior pattern composed of the input sequence S as $<S_1, S_2, S_1, S_3, S_4, S_5>$. Based on this, you can add weights to the directed edges according to the needs of modeling, such as key duration, key interval, etc.

The K-means algorithm is a centroid-based classification method. The centroid of a cluster is the center point of the cluster. This method uses the centroid of the cluster to represent the cluster. Multi-user data is clustered through K-means, and abnormal data is eliminated to distinguish whether the data source is from different users. In the keyboard behavior data of the account, randomly select a sample point, and calculate the variance of the Euclidean distance from the remaining sample points to the sample point. Since the data points of a single user's keyboard behavior are relatively concentrated when compared with the data under multiple user accounts, the variance is smaller when there is only one user, and the variance is larger when there are multiple users in a single account. Therefore, we can judge whether there are multiple users or not.

The K-means algorithm can be improved by adding variance discrimination conditions, thus the algorithm can determine whether there are multiple users under the account and whether clustering is required. Calculate the variance of the Euclidean distance from a sample point to a random point under the account, use this variance to determine whether clustering is required, and automatically identify the number of users under the account. By taking random sample points, the variance of the Euclidean distance from the remaining data points to that point is calculated, and the variance is used to determine whether the account is a multi-user account. Suppose the sample set is $\{D_1, D_2, D_3, \ldots, D_p\}$, $D_i = \{D_{i1}, D_{i2}, \ldots, D_{in}\}$. Among them, p represents the number of continuous sequences of keys in the sample set. One sample point $D_x = \{D_{x1}, D_{x2}, \ldots, D_{xn}\}$ is arbitrarily selected, and the variance of the distance from the remaining sample points to the x point in the sample set is calculated. The single account single user, and single account multi-user accounts respectively use this method to calculate the variance of the sample set, compare the difference between the two, and determine the variance discrimination threshold TH. TH is used to determine whether there are multiple users under the account. In the improved k-means algorithm, when the variance of all clusters is less than TH, the algorithm terminates. Judge the similarity between the estimated keyboard data and the established user model by Gaussian probability density function, and call it the evaluation standard of the model. The score of the model is a decimal distributed in the interval $[0, 1]$. The closer the value is to 1, the higher the degree of similarity between the estimated keyboard data and the user model, the higher the probability that the estimated keyboard data comes from legitimate users. On the contrary, it indicates that the degree of similarity is low and it may be an illegal user.

5.3.3   *User mouse sliding behavior analysis technology*

User behavior is a comprehensive manifestation of the long-term effects of the user's physiological characteristics and habits. It has the characteristics of uniqueness, features that are not easily stolen, and non-imitative. This section proposes an auxiliary method of identity authentication, which effectively authenticates the user identity in dynamic soft keyboard applications. Data mining is performed according to the mouse behavior data collected during the login process by the legitimate user using the soft keyboard to type the password information. The user's unique mouse behavior pattern is formed, which is used for identity legality authentication. The feasibility of using the mouse behavior mode to perform the auxiliary authentication method, thereby further protecting the user's account and fund security, is studied.

The characteristics of the user's mouse behavior are related to the speed of the person's hand, the familiarity with the computer equipment, age, gender, and so on. The basic premise of identity authentication based on mouse behavior is that for each different user, the mouse behavior habit, that is, the mouse usage mode, is significantly different from that of other users. The unique mouse behavior pattern of one user is difficult to be copied by others [26–34]. The biggest advantage of using mouse behavior mode for user identification is that no additional hardware auxiliary equipment is needed, and the user does not need to make any changes to the original operating habits. The mouse data is collected and assisted in the process of logging in with the soft keyboard. There is no intrusion on the normal operation of the user's use of the computer.

To build a user's mouse behavior pattern, the first thing is to select the appropriate mouse behavior characteristics as the basis for building the model, and then select the appropriate model construction technology and identification method. The main mouse actions are clicking and moving when a user operates the soft keyboard. Due to the time and displacement characteristics, the mouse behavior patterns can be well distinguished, and the time and displacement values have the advantage of easy extraction and processing. The mouse movement behavior mode mainly takes these two types of data as features. The specific steps of mouse behavior authentication include mouse behavior data acquisition, feature extraction, and feature selection, mouse behavior pattern construction, and identity authentication. The data collected by the mouse behavior authentication is mainly the mouse action type, the mouse coordinate value, the mouse action time stamp, and so on. In the existing research, the mouse behavior characteristics are generally divided into interactive layer features (also known as application layer features) and physiological layer features [35]. The characteristics of the interaction layer are related to the application environment operated by the user, and reflect the characteristics of the user's preference and habits, such as the operating frequency distribution, the moving direction frequency, the operating screen frequency distribution, the static time duty ratio, etc.; the physiological layer features, as the name suggests, reflect the unique characteristics of the user's physiology, such as mouse single-click time interval, average moving speed, average acceleration, moving speed extreme value, and so on. In the application scenario of the dynamic soft keyboard, the characteristics of the physiological layer are often used when calculating the feature quantity of the mouse behavior. Then, based on the L-to-R selection algorithm, the mouse behavior pattern under the non-fixed trajectory is constructed. By simulating the dynamic soft keyboard application scenario, the user mouse behavior under the relatively free trajectory is captured, and new feature attribute values are proposed according to the behavioral characteristics. Meanwhile, the traditional feature values are classified and refined, and the cumulative function distribution and the L-to-R selection method are combined. By simulating the application scenario of a dynamic soft keyboard, the mouse behavior feature vector is obtained, and the SVM support vector machine classifier is used to classify the feature vector to obtain the user mouse behavior pattern, adopting a majority vote method to legalize the identity of the user.

The user mouse behavior authentication method can be subdivided into the following modules specifically: the user mouse behavior data acquisition module, which implements interception and storage of data generated by the user operating the mouse, including basic data items such as coordinate axes, time stamps, and mouse action types. The data preprocessing module is mainly responsible for cleaning the dirty data, processing the original data, and calculating the mouse behavior characteristic attribute through the mathematical formula; the feature vector selection module selects and forms the best feature vector from all the feature attribute sets; the behavior pattern construction and storage module uses the best feature vector for the construction and storage of the mouse behavior pattern; the user identity authentication module is used to authenticate the

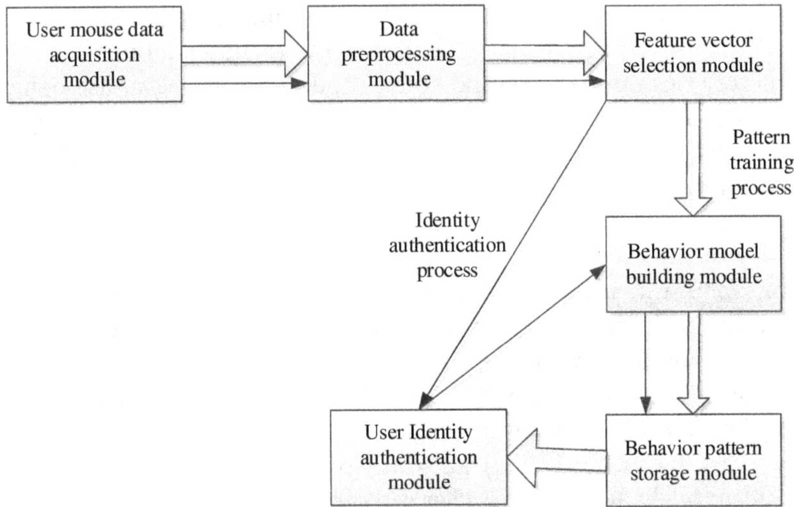

Figure 5.5   Mouse behavior authentication method function module diagram.

identity of the user. Figure 5.5 shows the various functional modules of the user's mouse behavior authentication method.

The main function of the mouse behavior data acquisition module is to use the designed random dynamic soft keyboard, simulate user input password scenario, collect and store data generated by using the mouse during user password operations. The recorded data tuple includes the time stamp, X and Y axis information, Basic data items such as action types.

The data preprocessing module must first clean the dirty data, mainly including the recording tuple that does not conform to the rules and the recording tuple with abnormal data size. At the same time, the cross-platform data is calibrated to eliminate the influence of platform differences as much as possible. Then, through mathematical formula processing, an alternative mouse behavior feature attribute is obtained, which is used to generate a feature vector required for subsequent modeling.

The feature vector extraction module uses the feature vector selection algorithm, and the evaluation function compares the classification accuracy, before finally selecting the best feature vector for pattern construction.

The user behavior pattern construction and storage module use the SVM support vector machine method to train the mouse behavior characteristics obtained by the above modules. For the mouse behavior data under each account, the pattern building module analyzes and models the processed data by using the specified pattern construction method, and stores the relevant parameters of the behavior pattern in the database, to facilitate the subsequent mouse behavior identity authentication operation.

In the user identity authentication module, the main function is to calculate the feature attributes of the new data to be tested and use the stored model parameters to identify the identity of the unknown user using the SVM classifier and the majority vote method. For data that matches the user's mouse behavior pattern, the user is allowed to log in, and this legal data is added to the model library to continuously update the user's mouse behavior pattern. If it is determined to be illegal data, the user is prevented from performing the login operation.

In different platforms, the inconsistency of the operating environment and equipment will affect the accuracy of the user's mouse behavior authentication. Aiming at the influence of factors such as display resolution and mouse pointer sensitivity, it is proposed to select feature quantities that do not depend on the operating environment, such as time, angle, and ratio features. For feature quantities that depend on the operating environment, the variance discrimination calibration operation can be used. At the same time, from the aspect of the user's habits of operating the mouse, the change of the characteristic attributes of passwords of different lengths entered by users is studied, and the impact of different lengths of passwords on the authentication effect is analyzed through experimental data. According to the different mouse behavior habits when the user enters passwords of different lengths, the value of the judgment attribute parameter is dynamically adjusted to eliminate the adverse effect of the behavior difference on the final authentication effect, thereby improving the accuracy of mouse behavior authentication.

5.4 User Behavior Certificate Method

A digital certificate, as an effective identity authentication mechanism in the network environment, has been widely adopted. It can basically solve the problem that both the buyer and the seller of a online transaction must have a legal identity, and be able to effectively and accurately verify on the Internet. Digital certificates, as a static authentication mechanism, have gradually exposed their shortcomings. First, they cannot solve problems such as "identity theft" and "use of legal identities to do illegal things". Once this kind of situation happens, generally one can only carry out post-mortem analysis and offline detection. Digital certificates provide guarantees for the identification of online payment participants, but there is currently no good mechanism for authenticating participants' transaction behaviors. Therefore, a corresponding behavior certificate can be generated for each user's behavior, and the behavior authentication on the client-side can effectively monitor the "illegal behavior of legitimate users" by analyzing user behavior. The user behavior certificate method is mainly used to monitor and analyze the user's transaction behavior, thereby identifying the user's identity, avoiding identity theft and fraud, and preventing the occurrence of transaction risks.

The basic design framework for a user behavior certificate can be shown in Figure 5.6. The figure shows the overall design framework for user identity authentication with behavior certificates. The figure shows that the client is responsible for collecting and uploading user behavior data. In the certification center, the collected user behavior data will produce the corresponding user's behavior certificate according to the behavior data processing model. If the user's behavior certificate already exists, the user's behavior model certificate will be dynamically adjusted incrementally to adapt to the dynamic migration of user behavior. After the user behavior certificate is generated or updated, the certificate file will be sent to the client, the authentication of the end-user identity information will be completed at the client. The authentication center will take corresponding release or warning measures according to the authentication result of the client [36–39].

User behavior mode authentication can collect normal web browsing records of normal users, extract behavior information that is most representative of the user, and construct a user behavior certificate to further determine whether the web browsing behavior of the user is consistent with the user based on the original authentication method. Furthermore, users are double-authenticated to better ensure the safety of user property.

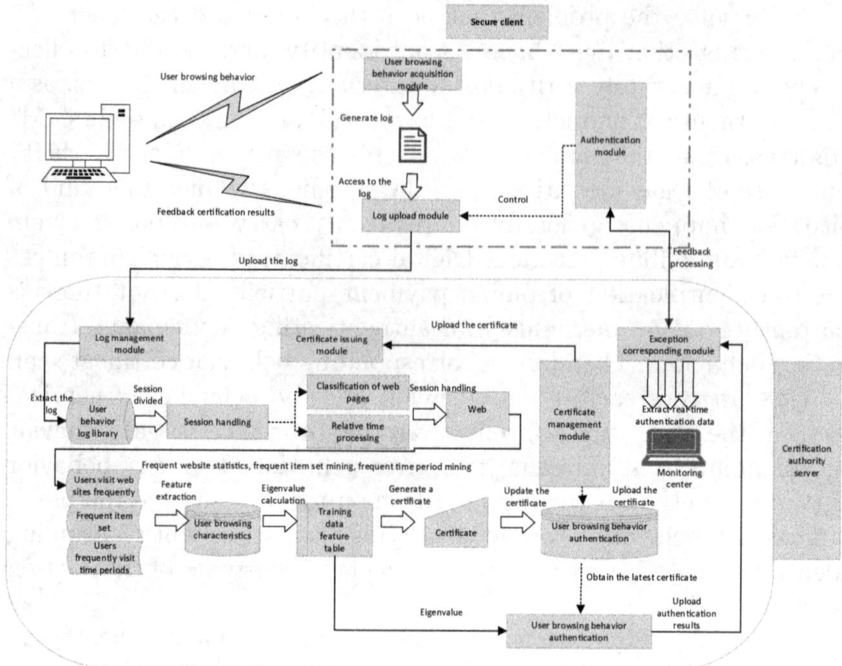

Figure 5.6   Behavior certificate design framework.

User behavior mode authentication can collect normal web browsing records of normal users, extract behavior information that is most representative of the user, and construct a user behavior certificate to further determine whether the user's web browsing behavior is consistent with the user behavior certificate based on the original authentication method or not, and then perform double authentication for the user to better ensure the safety of user property.

Every time a user opens a webpage, while browsing the webpage, a browsing record Rec containing a five-dimensional vector is generated to store the webpage-related information.

$$\boldsymbol{Rec} = (UserID, TimeStamp, LastingSeconds, URL, Reference)$$

Among them, $UserID$ identifies the user identification that generates this web browsing record; and $TimeStampLastingSeconds$ records the date and duration of this web browsing; besides, $URLReference$ records the web address of the user's current

Table 5.1   Sample *Recd* data record format.

Label	Content
UserID	user1
URL	http://123.duba.net/dbtj
Reference	http://weibo.com/u/1652598533?c=spr_web_sq_kings_weibo_t001
TimeStamp	2013/12/11 21:07:17
LastingSeconds	60

browsing and the forward link of the web address (NULL if there is no forward link). The user's raw data records collected by the data collector can be shown in Table 5.1.

The user's web browsing behavior authentication mainly includes two stages: offline and online. The main work of the offline phase is to build a user behavior model. The online phase mainly includes the observation sequence for monitoring and the use of behavior certificates for user behavior authentication. At the same time, the modeling and identity authentication of users' web browsing behaviors are based on the existing behavior stability assumptions, which are mainly reflected in the following two aspects: First, in a short period, users' web-browsing preferences will not change a lot (i.e., the type of web browsing and online time), and most of the web browsing information of the user during each web browsing is gathered in a specific part of the web category; Second, if a normal account is stolen by a malicious attacker, then the web browsing behavior of the attacker is less similar to that of the account owner. This stability hypothesis has been proved to be reasonable in a large number of scientific studies.

After collecting the user behavior data, the constructed user behavior model can be expressed in the form of the user Markov model. The build process has the following steps. Step one is the process of data mining: collect web users' web browsing records for at least 30 days, and obtain the order of web links and the order of web browsing. Step two is the information presentation process: according to the collected data, extract key information of the webpage, such as the content of the webpage description and the information about the link in and out of the webpage, and cluster the webpage based

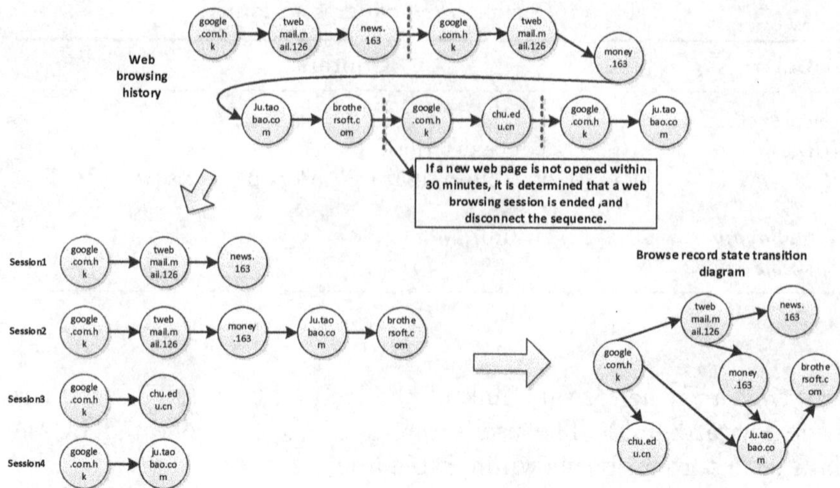

Figure 5.7   User browsing behavior sequence extraction process.

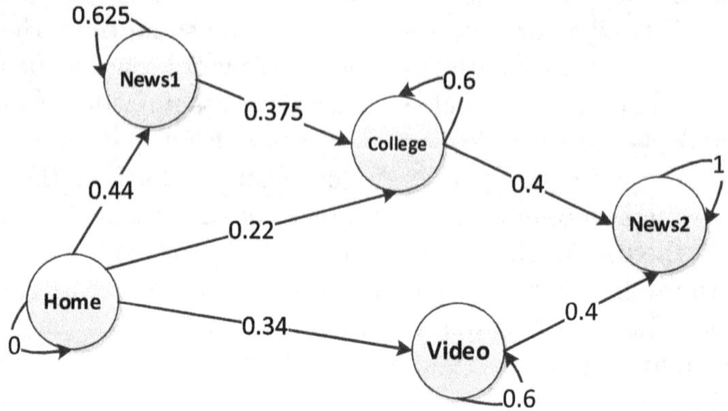

Figure 5.8   Simplified user browsing Markov Chain example.

on the content and time of the webpage to form webpage nodes; Step three is to add weights to the edges of the graph according to the number of links between the nodes of the web page class: form the user behavior pattern graph (as shown in Figure 5.7); Step 4 is the construction of a Markov model: it includes generation of initialization probability vector and state transition probability (as shown in Figure 5.8).

In addition to the Markov model, other data analysis models such as association rules and frequent tree mining can be used for user behavior analysis. Besides, in addition to the mining of the sequence of browsing URL types, the behavior characteristics of browsing content can be further studied to identify users [40–44].

5.5 Complex Event Processing

If considering user behavior as an event in business flow, complex event processing (CEP) technology can also be used for risk prevention and control of network transaction systems. CEP is based on event flow, which can realize high-speed access to real-time information and provide advanced query function. It is a technology to build and manage the event-driven information system. It regards the system data as different types of events. By analyzing the relationship between single or simple events, establishing different event relationship sequence libraries, using filtering, correlation, aggregation, and other technologies, it discovers and organizes valuable and meaningful complex events, and finally generates advanced events or business processes by simple events.

An event in CEP refers to the occurrence of any activity in the system which is significant, transient, and atomic. Data are closely associated with the occurrence of an event, and the data item associated with an event is referred to as an attribute. CEP uses the event hierarchy to define a set of rules to step up the lower-level event to a high-level event. CEP identifies important event patterns in real-time systems through event pattern matching. Different from the traditional database query, the CEP event query is a continuous and long-term query against infinite event flow. Because the data arrives continuously, the event query needs to use a sliding window to deal with the infinite data flow.

CEP technology captures events by analyzing the real-time data stream of the system, processes all input events in real-time according to the pre-formulated event processing rules or patterns, obtains the information contained in them, deduces meaningful complex events, and responds in real-time. CEP techniques include event pattern recognition, association, and abstraction of events, event levels, relationships between events, and complex event handling.

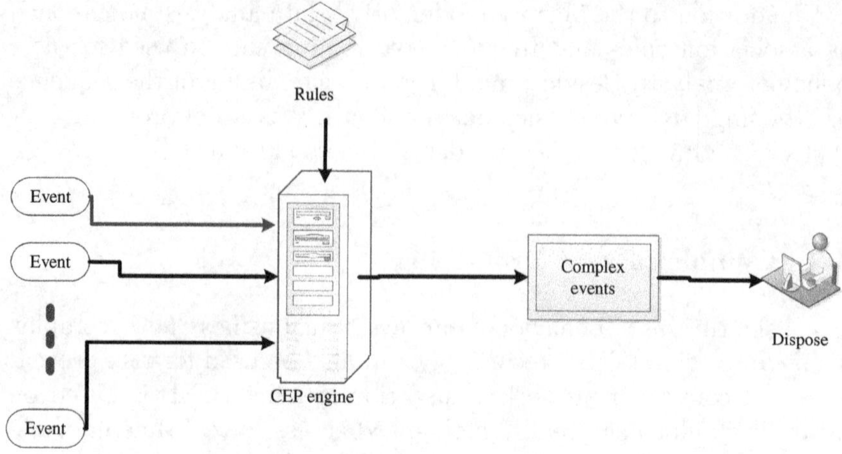

Figure 5.9   Basic process flow chart of the CEP system.

Accordingly, the CEP system includes some core modules, such as EPL resolver, rule management, event access, preprocessing, CEP engine, data model, event dispatch, and action module.

Among them, EPL is the language used to describe compound events, which will be processed by EPL parser and become a rule that can be used internally. These event processing rules are described by SQL-like event processing language, which can facilitate users to make complex processing rules, and can also be run in memory to process and query input events; The preprocessing module processes events, including field filtering, field filling, event filtering, event shunt, event confluence, etc.; CEP engine is the core of CEP platform, which provides CEP function. CEP engine is a platform for real-time processing, analyzing massive events, receiving events from different event sources, and processing each received event; Event handling rules describe how to handle original input events and generate complex events [45–49].

If CEP technology is applied to the risk control of the online transaction system, it should be considered from the perspective of user behaviors. In the face of massive user transaction data and behavior, how to collect information and judge the transaction risk is a great challenge. The transaction event of legitimate users can be abstracted as user behavior. Through the analysis and processing of a large number of simple user behaviors, useful information (complex event

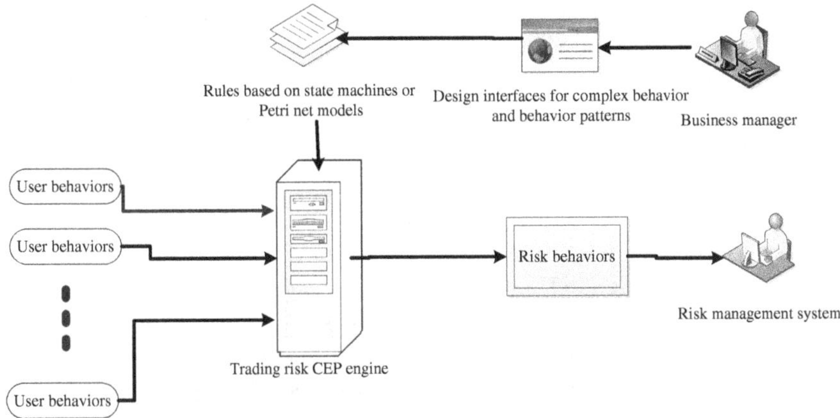

Figure 5.10   Basic processing flow chart of the CEP system for online transaction risk control.

or risk behavior) can be deduced, and the transaction risk can be finally discovered and processed in time. Among them, the design of the CEP engine is the key. The bottom of many CEP engines is a database, and online transaction risk control pays more attention to the behavior mode of users. Therefore, the underlying rule base of the online transaction risk control CEP platform should be implemented by a state machine or Petri net, which is beneficial to improve the efficiency and false alarm rate of the system. At the same time, the behavior definition based on a state machine or Petri net is based on strict formal modeling and verification, which can ensure the correctness and integrity of the behavior model. Alipay Governor System is a transaction risk control system based on CEP and state machine model [50].

As shown in Figure 5.10, the transaction risk control CEP system collects and processes the real-time transaction data of a large number of users through the window mechanism, abstracts as user behavior, and acts as the input of the transaction risk control CEP engine. The CEP engine analyzes these user behaviors and matches them with the state machine or Petri net model. Through hierarchical recurrence, more complex and meaningful events, that is, risk behavior is obtained. Finally, it is handed over to the relevant departments or systems for early warning and processing to avoid the huge losses caused by transaction risk. Note here that business managers are responsible for designing and managing behavior patterns. Business managers can be domain experts or model analysts to design and manage models and rules through relevant graphical interfaces.

The CEP is a real-time processing technology that stores data first and processes it later. It has changed the conventional data mining approach, to reduce the processing time of refinement of the data streams. At the same time, the technology provides the specified time-based or length-based query methods. For example, using a time-based window, CEP can create an average shopping amount for a user over some time. The Esper is an open-source implementation framework of CEP, which monitors users' shopping information and triggers monitoring when a risk event occurs. The Esper is a rule-based CEP engine, which can store the monitored risk information in the database or display it on the user interface.

According to the risk category of shopping information, the system administrators will define corresponding processing rules in advance. There is an event flow that goes into the Esper and matches it to the event rules base, and when the rule match is successful, the engine triggers the listeners and finally catches the risk event. At the same time, the risk events are sent into the database or displayed on the user interface.

We firstly obtain data streams of the online shopping process and convert unstructured data into structured data by byte filling, filtering, and aggregation, etc.; then use them as the input event streams of the CEP engine; finally, the online shopping risks are identified by the CEP platform. Here, according to the typical user malicious behavior patterns, we define the relevant variables, atomic events, and the relevant event patterns as follows [51].

userID: ID number of a user
money: Shopping amount of a user
orderID: Order ID of a user
tradeway: Payment way of a user
tradeplace: Trading address of a user(1-paid, 0-unpaid)
tradetime: Shopping time of a trading
tradestate: Shopping status of a user

E is the set of events in risk detection of the online shopping process:

$$E = \{e_n | n = 1, 2, 3, \ldots, N+\}, \quad e_n = \{a, t_1, t_2\}$$

TE is the set of events that capture user shopping behavior in real-time:

$$TE = \{e_n | n = 1, 2, 3, \ldots, N+\}, \quad e_n = \{a, t_1, t_2\}$$

$$a = \{userID, money, orderID, tradeway, \ tradeplace,$$

$$tradetime, tradestate\}$$

The event patterns of the single account mainly analyze the shopping data streams of the same accounts and capture the user risk behavior by analyzing the shopping amount, transaction address, and payment way. Mainly includes event patterns 1, 2, 3, and 4.

The event patterns of the multi-user account mainly analyze that a person has different accounts for shopping. Order replacement means that a user uses different accounts to achieve the purchase of a high-priced item for a low price. These mainly include event pattern 5 and event pattern 6.

The risk behaviors of shopping are characterized by algebraic expressions, which are easy to read and understand. At the same time, the correctness of semantics is guaranteed. Algebraic expressions construct atomic events for complex events through operators. The threshold t is settled according to the event pattern of the user's online shopping process.

Event pattern 1 In the time period T, the user m, whose shopping amount exceeds the average amount v, is algebraically expressed as follows:

$$C_1 = \sigma(TE)T;$$

$$\theta = (userID = m) \wedge (money > v) \wedge (tradestate = 1);$$

Event pattern 2 For user m, the four consecutive shopping sessions are o_1, o_2, o_3, o_4, and the shopping times are t_1, t_2, t_3, and t_4, respectively. The shopping amount shows an increasing trend and the fourth shopping amount is more than four times of the first shopping amount. The algebraic expression is as follows:

$$C_2 \rightarrow C_3;$$

$$C_3 \rightarrow C_4;$$

$$C_4 \rightarrow C_5;$$

$$C_2 = \sigma\theta_1(TE)t_1;$$

$$C_3 = \sigma\theta_2(TE)t_2;$$

$$C_4 = \sigma\theta_3(TE)t_3;$$

$$C_5 = \sigma\theta_4(TE)t_4;$$

$$\theta_1 = (userID = m) \wedge (tradestate = 1) \wedge (money = m_1)$$
$$\wedge\, (tradedate = t_1) \wedge (orderID = o_1);$$

$$\theta_2 = (userID = m) \wedge (tradestate = 1) \wedge (money = m_2)$$
$$\wedge\, (tradedate = t_2) \wedge (orderID = o_2);$$

$$\theta_3 = (userID = m) \wedge (tradestate = 1) \wedge (money = m_3)$$
$$\wedge\, (tradedate = t_3) \wedge (orderID = o_3);$$

$$\theta_4 = (userID = m) \wedge (tradestate = 1) \wedge (money = m_4)$$
$$\wedge\, (tradedate = t_4) \wedge (orderID = o_4);$$

$$m_1 < m_2 < m_3 < m_4;$$

$$m_4 >\, = 4 \times m_1;$$

$$o_1 < o_2 < o_3 < o_4.$$

It is important to note that the operator "→" indicates that there is a sequence among different events and that one event can occur after another.

Event pattern 3 The payment way and shopping status (paid) of the user m at time t_1 are the same as the time t_2, respectively, p and 1 (paid). However, the trading addresses of the two are different as $p1$ and $p2$, respectively. It should be noted that the shopping interval of the same user account is less than the threshold t.

The algebraic expression is as follows:

$$C_6 \rightarrow C_7;$$

$$C_6 = \sigma\theta_5(TE)t_1;$$

$$C_7 = \sigma\theta_6(TE)t_2;$$

$$\theta_5 = (userID = m) \wedge (tradeplace = p_1) \wedge tradeway = w)$$
$$\wedge\, (tradestate = 1);$$

$$\theta_6 = (userID = m) \wedge (tradestate = p_2) \wedge (tradeway = w)$$
$$\wedge (tradestate = 1);$$
$$t_2 - t_1 < t.$$

Event pattern 4 The trading address and shopping status (paid) of the user m at time t_1 are the same as the time t_2, where the trading address is p and shopping status is paid. However, the payment way of the two is different as w1 and w2, respectively. Besides, the time interval between the two signals is less than the threshold value t.

The algebraic expression is as follows:

$$C_8 \rightarrow C_9;$$
$$C_8 = \sigma\theta_7(TE)t_1;$$
$$C_9 = \sigma\theta_8(TE)t_2;$$
$$\theta_7 = (userID = m) \wedge (tradeplace = p) \wedge (tradeway = w_1)$$
$$\wedge (tradestate = 1);$$
$$\theta_8 = (userID = m) \wedge (tradeplace = p) \wedge (tradeway = w_2)$$
$$\wedge (tradestate = 1);$$
$$t_2 - t_1 < t.$$

Event pattern 5 Obtaining online shopping information with the user name m_1 at the time t_1, specifically: the order ID o_1, the trading address p; and the online shopping information with the user name m_2 are obtained at time t_2, the order ID o_2, the trading address is p. The time interval between the two signals is less than the threshold value t. Two user accounts (actually the same person) place two orders at the same time, and the algebraic expression is as follows:

$$C_{10} \rightarrow C_{11};$$
$$C_{10} = \sigma\theta_9(TE)t_1;$$
$$C_{11} = \sigma\theta_{10}(TE)t_2;$$
$$\theta_9 = (userID = m_1) \wedge (orderID = o_1)$$
$$\wedge (tradeplace = p) \wedge (tradestate = 0);$$
$$\theta_{10} = (userID = m_2) \wedge (orderID = o_2)$$
$$\wedge tradeplace = p) \wedge (tradestate = 0);$$
$$t_2 - t_1 < t.$$

Event pattern 6 On the basis of the event pattern 5, one of the two orders was not paid for, whose algebraic expression is

$$C_{12} \to C_{13};$$
$$C_{12} = \sigma\theta_{11}(TE)t_1;$$
$$C_{13} = \sigma\theta_{12}(TE)t_2;$$
$$\theta_{11} = (userID = m_1) \wedge (orderID = o_1)$$
$$\wedge (tradeplace = p) \wedge (tradestate = 0);$$
$$\theta_{12} = (userID = m_2) \wedge (orderID = o_2)$$
$$\wedge (tradeplace = p) \wedge (tradestate = 1);$$
$$t_2 - t_1 < t.$$

According to the relevant definitions and event descriptions of online shopping risk, the corresponding rules are constructed by Event Processing Language (EPL), a subset of SQL, extended with features for stream processing. Thus, rules can be established in a familiar, easy-to-learn, high-level language. When building user online shopping structured data streams, we need to filter the invalid data streams, such as the types of products purchased by users, non-existent user names, and invalid shopping records, etc. Esper has special data structure conventions for events. The event structures can be handled by Plain Ordinary Java Object (POJO), MAP, Object Array, Extensible Markup Language (XML). Esper's event object could be a container to send events to Esper's engine. The event class of online shopping risk identification is defined as TranEvent (event object), a standard Java class, which mainly includes userID, money, orderID, tradeway, tradeplace, tradetime, and tradestate.

The event streams of user online shopping are arranged based on the time stamp and sent to the engine for further processing. Then EPLs are constructed to implement flow quires and pattern matching based on the risk that may arise in the shopping process. Once the query is registered, the incoming shopping user data will be processed. Meanwhile, it is worth noting that all EPLs must be registered at the beginning. Next, we need to add listeners to receive risk results. Whenever a risk event (complex event) occurs, as long as it matches the rules, a response will be sent to the appropriate listener. Esper handles the streaming data by using POJO, because it is a good way to represent trading events to better predict the risk of the user's trading behaviors. The shopping information that enters the Esper engine mainly includes user name, trade way, amount, and other information.

To sum up, CEP can fix the problem of risk identification in real-time trading to some extent by designing relevant user trading scenarios and constructing complex event patterns (EPL rules). The proposed method can play an important role in early real-time warning when risks occur in the online shopping process [51].

5.6　Chapter Summary

With the increasing attention on the security of web applications, it is difficult to attack web applications from a technical perspective, such as cross-site script attacks. However, due to the general lack of computer expertise of web users, network fraud, a social engineering method of deceiving web users of their online silver account passwords through phishing websites, can be successful over and over again. A digital certificate, that is, a series of data that marks the identity information of online users, is a widely used means of user authentication in online transactions at present. The biggest drawback of this mechanism is that the password and other information are easy to divulge, so there are serious security risks. When the password is relatively simple, it can be cracked by violence based on the dictionary, and people familiar with it can even guess the password. At the same time, due to phishing and information disclosure of regular websites, hackers can obtain users' digital certificates and then impersonate user identity for business activities. Therefore, the use of digital certificates containing user information and encryption keys cannot perfectly solve the problem of user identity trust. How to effectively identify a person's true identity and behavior is an important challenge. As each person's behavior pattern is different, and it is difficult to be stolen by others, by studying user behavior the recognition rate of the real identity of the user can be greatly improved. Therefore, by collecting users' usual online habits, collecting their browsing logs, and mining out the unique behavior patterns of each user, we can achieve the purpose of more effective identification of the true identity of users, reduce the possibility of the success of network fraud; and reduce the probability of transaction risk.

References

[1] Wang, R., Chen, S., Wang, X. F. *et al.* How to Shop for Free Online–Security Analysis of Cashier-as-a-Service Based Web Stores. In *32th IEEE Symposium on Security and Privacy (S&P)*, IEEE, Oakland, USA, pp. 465–448, (2011).

[2] Peng, A., Han, L., Yu, Y. *et al.* Algebra-Based Behavior Identification of Trojan Horse. In *5th International Symposium on Cyberspace Safety and Security (CSS)*, China, pp. 323–337, (2013).

[3] Chen, E. Y., Chen, S., Qadeer, S. *et al.* Securing Multiparty Online Services via Certification of Symbolic Transactions. In *36th IEEE Symposium on Security and Privacy (S&P)*, San Jose, USA, pp. 833–849, (2015).

[4] Sun, F. Q., Xu, L., and Su, Z. D. Detecting Logic Vulnerabilities in E-Commerce Applications. In *21st Network and Distributed System Security Symposium (NDSS)*, Internet Society, San Diego, USA, pp. 1–16, (2014).

[5] Jain, A., Ross, A., and Prabhakar, S. An Introduction to Biometric Recognition. *IEEE Transactions on Circuits and Systems for Video Technology*, 14: 4–20 (2004).

[6] Abaza, A., Ross, A., Hebert, C. *et al.* A Survey on Ear Biometrics. *ACM Computing Surveys*, 45(2): 1–35 (2013).

[7] Sharif, M., Bhagavatula, S., Bauer, L. *et al.* Accessorize to a Crime: Real and Stealthy Attacks on State-of-the-Art Face Recognition. In *Proceedings of the 2016 ACM SIGSAC Conference on Computer and Communications Security (CCS'16)*, New York, NY, USA: ACM, pp. 1528–1540, (2016).

[8] Song, C., Qu, Z., Blumm, N. *et al.* Limits of Predictability in Human Mobility. *Science*, 327: 1018–1021 (2010).

[9] de Montjoye, Y. A., Radaelli, L., Singh, V. K. *et al.* Unique in the Shopping Mall: On the Reidentifiability of Credit Card Metadata. *Science*, 347: 536–539 (2015).

[10] Iglesias, J., Angelov, P., Ledezma, A. *et al.* Creating Evolving User Behavior Profiles Automatically. *IEEE Transactions on Knowledge and Data Engineering*, 24: 854–867 (2012).

[11] Antwarg, L., Rokach, L., and Shapira, B. Attribute-Driven Hidden Markov Model Trees for Intention Prediction. *IEEE Transactions on Systems, Man, and Cybernetics, Part C: Applications and Reviews*, 42: 1103–1119 (2012).

[12] Neverova, N. Learning Human Identity from Motion Patterns. *IEEE Access*, 4: 1810–1820 (2016).

[13] Leiva, L. A. and Vivo, R. Web Browsing Behavior Analysis and Interactive Hypervideo. *ACM Transactions on Web*, 7(4): 1–28 (2013).

[14] Canali, D., Bilge, L., and Balzarotti, D. On the Effectiveness of Risk Prediction Based on Users Browsing Behavior. In *ASIA CCS'14*, ACM, New York, USA, pp. 171–182, (2014).

[15] Ceccarelli, A., Montecchi, L., Brancati, F. *et al.* Continuous and Transparent User Identity Verification for Secure Internet Services. *IEEE Transactions on Dependable and Secure Computing*, 12: 270–283 (2015).

[16] Mondal, S. and Bours, P. Continuous Authentication in a Real World Settings. In *8th International Conference on Advances in Pattern Recognition (ICAPR)*, IEEE, Kolkata, India, pp. 1–6, (2015).

[17] Xing, Z., Pei, J., and Keogh, E. A Brief Survey on Sequence Classification. *ACM SIGKDD Explorations Newsletter*, 12: 40–48 (2010).

[18] Radinsky, K., Svore, K. M., Dumais, S. T. *et al.* Behavioral Dynamics on the Web: Learning, Modeling, and Prediction. *ACM Transactions on Information Systems*, 31(3): 1–37 (2013).

[19] Manjusha, R. and Ramachandran, R. Web Mining Framework for Security in E-Commerce. In *ICRTIT'11*, IEEE, Chennai, Tamil Nadu, pp. 1043–1048, (2011).

[20] Srivastava, A., Kundu, A., Sural, S. *et al.* Credit Card Fraud Detection Using Hidden Markov Model. *IEEE Transactions on Dependable and Secure Computing*, 5: 37–48 (2008).

[21] Zhang, H. B. *Research on Identity Authentication Method Based on Keyboard Behavior of Mobile Users*, Shanghai, China, Tongji University, (2016).

[22] Zhang, X. M. *Research on the Construction Method of User Keyboard Behavior Pattern*, Shanghai, China, Tongji University, (2015).

[23] Zhang, X. M., Zhao, P. H., and Wang, M. M. Keystroke Dynamics in Password Authentication for Multi-User Account. *Journal of Computational Information Systems*, 11(1): 321–331 (2015).

[24] Gamboa, H. and Fred, A. A Behavioral Biometric System Based on Human-Computer Interaction. *Defense and Security. International Society for Optics and Photonics*, 5404: 381–392 (2004).

[25] Gamboa, H. and Fred, A. L. N. An Identity Authentication System Based on Human Computer Interaction Behaviour. In *Pattern Recognition in Information Systems (PRIS)*, ICEIS Press, Angers, France, pp. 46–55, (2003).

[26] Hamdy, O. and Traore, I. Homogeneous Physio-Behavioral Visual and Mouse-Based Biometric. *ACM Transactions on Computer-Human Interaction*, 18(3): 1–30 (2011).

[27] Pao, H. K., Fadlil, J., Lin, H. Y. *et al.* Trajectory Analysis for User Verification and Recognition. *Knowledge-Based Systems*, 34: 81–90 (2012).

[28] Shen, C., Cai, Z., Guan, X. *et al.* User Authentication Through Mouse Dynamics. *IEEE Transactions on Information Forensics and Security*, 8: 16–30 (2013).

[29] Shen, C., Cai, Z., Guan, X. *et al.* User Authentication and Monitoring Based on Mouse Behavioral Features. *Journal on Communications*, (7): 68–75 (2010).

[30] Shi, Y. X. The Data Collection of Imitating Dynamic Digital Input by Mouse. *Natural Science Journal of Xiangtan University*, (4): 23–27 (2001).

[31] Cai, Z., Shen, C., and Guan, X. Mitigating Behavioral Variability for Mouse Dynamics: A Dimensionality-Reduction-Based Approach. *IEEE Transactions on Human-Machine Systems*, 44(2): 244–255 (2014).

[32] Zheng, N., Paloski, A., and Wang, H. An Efficient User Verification System via Mouse Movements. In *Proceedings of the 18th ACM Conference on Computer and Communications Security*, ACM, pp. 139–150, (2011).

[33] Ahmed, A. A. E. and Traore, I. A New Biometric Technology Based on Mouse Dynamics. *IEEE Transactions on Dependable and Secure Computing*, 4(3): 165–179 (2007).

[34] Nakkabi, Y., Traoré, I., and Ahmed, A. A. E. Improving Mouse Dynamics Biometric Performance Using Variance Reduction via Extractors with Separate Features. *IEEE Transactions on Systems, Man and Cybernetics, Part A: Systems and Humans*, 40(6): 1345–1353 (2010).

[35] Chandola, V., Banerjee, A., and Kumar, V. Anomaly Detection for Discrete Sequences: A Survey. *IEEE Transactions on Knowledge and Data Engineering*, 24: 823–839 (2012).

[36] Jiang, C. J., Chen, H. Z., Yan, C. G. *et al.* Sequential Pattern Mining Method Based on Web User Time Attribute, Patents (CN 201410004623.6), 2014.04.23.

[37] Jiang, C. J., Chen, H. Z., Yan, C. G. *et al.* Identity Authentication Method Based on Web User Behavior Pattern, Patents (CN201210445681.3), 2015.11.04.

[38] Jiang, C. J., Chen, H. Z., Yan, C. G. *et al.* User Behavior Pattern Mining System and Its Method, Patents (CN 201210448617.0), 2015.11.04.

[39] Zhao, P. H., Yan, C. G., and Jiang, C. J. Authenticating Web User's Identity Through Browsing Sequences Modeling. In *ICDM Workshops*, IEEE, Barcelona, Spain, pp. 335–342, (2016).

[40] Mayil, V. Web Navigation Path Pattern Prediction Using First Order Markov Model and Depth First Evaluation. *International Journal of Computer Applications*, 45: 26–31 (2012).

[41] Yang, Y. C. and Padmanabhan, B. Toward User Patterns for Online Security: Observation Time and Online User Identification. *Decision Support Systems*, 48: 548–558 (2010).

[42] Abramson, M. and Aha, D. W. User Authentication from Web Browsing Behavior. In *FLAIRS'13*, AAAI Press, USA, pp. 268–273, (2013).

[43] Awad, M. and Khalil, I. Prediction of User's Web-Browsing Behavior: Application of Markov Model. *IEEE Transactions on Systems, Man and Cybernetics, Part B: Cybernetics*, 42: 1131–1142 (2012).

[44] Ahmed, A. A. E. and Traore, I. Detecting Computer Intrusions Using Behavioral Biometrics. In *3rd Annual Conference on Privacy, Security and Trust*, IEEE, New Brunswick, Canada, pp. 91–98, (2005).

[45] Jiao, Y. *Research on the Application of Complex Event Processing in Financial Industry*, Shanghai, China, Shanghai University, (2012).

[46] Jiang, L. F. and Zhao, J. B. The Summary of the Complex Event Processing Technology and Its Application. *Software*, 35(2): 188–192 (2014).

[47] Luckham, D. *The Power of Events: An Introduction to Complex Event Processing in Distributed Enterprise Systems*, Reading, MA, USA: Addison-Wesley, (2002).

[48] Luckham, D. *Event Processing for Business: Organizing the Real-Time Enterprise,* Hoboken, NJ, USA: Wiley, (2012).

[49] EsperTech. Esper-Complex Event Processing, accessed on November 3, 2016. Available at http://www.espertech.com/esper/.

[50] Cai, X. Y. Easy Understanding of Composite Event Handling. *Programmer*, (6): 112–113 (2010).

[51] Ma, Z. J., Yu, W. Y., Zhai, X. J. *et al.* A Complex Event Processing-Based Online Shopping User Risk Identification System. *IEEE Access*, 7: 172088–172096 (2019).

Chapter 6

Online Monitoring of Transaction Systems

6.1 Introduction

The preceding chapters mainly introduced the main theories, methods, and technology of risk prevention in the online transaction system. Based on the above content, research, and development of online transaction system, online monitoring platforms can realize the risk prevention and control of demand analysis, construction, validation, monitoring and evaluating the effective integration of theory and technology of online transaction system. By analyzing the existing problems in the business process, payment tools, and credit system of the existing online transaction system, a credible online transaction environment is constructed, and the behavior of each participant in the online transaction is restrained and standardized. The online monitoring platform of online transactions monitors and records the main transaction entities (buyers, sellers, third-party payment platforms, etc.) and the whole transaction process based on the behavior certificate, analyzes and processes the monitoring records from the monitoring center of online transactions, and then excavates the user behaviors of corresponding users. The monitoring records are classified according to the period, and then the transaction process of each transaction subject in a certain transaction are mined and analyzed accordingly. As a trusted and independent party in the online transactions, the fourth party certification center is responsible for constructing, updating, and issuing the behavioral certificates of the online transaction subject, thus certifying the online transaction behavior of the transaction subject. If any abnormality is found, an alarm will be issued to the corresponding transaction subject.

6.2   Composition and Architecture of the Monitoring System

The monitoring center developed by the research group belongs to the project "Test environment and demonstration application of trusted online transaction software system", which is used to monitor the behavioral data generated by users, merchants, and third-party payment platforms during transactions, and display the data and status in the transaction process utilizing tables and charts. Based on the fourth-party certification center, the monitoring center monitors and authenticates the three parties through the authentication technology of software behavior and user behavior, and can find abnormal behaviors in the transaction process. The preliminary work of the monitoring center includes the security client (which collects the data of online transaction behaviors of the system and users and uses it to mine behavior certificates) and the behavior authentication mechanism. The monitoring center mainly consists of four parts: interactive information display of client user behavior, information display of validation process of client software behavior, verification information display of e-commerce platform, and verification information display of third-party payment platform. The interactive display of client user behavior is used to present the interactive information between the user and the fourth-party certification center, such as user login, user behavior certificate download, log upload, and logout. The other three parts are used to display the software behaviors of users, e-commerce, and payment platforms, respectively, the software behaviors in the three-party interaction, and the results of certificate verification of software behaviors [1]. The architecture is shown in Figure 6.1.

Through the deployment of behavior monitors in user security clients, e-commerce websites, and payment platforms, the online transaction trusted authentication system platform is formed, and the online transaction trusted authentication protocol is developed. In the online transaction trusted authentication system, the

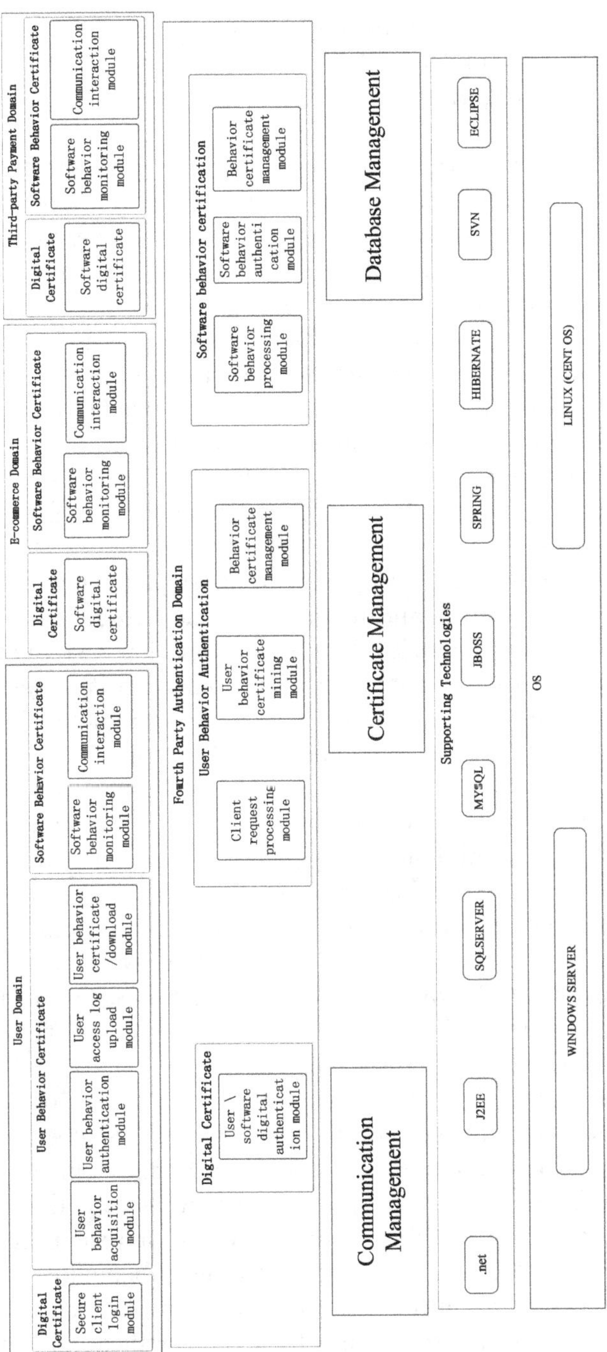

Figure 6.1 The architecture of trusted authentication center for online transactions [1].

authentication center is mainly responsible for the management of the user behavior and the software behavior certificate and can authenticate the credibility of software and user behavior in real-time simultaneously.

Online transaction trusted certification center supports a variety of operating systems, with good cross-platform capabilities. The supporting technology on the system provides good support for the application development of the upper layer. The communication management module, certificate management module, and database management module are designed based on supporting technology. The communication management module can encapsulate the network communication function according to the specific requirements of the system and provide communication services such as data exchange for the upper layer. The certificate management module provides unified management of software behavior certificates, user behavior certificates, and digital certificates, including the search, update, and release of certificates. The database management module is responsible for updating and maintaining the database to improve data access efficiency. There is a trusted certification system of online transactions' fourth-party authentication domain on the basic management module and its main function is to monitor and authenticate the online transaction process, to carry on the digital authentication to the three parties of the transaction, to verify the credibility of the user identity through the user behavior certificate, and to verify the credibility of the online transaction behavior of the three parties through the software behavior certificate.

The authentication protocol process of online transaction trusted certification center is as follows: when the online transaction occurs, the user uploads the digital certificate for digital authentication by logging in the security client, and the e-commerce and third-party payments also upload their digital certificate for corresponding digital authentication. After the digital authentication is passed, the user downloads the behavior certificate through the user behavior certificate download module, and the three parties officially enter the transaction process. In the process of transaction, the security client collects the user behavior in real-time through the user behavior acquisition module and gives it to the user behavior authentication module, which verifies the credibility of the user's current access behavior according to the user behavior certificate downloaded from the fourth-party certification center. If the authentication is approved, then the process continues to collect the user's access behavior for authentication; If the certification fails, the detailed certification results will be uploaded to the certification center, which will be reviewed and determined. At the same time, the software behavior is collected through the software behavior acquisition module and uploaded to the certification center by the communication interaction module. Meanwhile, e-commerce and third-party payment also collect their software behaviors in real-time through the software behavior monitoring module, which is uploaded to the certification center by the communication interaction module. If the software behavior certification is approved, the certification center will send back feedback information to continue the transaction process, and the monitoring of the three parties' software behavior will continue to be collected in real-time. If the certification is not passed, the certification center will broadcast an abnormal transaction process and terminate the transaction. When the transaction is completed, the security client will upload the new access log to the authentication center by the user access log. When the authentication center receives the new access log, it will send back the feedback information, and the user will exit the security client. After that, the certification center calls the user behavior certificate mining module through the certificate management module to mine the new user access log and update the user behavior certificate. When a new e-commerce or third-party payment platform is added, the digital certificate will be issued after it is approved. Then, by analyzing the source code of its website, the corresponding software behavior certificate is excavated and uploaded to the certification center for unified management by the behavior certificate management module [2–6].

6.3 System Optimization Management

At present, the strict risk control and verification methods of online transactions tend to cause higher false positives and lower the user experience. The large number of actual transactions also directly leads to a high number of false positives. False identification of normal transactions as fraudulent transactions will bring greater costs to the operators of the company. When the model identifies the transaction with fraud risk, the system will send confirmation messages, emails, and even manual phone calls to confirm the transaction, which requires the enterprise to pay a lot of extra capital and labor costs. Besides, SMS confirmation and manual confirmation of users will confuse users, increase the security concerns of users' use of the electronic payment, and interfere with the normal payment business process of users. It easily leads to users' operation failure, and even leads to the loss of users, resulting in additional costs. Therefore, for the online transaction system, how to optimize the existing risk system and reduce the interference to the normal users of the transaction platform needs to be solved urgently. The research group puts forward a risk control optimization scheme, which preliminarily verifies the online transaction by a simple model at first. If the verification is successful, it is considered a normal transaction; otherwise, strict model verification will be carried out. In this way, the problem of the high false alarm rate caused by the use of the classification model alone can be reduced. At the same time, by releasing a large number of normal transactions, the proportion of abnormal transaction samples in the classification stage can be increased, and the problem of unbalanced samples in the classification model can be improved [7].

The two-layer risk control method consists of two parts: risk transaction filtering method and risk identification model method. According to the trusted model of the transaction, the risk transaction filtering method can release the normal transaction quickly before the strict model verification, to improve the response speed of the normal transaction and reduce the false alarm rate of the transaction. The transaction after the risk filtering model still contains abnormal transactions, so it is necessary to use the risk identification model to further classify the remaining transaction samples and identify the abnormal transaction. Different from searching for a more effective model classification method and distinguishing features blindly, the two-layer risk control method solves and improves the risk problem in online transactions from two angles. The first layer focuses on the normal transaction, reducing subsequent rigorous model misreporting of the normal transaction and excessive computer performance losses by releasing normal trades. The second layer focuses on abnormal transactions, which are classified and identified through the selection of effective data features and classification models. The

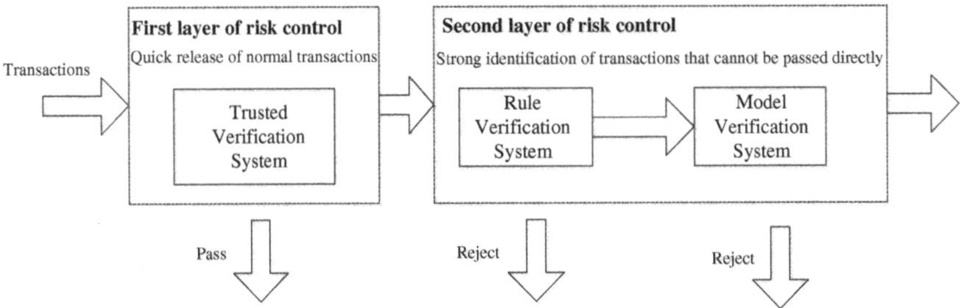

Figure 6.2   Transaction data flow diagram of the two-tier risk filtering system.

trade data flow diagram for the two-tier risk filtering system is shown in Figure 6.2.

6.4   System Online Monitoring

The data visualization system of user and software behavior monitoring in online transactions is composed of data acquisition and processing and data display systems. Data acquisition and processing are mainly responsible for obtaining the key software behavior information, platform transaction data, and end-user behavior and habit data in the transaction process, preprocessing these data, and processing the data according to the requirements of the presentation. The data presentation part shows the data of the data acquisition system and the authentication system in a multi-directional and multi-dimensional way, which includes three sub-modules: the visualization of the software behavior monitoring data of the quadrangle platform, platform transaction data monitoring visualization, and platform user behavior monitoring data visualization. They describe the monitoring data of user and software behavior in online transactions in three-dimensions. The architecture of the data visualization system for monitoring user and software behavior in online transactions is shown in Figure 6.3 [1].

The behavioral monitoring data visualization system is deployed in an unlimited target environment and can be deployed on Windows server systems or Linux server systems. The supporting technologies at the upper level adopt some mature technical frameworks in the industry, such as the mature MVC software development pattern, which provides services externally in the form of web service,

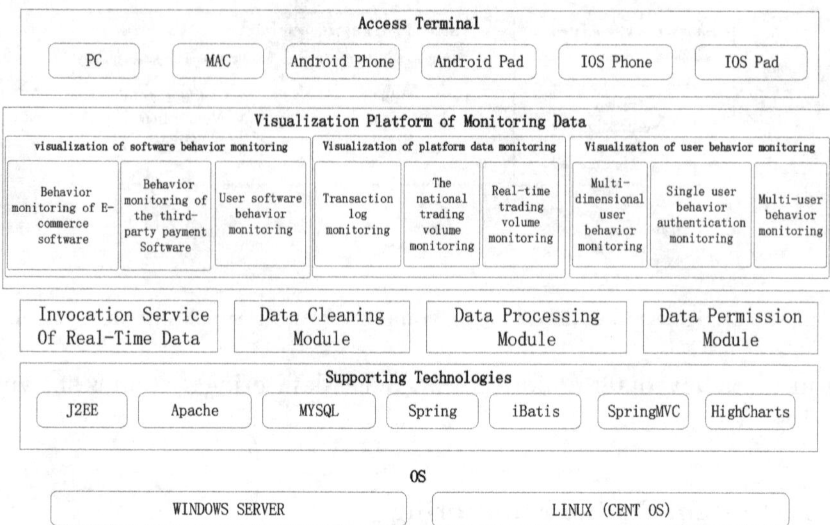

Figure 6.3   The architecture diagram of user and software behavior monitoring data visualization system in online transactions.

to support multi-terminal access to monitor interface. The overall system is based on the cross-platform Java implementation, in which the MVC framework adopts SpringMVC, which has good support for Restful, the data persistence layer adopts iBatis, and the view layer adopts Velocity. The visualization uses the javascript-based chart presentation tool HighCharts, so with the Internet access function, the browser supports Javascript terminal devices to access the monitoring visualization system. The entire system is deployed to an Apache server, and the server software is available on every operating system. On top of the supporting technologies are four lower-level middleware modules, namely real-time data invocation service, data cleaning module, the data processing module, and data authority module. The monitoring system emphasizes real-time data. The purpose of providing real-time data from the bottom up to call the service is to provide real-time data from the middle layer to the upper layer. Since the source of the data is not necessarily a local database, but also a third-party system, this part of the service will have access to both external and internal data sources. The data cleaning module is to carry out necessary preprocessing for irregular source data, such as partial fields being empty, conversion of discrete data and continuous data, etc. The main function of the data processing module is to further process the data and present it in the upper layer, such as data classification and data format filling. The main function of data authority is to protect the data of monitoring platforms and ensure the security of transaction data monitoring by controlling data granularity authority.

On the middleware module is the visual presentation platform of the monitoring system platform, which consists of three parts and each part consists of three sub-parts. The first part is the platform software behavior monitoring, which mainly includes the software behavior monitoring of e-commerce, third-party payment, and users, and is presented in three sub-parts, respectively. The presentation is done by scrolling through the list, showing the log of the software behavior, and highlighting the same exception transaction from multiple platform perspectives to help business people analyze the exception transaction. The second part is the visualization of platform transaction data. This part is used to display the transaction data through the platform, which is obtained from the monitored external e-commerce platform through real-time data service. The sub-parts are transaction log monitoring (displaying the transaction log of each key business process in a rolling way, linked to the software behavior log); the national transaction volume monitoring (showing the national transaction volume by heat map based on the national map and the bar chart distributed by province); real-time transaction volume monitoring (real-time transaction data of external service calls, including the number of real-time transaction strokes and real-time transaction volume, through the line chart display, you can also choose to present the transaction data for two hours, the previous day and the same period). The last part is the user behavior visual monitoring platform and this part is on the platform of user behavior monitoring data visualization. Its sub-part contains multi-dimensional user behavior monitoring (according to the user's online time distribution and the composition of the website class visited by the user, the multi-dimensional single-user behavior habit is formed, in which the distribution of the online time period is based on the area map, and the website class visited by the user is displayed at the same time as the column chart and the pie chart); Single-user behavior monitoring (display the visit log of users browsing the web in the way of scrolling, and display the real-time score of user

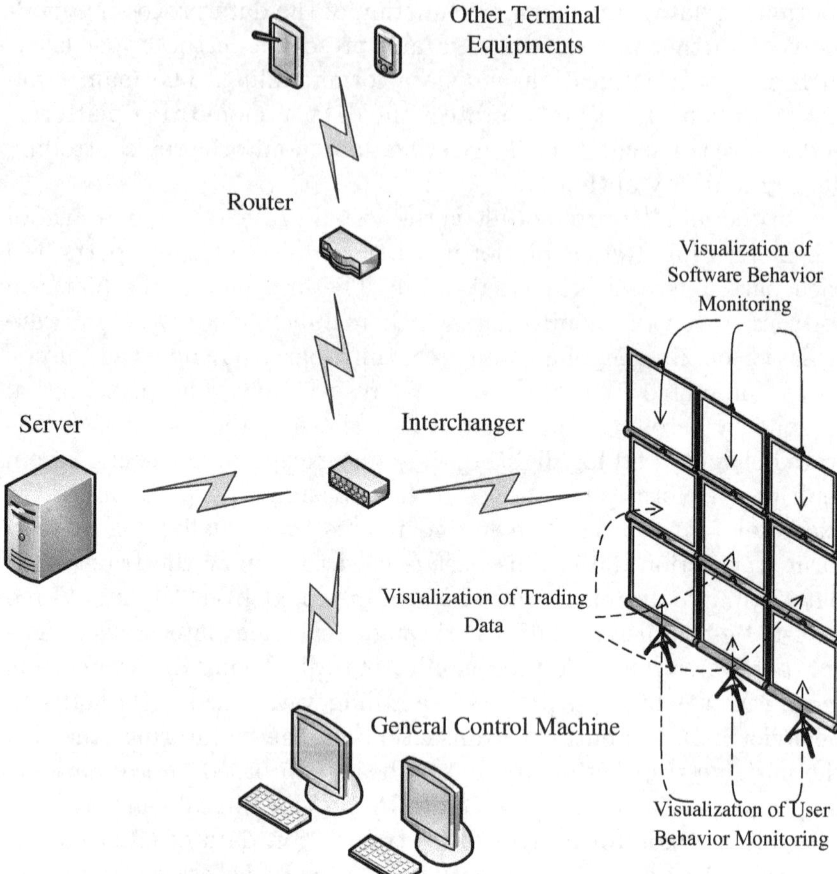

Figure 6.4   The deployment diagram of the data visualization system of user and software behavior monitoring.

identity authentication based on user behavior authentication technology, which is displayed inline graph); Monitoring of multi-user behavior (show the visiting log of multi-user browsing web pages in the way of scrolling, and show the real-time score of user identity authentication obtained by the authentication technology of user behavior when multi-users visit the website at the same time, which is updated in the column chart in real-time).

Figure 6.4 is the deployment diagram of the behavioral monitoring data visualization system. Figures 6.5 and 6.6 show the sever and monitoring interface. User-oriented monitoring visualization is

Figure 6.5   The Dawn Cloud platform.

Figure 6.6   The monitoring interface.

divided into indoor monitoring and external equipment monitoring. Indoor monitoring shows most of the above three contents by nine screens. The master computer can focus on the alarm data on the screen, so as to better help business personnel analyze the causes of alarm. Outdoor monitoring service is provided by the server, and real-time monitoring information can be directly viewed through handheld devices. All monitoring visualizations are provided by the visualization system software deployed on the server. (Note that all the data in the following sections are simulated experimental data, not real data).

6.4.1 *Real-time transaction volume monitoring*

Figure 6.7 is the real-time transaction volume and number of transactions protected by the risk control platform. The chart of this screen is drawn based on the combined chart function of HighChart, which combines the line chart and bar chart, among which the line chart shows the transaction information of the previous hour compared with the same period last year. The screen is refreshed at an interval of five seconds, and AJAX requests are periodically initiated to the server through the setInterval method of JS to obtain the data information cleaned in the server and display it. The display method is appended by scrolling in the last column.

6.4.2 *National transaction volume monitoring*

Figure 6.8 is the real-time national transaction volume distribution information protected by the risk control platform. It is the volume bar chart of the top 10 provinces with the largest transaction volume and the pie chart of their respective share of the total transaction volume.

6.4.3 *Transaction log monitoring*

Figure 6.9 is the transaction log information protected by the risk control platform. This screen displays the log information of participating users and software in online transactions from three aspects, respectively. The interface is also regularly refreshed for 5 seconds by appending data from the bottom of the table.

6.4.4 *Risk filtering transaction credibility verification display*

Figure 6.10 shows the risk-filtered transaction information, shown in two columns by time. The interface is refreshed by scrolling at regular intervals and the animation of scrolling and the purpose of

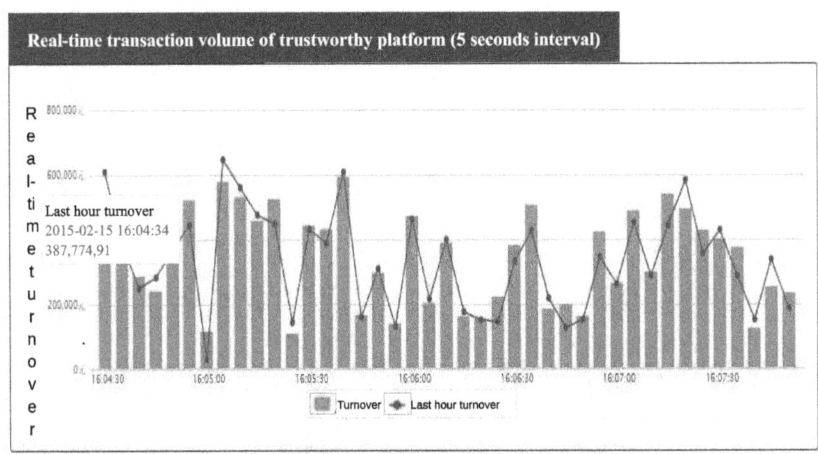

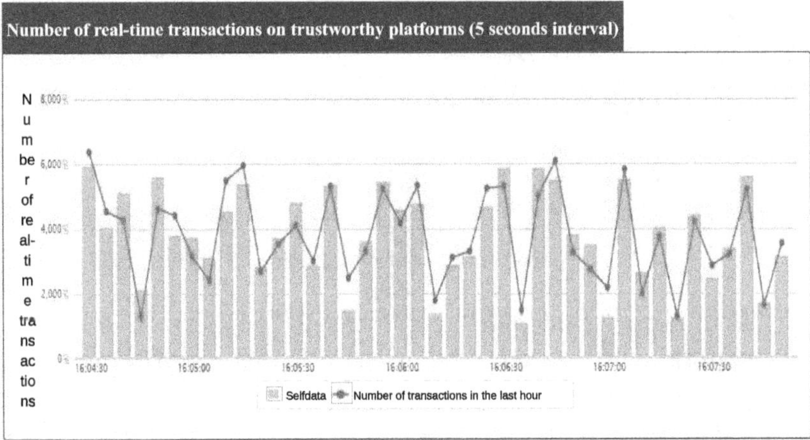

Figure 6.7 Display diagram of real-time transaction volume monitoring interface.

Figure 6.8   Display diagram of national transaction volume monitoring interface.

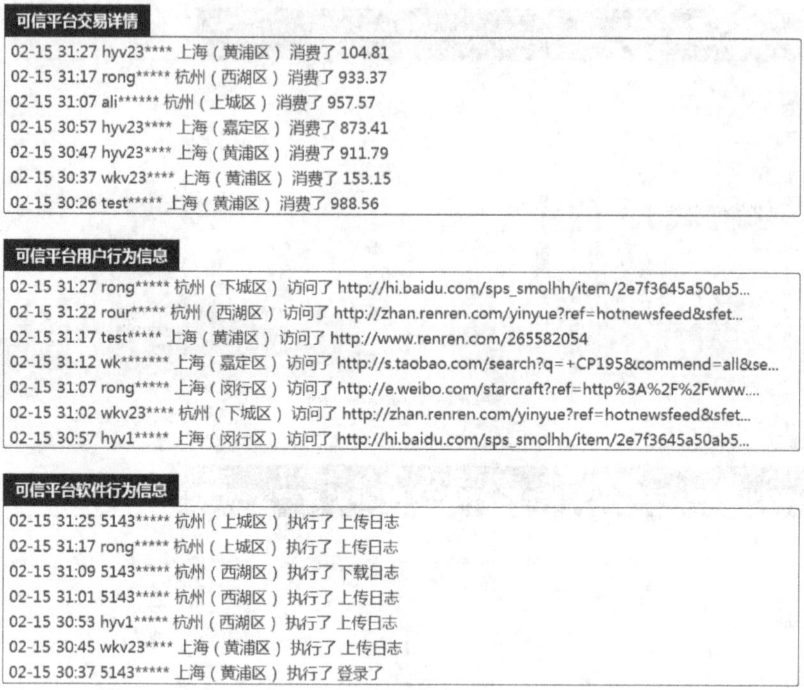

可信平台交易详情

02-15 31:27 hyv23**** 上海（黄浦区）消费了 104.81
02-15 31:17 rong***** 杭州（西湖区）消费了 933.37
02-15 31:07 ali****** 杭州（上城区）消费了 957.57
02-15 30:57 hyv23**** 上海（嘉定区）消费了 873.41
02-15 30:47 hyv23**** 上海（黄浦区）消费了 911.79
02-15 30:37 wkv23**** 上海（黄浦区）消费了 153.15
02-15 30:26 test***** 上海（黄浦区）消费了 988.56

可信平台用户行为信息

02-15 31:27 rong***** 杭州（下城区）访问了 http://hi.baidu.com/sps_smolhh/item/2e7f3645a50ab5...
02-15 31:22 rour***** 杭州（西湖区）访问了 http://zhan.renren.com/yinyue?ref=hotnewsfeed&sfet...
02-15 31:17 test***** 上海（黄浦区）访问了 http://www.renren.com/265582054
02-15 31:12 wk******* 上海（嘉定区）访问了 http://s.taobao.com/search?q=+CP195&commend=all&se...
02-15 31:07 rong***** 上海（闵行区）访问了 http://e.weibo.com/starcraft?ref=http%3A%2F%2Fwww....
02-15 31:02 wkv23**** 杭州（下城区）访问了 http://zhan.renren.com/yinyue?ref=hotnewsfeed&sfet...
02-15 30:57 hyv1***** 上海（闵行区）访问了 http://hi.baidu.com/sps_smolhh/item/2e7f3645a50ab5...

可信平台软件行为信息

02-15 31:25 5143***** 杭州（上城区）执行了 上传日志
02-15 31:17 rong***** 杭州（上城区）执行了 上传日志
02-15 31:09 5143***** 杭州（西湖区）执行了 下载日志
02-15 31:01 5143***** 杭州（西湖区）执行了 上传日志
02-15 30:53 hyv1***** 杭州（西湖区）执行了 上传日志
02-15 30:45 wkv23**** 上海（黄浦区）执行了 上传日志
02-15 30:37 5143***** 上海（黄浦区）执行了 登录了

Figure 6.9   Display diagram of transaction log monitoring interface.

the column purpose are implemented based on Jquery. Among them, the transaction that needs to be further identified by risk is marked red. All transactions of that user can be further monitored by clicking on the user name.

6.4.5   *Transaction risk identification model verification and monitoring*

Figure 6.11 is the transaction details verified by the transaction risk model. The mechanism shown in the part is consistent with the credible verification screen. Similarly, clicking on the user name displays the historical transaction log and details of the risks under that user.

6.4.6   *User risk transaction details monitoring*

In this section, the operator can query the risk of the user's historical transaction by entering a specific user name. The data detail section

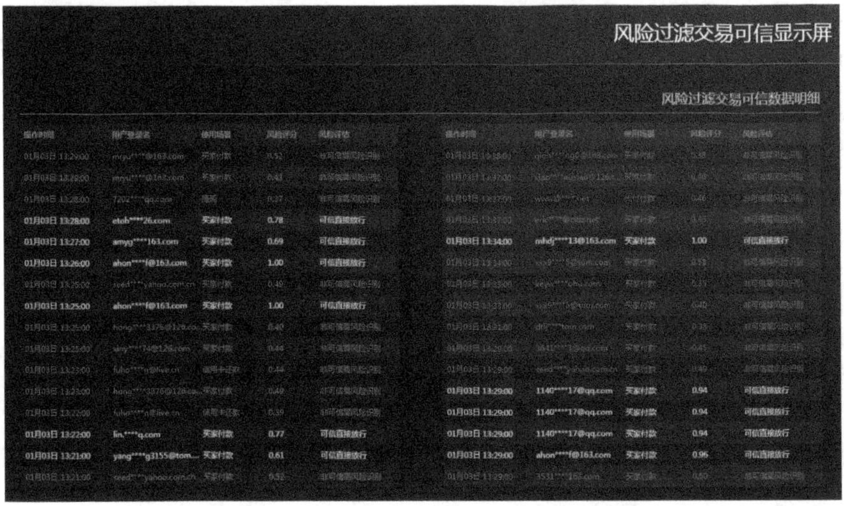

Figure 6.10　Display diagram of risk filtering.

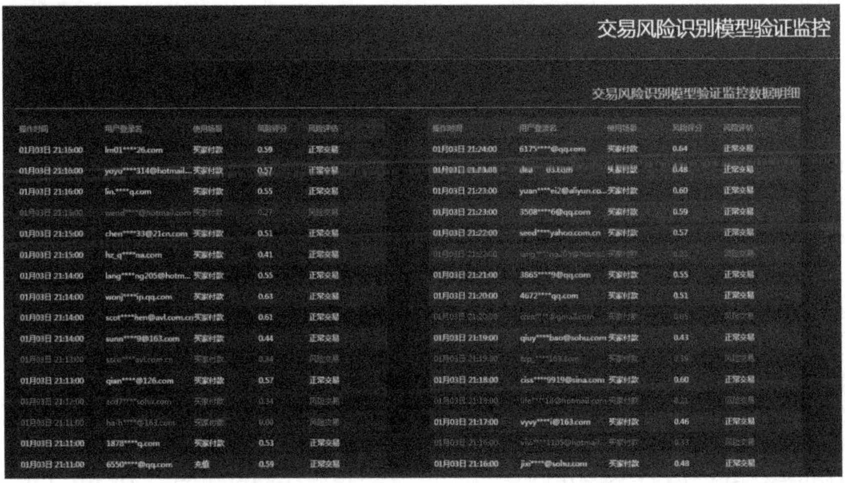

Figure 6.11　Display diagram of risk identification.

is consistent with the first two screens, which will capture the user's latest transaction situation in real-time for analysis and display, as shown in Figure 6.12.

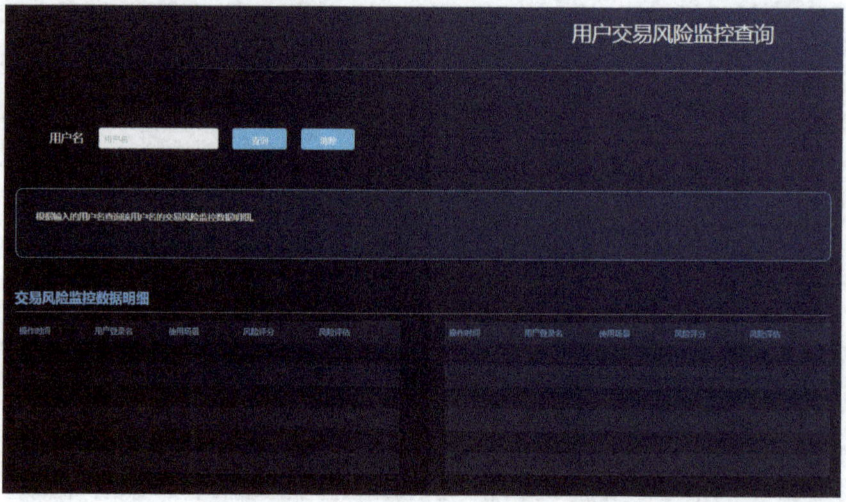

Figure 6.12   Display diagram of user risk trading details.

6.5   Exception Handling in the Online Transaction Process

With the wide application of online shopping, electronic transfer, and other forms of e-commerce, online transaction anomaly detection technology develops rapidly, and it is a new research direction to ensure the trustworthy [8,9]. Traditional anomaly detection technology usually extracts and preserves normal habitual behavior characteristics, and then compares the current behavioral characteristics with the preserved normal characteristics, according to the degree of difference between the two, to achieve the purpose of anomaly detection [10–15]. Based on the traditional abnormal detection technology, the research team based on the actual situation of the online transaction process, and based on the three mechanisms of immune self-stability of the biological immune system, immune monitoring, and immuno-updating [16–26], give a kind of immune method of abnormal detection in the course of the online transaction. In this method, the log which can reflect the behavior habit of the user in the process of online transaction is represented as an antibody. According to the mechanism of biological immune self-stabilization, the antibody update is realized by cleaning up the "aging" log, to ensure that the processed log can reflect the users' recent behavior habits, and detect whether the newly generated transaction log sequence is abnormal according to the immune monitoring mechanism, to achieve the purpose of detecting whether the user's online transaction process behavior pattern is normal.

The immune method for abnormal detection of the online transaction process is to extract the normal sequence library that can best reflect the recent behavior of users according to the transaction sequence of users' history and the evolution process of their age. When a new transaction sequence is generated, the abnormal sequence library and normal sequence library are used to detect whether the newly generated sequence has "mutation". When the detection result is the normal sequence, the normal sequence library should be updated in time. Its architecture consists of data preprocessing module, training module, detection module, and update module. The data preprocessing module mainly processes the user's operation process into a sequential format and cleans the relevant repetitive data. The training module mainly calculates the age value of each sequence according to the time smoothly and the age evolution process extracts the normal sequence library according to the age value and generates the abnormal sequence library by reverse selection. The detection module is mainly used to detect whether the newly generated transaction sequence has a mutation. The update module is to update the normal sequence library and abnormal sequence library in time.

The detection method takes the normal transaction history of the user as the starting point, processes the normal transaction sequence database that can reflect the user's recent behavior habits, and generates an abnormal transaction sequence database by the immune reverse selection algorithm. When a new transaction sequence is generated, two-step detection is required. First compared with the exception sequence library, the alarm is determined to be abnormal and further detected; on the contrary, compared with the normal sequence library, the update operation is carried out if the alarm is determined to be normal, otherwise the alarm is further detected. The architecture is shown in Figure 6.13.

The generation process of the abnormal transaction sequence library is shown in Figure 6.14. The source of allogeneic transaction sequence libraries mainly includes two aspects. On the one hand, it

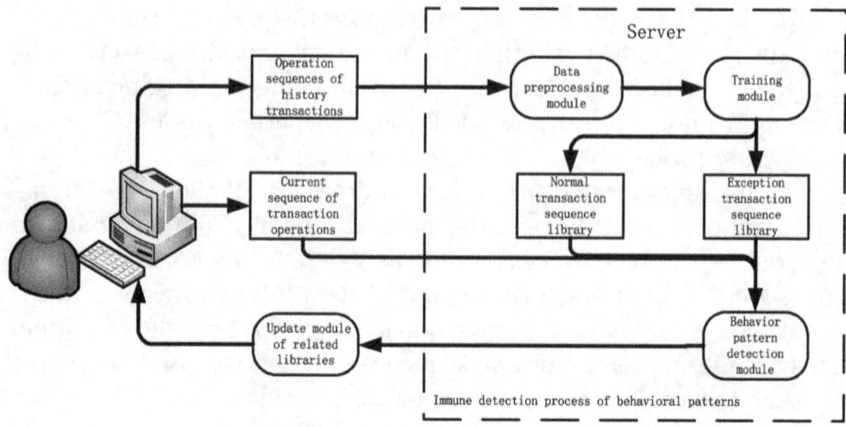

Figure 6.13   Overall architecture of immune detection method [9].

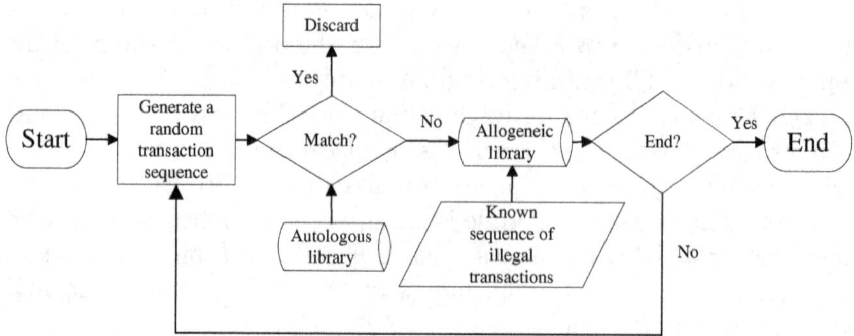

Figure 6.14   The generation process of abnormal transaction sequence library [9].

is known as an illegal transaction sequence; on the other hand, it selects the sequence that is greatly different from the normal transaction database through the reverse selection algorithm.

Among them, the reverse selection algorithm, also known as the negative selection algorithm, starts from the normal mode library and randomly generates the mode to compare with the normal mode. If it is similar to the normal mode, it is discarded; otherwise, if it is very different from all the modes in the normal mode library, it is added to the abnormal mode library.

Behavior pattern detection module: it is mainly the "mutation" detection for the newly generated transaction sequence Ag, which is

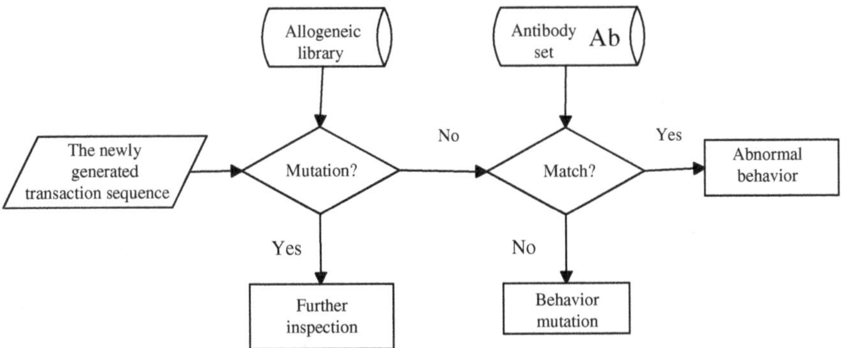

Figure 6.15   User behavior pattern detection process [9].

divided into two steps. Figure 6.15 shows the main functions of this module.

The first step is to compare it with the allogeneic library. If the "mutation" log condition is met, the alarm will be given for further verification; otherwise, the second step will be entered.

In the second step, the newly generated transaction sequence Ag is compared with the normal transaction sequence (that is, the antibody set Ab). If the affinity degree with all antibodies is very low, it indicates that the sequence has the possibility of "mutation" and needs to be further examined; otherwise, it is detected as the normal behavior pattern.

Two-step detection not only improves the detection accuracy but also improves the detection efficiency. Because the first step is based on the abnormal pattern library, most abnormal conditions can be found in time, and only a few abnormal conditions need to be compared with the normal pattern library for further determination.

Update module: based on immune detection, this module has the immune function for the next similar abnormal situation. Its function is mainly to update the normal pattern library and abnormal pattern library. Figure 6.16 is the overall flow chart of the system. It can be seen that the two pattern libraries play a great role in the detection process, and timely updates are particularly important.

According to the test results, if the results are normal behavior patterns, the normal pattern library (antibody set Ab) will be updated with age, and the "aging" log will be deleted to ensure that the antibody set Ab can reflect the user's recent behavior habits.

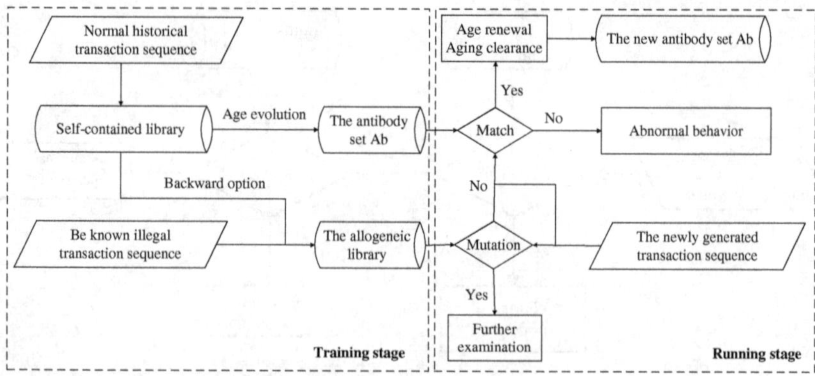

Figure 6.16   Overall flow chart of immunization [9].

If the result is an exception behavior pattern, it is compared to the pattern in the exception library, and if it is a new pattern, it is added to the exception pattern library.

6.6   Chapter Summary

The online transaction software system is a kind of typical human–computer interaction system and the software behavior and user behavior of this kind of system are interlaced and interactive. Therefore, it is necessary to synthesize and integrate software behavior and user behavior to form an overall system behavior pattern, to depict the online behavior of online transaction software systems completely and accurately. Users' behaviors are collected and normal behavior patterns of users are mined through data mining methods to realize online authentication of user behaviors, which can effectively monitor "illegal behaviors of legitimate users" and prevent fraudulent behaviors caused by information disclosure. This chapter mainly introduces the relevant technology of the online transaction platform and architecture. The monitoring center is used to monitor the user behavior data and software behavior data produced by users, businessmen, and third-party payment companies when online transactions are carried out, and adopt many forms of multi-dimensional tables and intuitive graphical ways to dynamically display the data. The purpose of the monitoring center is to add the fourth-party authentication mechanism into the original three-party transaction process. Based on the authentication technology of software behavior and user behavior, it provides authentication for the system software behavior and user identity of merchants and third-party payment companies.

References

[1] Jiang, C. J., Chen, H. Z., Yan, C. G., Ding, Z. J., and Zheng, Y. W. User and Software Behavior Monitoring Data Visualization System in Network Transactions, Patents (CN201410513131.X), 2017.08.25.

[2] Jiang, C. J., Chen, H. Z., Yan, C. G., Ding, Z. J., Yu, W. Y., and Zhong, J. Z. Software Behavior Monitoring and Verification System, Patents (CN 201410014450.6), 2015.08.19.

[3] Jiang, C. J., Chen, H. Z., Yan, C. G., Ding, Z. J., Yu, W. Y., and Ge, Y. L. Trusted Authentication System and Method of Network Transaction, Patents (CN201410499859.1), 2015.01.07.

[4] Jiang, C. J., Chen, H. Z., Yan, C. G., Ding, Z. J., Yu, W. Y., and Chen, Y. H. Sequential Pattern Mining Method Based on Web User Time Attribute, Patents (CN 201410004623.6), 2014.04.23.

[5] Jiang, C. J., Chen, H. Z., Yan, C. G., Ding, Z. J., Yu, W. Y., and Zhao, P. H. Identity Authentication Method Based on Web User Behavior Pattern, Patents (CN201210445681.3), 2015.11.04.

[6] Jiang, C. J., Chen, H. Z., Yan, C. G., Ding, Z. J., Yu, W. Y., and Ge, Y. L. User Behavior Pattern Mining System and Its Method, Patents (CN 201210448617.0), 2015.11.04.

[7] Zheng, W. Y. *A Two-Layer Risk Control Model for Electronic Transactions and Its Methods*, Shanghai, China, Tongji University, (2015).

[8] Jiang, S. P., Yan, C. G., Zhao, P. H. *et al.* An Immune Approach for Detecting the User's Behavior of Electronic Transaction Process. *Journal of Computational Information Systems*, 11(2): 683–692 (2015).

[9] Jiang, S. P. *Study on Immune Method of Abnormal Detection in Electronic Transaction*, Shanghai, China, Tongji University, (2015).

[10] Modi, C., Patel, D., Borisaniya, B. *et al.* A Survey of Intrusion Detection Techniques in Cloud. *Journal of Network and Computer Applications*, 36(1): 42–57 (2013).

[11] Chandola, V., Banerjee, A., and Kumar, V. Anomaly Detection: A Survey. *ACM Computing Surveys (CSUR)*, 41(3): 15 (2009).

[12] Chandola, V., Banerjee, A., and Kumar, V. Anomaly Detection for Discrete Sequences: A Survey. *IEEE Transactions on Knowledge and Data Engineering*, 24(5): 823–839 (2012).

[13] Chen, B., Chen, S. C., Pan, Z. S. *et al.* Survey of Outlier Detection Technologies. *Journal of Shandong University (Engineering Science)*, 39(6): 13–23 (2009).

[14] Xie, Y. and Yu, S. Z. Anomaly Detection Based on Web Users' Browsing Behaviors. *Journal of Software*, 18(4): 967–977 (2007).

[15] Lu, Y., Li, W., Luo, J. Z. *et al.* A Network Users' Abnormal Behavior Detection Approach Based on Selective Collaborative Learning. *Chinese Journal of Computer*, 37(1): 28–40 (2014).

[16] Mo, H. W. and Zuo, X. Q. *Artificial Immune System*, Beijing: Science Press, (2009).

[17] Tuo, J. W., Li, X., Ren, S. J. *et al.* Fraudulent Customer Analysis Based on Artificial Immune Clustering. *Journal of TsingHua University: Science and Technology*, 51(7): 893–897 (2011).

[18] Ivanov, I. I. and Littman, D. R. Modulation of Immune Homeostasis by Commensal Bacteria. *Current Opinion in Microbiology*, 14(1): 106–114 (2011).

[19] Ransohoff, R. M. and Engelhardt, B. The Anatomical and Cellular Basis of Immune Surveillance in the Central Nervous System. *Nature Reviews Immunology*, 12(9): 623–635 (2012).

[20] Aickelin, U., Dasgupta, D., and Gu, F. *Artificial Immune Systems, in Search Methodologies*, US: Springer, pp. 187–211, (2014).

[21] Chen, Y. B., Feng, C., Zhang, Q. *et al.* Integrated Artificial Immune System for Intrusion Detection. *Journal on Communications*, 33(2): 125–131 (2012).

[22] Iyer, D., Mohanpurkar, A., Janardhan, S. *et al.* Credit Card Fraud Detection Using Hidden Markov Model. In *2011 World Congress on Information and Communication Technologies (WICT)*, IEEE, Mumbai, India, pp. 1062–1066 (2011).

[23] Bhattacharyya, S., Jha, S., Tharakunnel, K. *et al.* Data Mining for Credit Card Fraud: A Comparative Study. *Decision Support Systems*, 50(3): 602–613 (2011).

[24] Soltani, N., Akbari, M. K., and Sargolzaei Javan, M. A New User-Based Model for Credit Card Fraud Detection Based on Artificial Immune System. In *2012 16th CSI International Symposium on Artificial Intelligence and Signal Processing (AISP)*, IEEE, Shiraz, Iran, pp. 029–033, (2012).

[25] Fang, X., Koceja, N., Zhan, J. *et al.* An Artificial Immune System for Phishing Detection. In *2012 IEEE Congress on Evolutionary Computation (CEC)*, IEEE, Brisbane, Australia, pp. 1–7, (2012).

[26] Wong, N., Ray, P., Stephens, G. *et al.* Artificial Immune Systems for the Detection of Credit Card Fraud: An Architecture, Prototype and Preliminary Results. *Information Systems Journal*, 22(1): 53–76 (2012).

Chapter 7

Credit System

7.1 Introductions

With the rapid development of the Internet finance industry, the credit assessment of individuals or SMEs has received increasing attention. Credit assessment is the credit rating agency's score on the "reliable" level based on the user's daily life, consumption habits, or corporate credit. The assessment of user credit in China is mainly by the credit evaluation of the People's Bank of China Credit Information Center. Besides, the sesame credit score of Alipay, a domestic third-party payment platform, is also a kind of credit evaluation for its users. The evaluation basis mainly depends on the consumer behavior data of users purchasing goods. The credit system, based on real-time analysis of the actual situation of individual users or SMEs, build a credit basis, integrate superior resources, can control the risk of Internet financial transactions, and promote the healthy development of the Internet finance industry.

7.2 Credit Rating Overview

The development of credit rating has gone through three main stages: the traditional credit scoring method, the comprehensive credit scoring method, and the modern credit scoring method. In the first stage, the traditional credit scoring method is also called the empirical method. This is a qualitative credit scoring method. Bank creditors rely on their experience and subjective judgment as of the basis for loan approval. This method is easier to implement and more flexible, but it is susceptible to subjective judgment, lack of objectivity, and easy to cause deviations and errors. In the second stage, the comprehensive credit scoring method, which is commonly used by present major rating companies in the world, is mainly based on qualitative analysis and supplemented by quantitative analysis. The third stage, the modern credit scoring method, is also called the credit risk measurement model. This method refers to a credit risk assessment system based on mathematical technology, which can measure credit risk more accurately. In the middle of the 20th century, to overcome the defects of the subjective setting of indicators and weights in the credit scoring method, the credit risk measurement model has been widely studied and applied. The credit risk measurement model uses statistical methods or operations research methods to find out the characteristics of customers with certain attributes based on a large amount of historical data, summarizes the classification rules, establishes mathematical models, and uses this model to predict the likelihood of an event with a certain nature, and provides a basis for consumer credit decisions. Currently, the application of such methods is the most effective [1–7].

Developed countries mainly have two modes in the social credit system, one is represented by the United States and the other is represented by the European continent.

The United States has a relatively complete credit information service industry. The legal system mainly including the Fair Credit Reporting Act (FCRA), the Truth in Lending Act, the Consumer Credit Protection Act, the Fair Credit Billing Act, the Equal Credit Opportunity Act (ECOA), and the Fair Debt Collection Practices Act.

The supply and demand of the credit product market are strong in the Unite states. The credit information service producers — credit information service agencies — can be roughly divided into three categories: (1) Credit intermediaries engaged in personal credit information services (credit bureau). At present, there are three large credit bureaus (also known as consumer credit bureaus). (2) Enterprise credit service organization. It mainly refers to credit intermediaries that conduct credit investigations, credit evaluations, and other credit information services for various enterprises. (3) A rating agency that serves corporate finance mainly refers to any credit intermediary that rates the credits of countries, banks, securities companies, funds, bonds, and listed companies [8,9].

In Europe, credit information services are established as a department of the central bank rather than by the private sector. Banks need to provide relevant credit information to the Credit Information Bureau following the law, and the central bank assumes the main supervisory functions.

Nowadays, more and more credit bureaus incorporate user behavior into the evaluation system and use data mining techniques to evaluate the credit value of a user or even a company; compared with the traditional manpower assessment, the application of data mining methods not only evaluates with high efficiency, but also does not introduce artificial cognitive bias, and reduces the cost of evaluation; what's more, with the accumulation of data and the maturity of mining technology, the credit evaluation using data mining methods will be more accurate.

7.3 Transaction Data Cleaning and Query

For effective credit evaluation, effective online transaction data cleaning and query methods are essential. The rapid development of online transactions has led to explosive growth in the volume of electronic transaction data. Therefore, to ensure the security and consistency of data, it is necessary to design a simple and efficient data representation and acquisition method on the condition of ensuring the secure transmission of transaction data; For the large-scale electronic transaction data that is stored, how to identify and clean the noise transaction data generated by means such as misappropriation and quickly locate each transaction's single transaction data is an issue that needs to be studied in electronic transaction data management.

Trading data cleaning mainly needs to solve two problems: noise data detection and data normalization.

Real-world data are generally incomplete, noisy, and inconsistent. Data cleaning routines through domain-related knowledge generate filter rules, identify problem data, and attempt to fill in missing values, smooth noise, identify outliers, and correct inconsistencies in the data. Data that cannot be repaired are directly filtered. It should be emphasized that the filtering rules in data cleaning must be targeted at specific domain knowledge. For example, the range of temperature data should be between $-20°C$ and $50°C$, otherwise, it is exception data; in the keyboard behavior, the value range of the user's button delay should be 0–600 ms, otherwise, it is a timeout exception, which needs smooth processing or direct.

Due to the different sources of data collection, the range and importance of the collected data are different. For example, a feature with a range of [0, 1] and a feature with a range of [−100, 100] have different weights in application technology and have different effects on the final data mining results. Therefore, it is recommended to normalize them and have the same weights for further analysis.

Most real-world data mining applications deal with high-dimensional data, but not all features are important. For example, high-dimensional data may contain a lot of uncorrelated interference information, which significantly reduces the performance of the data mining process. Even top-notch data mining algorithms can't handle a large number of weakly correlated and redundant features. This is usually attributed to Dimensionality Curse or because the non-correlated features reduce the Signal to Noise Ratio [10–12].

Besides, complex data analysis and mining for massive or large datasets will take a long time, making this analysis impractical or infeasible. The data reduction technique can be used to obtain a reduced representation of the dataset, which is much smaller in scale than the original dataset but still maintains the integrity of the original data basically. This will be more efficient for mining the reduced dataset, and produce almost identical results.

Data reduction can be divided into two main categories: feature selection and feature exaction. Feature selection can detect and delete unrelated, weakly correlated, or redundant attributes or dimensions, and reduce the possibility of overfitting. Feature extraction mainly maps high-dimensional feature vectors to low-dimensional vector spaces through a coding mechanism to achieve the role of reducing the dimension.

Main evaluation indicators for feature selection:

- **The statistical characteristics of the attributes:** Such as arithmetic average, weighted average, median, etc. reflect the central trend of the attribute, variance, quartile, etc., as well as reflect the degree of dispersion.

- **Information gain:** Entropy reflects the disorder degree of the dataset, that is, the amount of information. The binary test can divide the dataset into two sub-sets, reduce the data disorder, and obtain the information. Good attributes can maximize the classified information gain.
- **Mutual information:** Mutual information is a measure of information that refers to the correlation between two sets of events. For feature selection, those attributes that are highly relevant to a particular category are always hoped to be retained.
- **Pearson chi-square test:** The Pearson chi-square test can be used for the comparison of variables in two scenarios: the goodness of fit test, and the independence test. Among them, the goodness of fit test verifies whether the number of times a set of observations is assigned is different from the theoretical allocation; the independence verification verifies whether the paired observations extracted from the two variables are independent of each other.

7.4 Credit Evaluation Model

The traditional expert assessment method and the loan rating method are mainly on qualitative analysis. Experts analyze credit risk and make decisions based on their own professional knowledge and rich experience. This type of credit analysis and rating method is simple and feasible, while the requirements for data are not very strict. However, with this more subjective method, the analysis of the same object by different rating agencies or different experts may lead to different conclusions. The fairness of the rating results is also affected by many factors. Under this method, for the same loan business, different risk assessment results will be obtained because of different loan personnel, so that the consistency of the loan policy cannot be complied with [13, 14].

As the basis and core of credit risk management, the credit scoring model has an irreplaceable role in not only establishing social credit information systems but also credit asset management of financial institutions. Its main purpose is to integrate as much as possible the indicators that can predict the borrower's future behavior, and unify them into a single indicator that can be compared to show the possibility of the borrower defaulting at a specific time in the future. All credit scoring models, regardless of the theory or method used, are ultimately designed to classify the credit ratings of loan applicants. With the continuous development of the credit scoring model, credit scoring is not only a statistical method, but also operational research, such as mathematical programming, non-linear fuzzy mathematics (such as neural network methods), etc. Besides, the practical application of the credit score is closely related to the decision-making principle. The decision-making principle actually determines the degree to which the credit scoring model achieves its purpose and role [15–21].

There are several quantitative models used in international credit scoring:

(1) Linear probability model:

The linear probability model assumes that the relationship between the default probability Y and the credit variable X is linear, and the credit variable used to explain past credit behavior (default or non-default) and its importance (coefficient) are used to predict future credit behavior. This method is comparatively simple, but there are limitations to the handling of the dichotomous variable of credit behavior (default or non-default).

(2) Linear discriminant model:

The discriminant model divides the credit characteristics of borrowers who have been observed in the past into two risk categories: default and non-default. A Linear Discriminant Model is established under linear assumptions to fit the discriminant function. The credit of the judgment object is evaluated using the fitted discriminant function. However, the discriminant analysis gives a plurality of discriminant functions, and it is difficult to convert the discriminant result into a credit risk score, making it difficult to implement.

(3) Logistic credit scoring model:

For the binary response variable of credit behavior (default or non-default), the Logistic credit scoring model is very suitable. The method converts the estimated default probability into a credit score for easy implementation in the system.

In terms of credit model analysis, the existing decision tree model is a statistical technique that continuously segments the overall to predict the outcome of a certain target variable. In reality, to conduct corporate credit analysis, enterprise credit is selected as the goals attribute, and other attributes are used as independent variables. All customers are divided into two categories, good and bad customers, converting customer credit status to "whether good customers or not" and then using the dataset to generate a complete decision tree. The decision tree model is very intuitive and easy to interpret. It does not require any assumptions about the structure and distribution of the data, and it is easier to translate into business rules. However, the decision tree model has a large demand for sample size, and it is easy to over-adjust the sample data thereby lose stability and anti-vibration. On the other hand, the discriminant analysis method is a statistical analysis method for judging the category to which the research object belongs. For discriminant analysis, the classification of the observed object and a number of variable values indicating the characteristics of the observed object must be known. Discriminant analysis is to select from which to provide more information variables and establish a discriminant function so that the deduced discriminant function minimizes the misjudgment rate when classifying the observed samples. Multivariate discriminant analysis can find financial ratios with the discriminative ability and measure the overall performance of the company. However, this method requires the variable to conform to the assumption that the normal distribution, the variable, and the credit risk have a linear relationship, so that the multivariate discriminant analysis model is only applicable to companies with accurate financial data, that is, the company has a certain scale and the development is relatively mature. The applicability to SMEs is comparatively poor.

With the deep research in the field of credit scoring, some scholars have introduced some model algorithms in the field of artificial intelligence into credit scoring research. The artificial neural network model is a typical representative. The artificial neural network is an adaptive non-linear dynamic system composed of a large number of simple basic components — the neurons which are connected. It is an information processing structure that converts various input elements into outputs through a complex network. The problem solved by the neural network model is still the classification or pattern recognition problem, but its principle is quite different from its method. Artificial neural networks have many models, such as behavior profile (BP) neural network, radical basis function (RBF) neural network, Hopfield network, and so on. BP neural network is a neural network model with the most mature research, the most stable algorithm, and is the most widely used. The operational model of the neural network model is very useful for weakening the weighted human factors, has strong fault tolerance, and can deal with complex non-linear relationships. However, it takes a lot of manpower and time to get a better neural network structure. Therefore, the neural network model is generally applicable to the post-credit evaluation process and is less used in the early stage of credit evaluation [22–27].

Due to the shortcomings of the above-mentioned credit analysis model in commercial application, the regression analysis method has the characteristics of fast convergence and accurate model evaluation. It is still the most widely used credit scoring model in a commercial application, among which the famous logistic regression analysis is representative. Besides, methods such as linear regression analysis and Probit regression also fall into this category. Orgler *et al.*, who first used regression analysis, developed a credit card-like scorecard by using a linear regression model. The research shows that consumer behavior characteristics are more predictive of future default likelihood than application form material. The goal of regression analysis is to minimize the error between the target variable value and the actual target variable value. At present, the application of the credit score system based on Logistic regression is the most common. However, the regression analysis model can only perform static analysis on enterprise credit evaluation, and cannot make timely model adjustments according to the dynamic development of the enterprise and the prospects of its related industries. At the same time, the credit rating of the enterprise is not able to make a comprehensive credit risk assessment based on the credit process of the enterprise in the credit granting process, which has certain limitations.

7.5   Credit Mining and Evaluation

The main users of personal credit protect the transaction subject and identify the credibility of the counterparty. Therefore, in credit evaluation mining, the credit evaluation method based on the risk of the transaction subject can be used to verify the online transaction through a simple model. If the verification is passed, it is considered to be a normal transaction, and no strict verification is required later, so as to solve the drawbacks of the simple data mining model verification. What needs to be distinguished is that the model measures are normal transactions, that is, the purpose is to filter some normal transactions in the transaction process before the model is verified, while the transactions that cannot pass through the model also contain normal transactions, they require that the model further use rigorous model verification for risk identification.

In transaction risk control, rule verification has more accurate case-control effects according to domain knowledge, blacklist, and so on, so it is often at the entry point of transaction risk identification in the enterprise risk system. Model validation, as a supplement to rule filtering, builds models based on historically normal and abnormal transactions, and identifies and classifies risky transactions and normal transactions [28, 29]. According to the problems caused by the classification and identification of some obviously normal transactions in the model verification process, and the problems caused by a large amount of inclined data faced by the model verification, the risk filtering method is proposed, and the process of adding risk filtering between the rule verification and model verification of transaction risk enables the transactions that meet the filtering conditions to pass the risk certification directly, reducing the pressure on the subsequent model verification and the potential misclassification risk, and making the response of the normal transaction faster. The location of risk filtering at the system level is shown in Figure 7.1. Risk filtering has changed less among the risk control methods adopted by the industry and can be well integrated.

Firstly, it is necessary to select the characteristics of the original transaction data, and according to the information value, IV (Information Value), the importance degree of the extracted feature variables can be filtered [30]. The selection of features can refer to the general credit card fraud monitoring feature. The calculation of IV first requires the calculation of the weight of the evidence for each eigenvalue, Woe (Weight of Evidence). Woe can only indicate the importance of each optional eigenvalue for the target variable. If you want to measure the importance of the whole feature to the

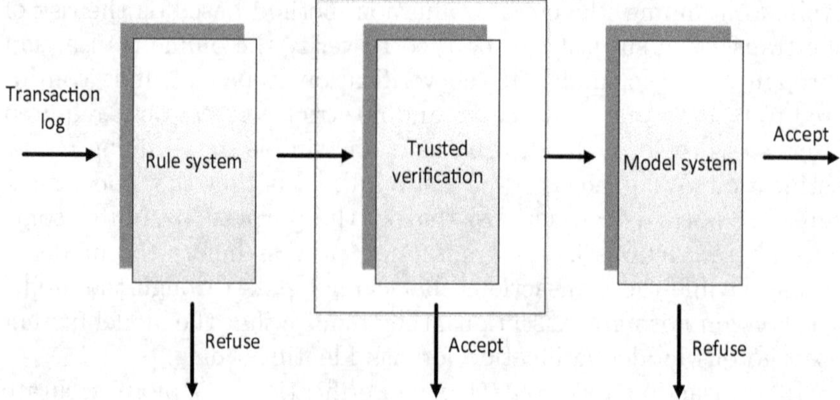

Figure 7.1   Hierarchical diagram of the credit assessment system.

target variable, you should introduce the IV calculation. Assume that the filtered feature vector is $E = \{X_1, X_2, X_3, \ldots, X_4, Y\}$, and Y is the category. To determine whether the sample is a normal transaction or not, a measure is needed. We define this measure as a transaction measurement function (E). We use the distance from the transaction sample to the centroid of the sample set to represent the transaction measurement function. The degree of discrimination between the feature vector and the case can be obtained by calculating the Euclidean distance from the feature vector to the center point of the case sample. We make this discrimination the distance measure of the sample, where each feature value X_{ti} of the case sample center point is calculated and taken from the average of each corresponding feature in the feature vector of all case samples, respectively. At the same time, to reflect the important difference between the features of the feature vector, it is necessary to additionally calculate the weight of each feature variable. We can calculate the feature weights of each feature based on the IV. Let IV of the feature variable X_i be v_i, then calculate the proportion w_i as the weight of the feature variable by calculating the v_i in the sum IV of all the feature variables participating in the calculation.

All samples are sorted by distance quantized values as keywords. At this time, the sample of the distance quantization may be selected according to a certain target condition, that is, the log smaller than the threshold is the sample that needs further distinction, and the

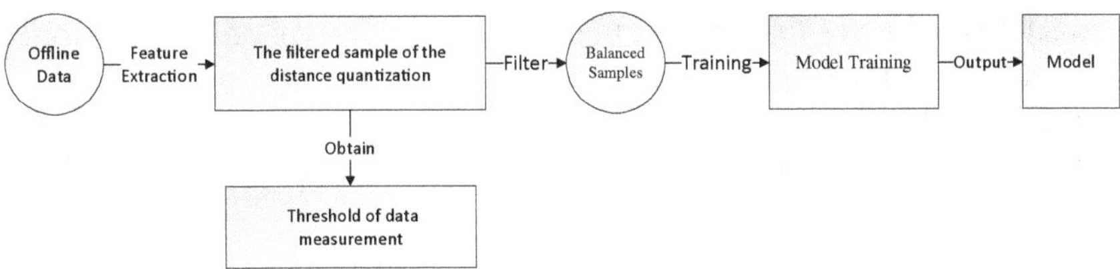

Figure 7.2 Flow chart of offline data processing based on distance discrimination.

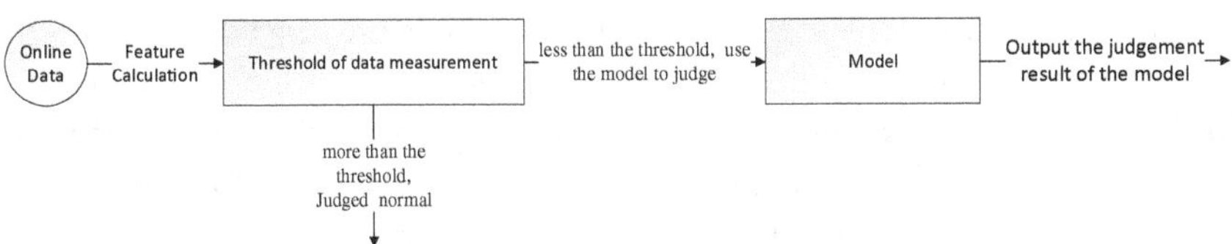

Figure 7.3 Online data classification flow chart based on distance discrimination-based risk filtering method.

log larger than the threshold may be regarded as a normal transaction. Therefore, according to the specific scenario requirements, giving the acceptance range of the case transaction that can be mistakenly excluded, thereby selecting an appropriate distance division threshold and dividing concentration equalization of the sample. For the balanced samples, a general classification model can be used for model training. This part of the process is shown in Figure 7.2.

Finally, in the model verification phase, for online data, first calculate the eigenvalues for distance measurement. Then, using the distance quantization threshold obtained in the offline training phase, determine whether the sample belongs to the normal transaction, if yes, directly predict the sample as a normal transaction, and return the classification result, if not, that is, it is less than the threshold, then use the model obtained after the equalization training in offline training to classify and the results of the classification are output. The partial process of online data verification is shown in Figure 7.3.

7.6 Credit Card Fraud Detection

Credit card fraud detection is an important part of the field of credit systems. With the rapid development of e-commerce, the number of transactions by credit cards is increasing rapidly. As online shopping becomes the most popular transaction mode, cases of transaction fraud are also increasing. This section presents several detecting methods based on machine learning which are from Refs. [31–34].

7.6.1 *A novel approach using aggregation strategy and feedback mechanism*

In this subsection, we illustrate a fraud detection method that composes of four stages. To enrich a cardholder's behavioral patterns, we first utilize the cardholders' historical transaction data to divide all cardholders into different groups such that the transaction behaviors of the members in the same group are similar. We thus propose a sliding-window-based strategy to aggregate the transactions in each group. Next, we extract a collection of specific behavioral patterns for each cardholder based on the aggregated transactions and the cardholder's historical transactions. Then we train a set of classifiers for each group based on all behavioral patterns. Finally, we use the classifier set to detect fraud online and if a new transaction is fraudulent, a feedback mechanism is taken in the detection process to solve the problem of concept drift.

There exist several problems when we use all transactions to build one classifier. For example, in the real-world, a cardholder has his/her behavioral patterns, but one classifier trained via all transactions ignores the personalized behaviors of the cardholder. More importantly, binary classification cannot label each behavioral pattern of a cardholder. Hence, a traditional method with one classifier cannot solve the concept drift problem due to the lack of classified label information. Instead, our proposed method extracts the behavioral patterns precisely from the aggregated data and labels each behavioral pattern by using a clustering method. Thus, we can build each cardholder's behavioral profile via these behavioral patterns and our online model can adapt to a cardholder's transaction behaviors in a timely manner. Our method contains four steps.

(1) Preprocessing data.
(2) Clustering behavioral patterns.
(3) Classifying behavioral patterns and assignments.

(4) Updating cardholders' behavioral profiles by a feedback mechanism.

We first use the clustering method k-means [35] to divide all cardholders into three similar groups which are, respectively, labeled as high (h), medium (m), and low (l) based on the transaction amount. Therefore, we assume that $V = \{l, m, h\}$ and $|V| = 3$. Note that l, m, and h can be viewed as three sets of IDs of all cardholders in the corresponding group and id is the identification of the cardholder. Transaction data of all cardholders in a group are more helpful to solve the sparse problem of data compared with the transaction data of a single cardholder. More importantly, in this way, each cardholder's behavioral patterns can be composed of two parts: his/her behaviors reflected by his/her historical transactions, and other behaviors recommended by other members in the same group which may happen in the future but are not reflected by his/her historical transactions. The latter can enrich a cardholder's behaviors and improve the adaptiveness of the individual model.

After dividing all users into three similar groups, we propose a sliding-window-based algorithm [36] to aggregate the transactions and then derive some new amount-related/time-related features from the aggregated data to characterize the behavioral patterns of a cardholder more precisely. The sliding-window-based algorithm is an incremental mining technique and is often used to detect image objects. Furthermore, due to the fixed window size, this algorithm can quickly drop the first element and append the next new element to do data statistics by using the partial information from the previous window.

Figure 7.4 illustrates the method to aggregate transactions and derives new features. Each block represents one transaction of a cardholder. Let $t^{\mathrm{id}} = \{t_1^{\mathrm{id}}, \ldots, t_n^{\mathrm{id}}\}$ be a transaction sequence of the cardholder, where n is the number of the cardholder's transactions in history. The process of aggregating transactions is to select those transactions in a fixed window size p

$$T_i^{\mathrm{id}} = \mathrm{WINDOW}(id, i, p) = \{t_j^{\mathrm{id}} | j \in [i, i + p - 1]\}, \quad i < n - p + 1$$

where WINDOW is a function that creates a new window of a transaction sequence which is denoted as T_i^{id}, i is the new window index, and p is the size of the new window. Individual behavioral patterns

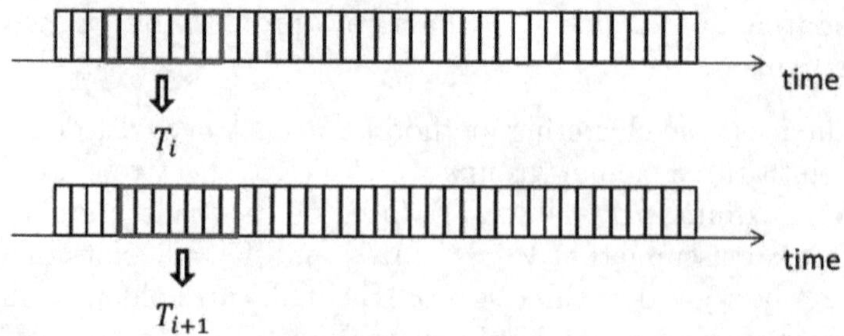

Figure 7.4   Sliding window algorithm for aggregating transactions and deriving features [31].

have strong weekly and monthly periodic structures and it is important to decide the size of a sliding window. We can analyze the frequency of transactions in a fixed time to choose a period such as a week or a month and decide p by human choice. For example, we can choose 50 transactions as a window size if the average number of each cardholder's transactions in a month is 50 (note that this can be obtained from the statistics of the data).

After the aggregation process, we use these new windows to derive some new features. It is important to assume that some fraudsters are not familiar with the transaction behaviors of a cardholder. They are trying to get the most profits by performing high-value transactions. Hence, four features we need to extract is the maximum, minimum, average amount of T_i^{id}, and the amount of the last transaction in a window:

(1) Maximum function: $x_{i1}^{\mathrm{id}} = \text{MAX\_AMOUNT}(T_i^{\mathrm{id}})$;

(2) Minimum function: $x_{i2}^{\mathrm{id}} = \text{MIN\_AMOUNT}(T_i^{\mathrm{id}})$;

(3) AVERAGE function: $x_{i3}^{\mathrm{id}} = \text{AVG\_AMOUNT}(T_i^{\mathrm{id}})$;

(4) Last transaction amount: $x_{i4}^{\mathrm{id}} = \text{AMOUNT}(T_i^{\mathrm{id}})$.

Besides, more cautious fraudsters try to imitate a cardholder's transaction behaviors and perform low-value transactions in a short time. Therefore, we are interested in analyzing some time-related features. We set $p-1$ time intervals which are, respectively, calculated from a transaction and its previous transaction in a window. For example, with the window size $p = 50$, amount-related features are $\{x_{i5}^{\mathrm{id}}, x_{i6}^{\mathrm{id}}, \ldots, x_{i53}^{\mathrm{id}}\}$. We denote $X_i^{\mathrm{id}} = (x_{i5}^{\mathrm{id}}, x_{i6}^{\mathrm{id}}, \ldots, x_{i53}^{\mathrm{id}})$ as a vector constructed by these derived features. Finally, we label each window

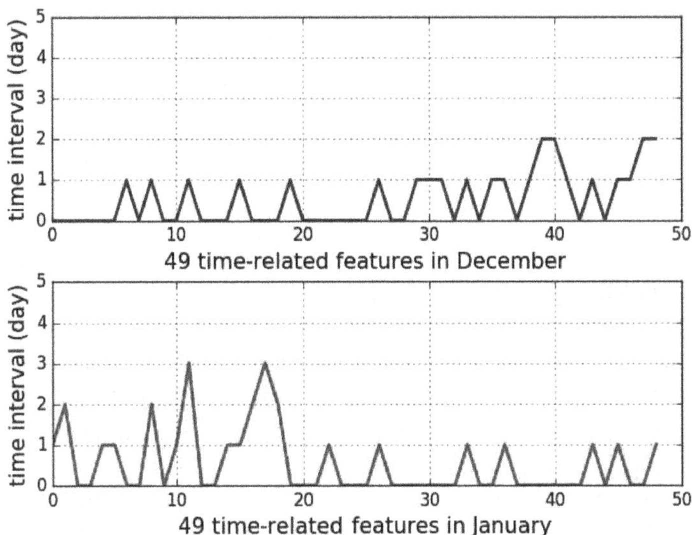

Figure 7.5   One cardholder with two different time-related curves in two different months [31].

as normal or abnormal by using the label of the last transaction and the label function is $y_i^{\mathrm{id}} = \mathrm{gABEL}(T_i^{\mathrm{id}})$. For each cardholder, we can obtain two datasets

$$G^{\mathrm{id}} = \{X_i^{\mathrm{id}} | y_i^{\mathrm{id}} = 0, i \in [0, n - p + 1]\}$$

$$F^{\mathrm{id}} = \{X_i^{\mathrm{id}} | y_i^{\mathrm{id}} = 1, i \in [0, n - p + 1]\}$$

where G^{id} is the normal feature set of the cardholder and F^{id} is the abnormal feature set.

After extracting new features from each window, X_i^{id} can be regarded as a single behavior pattern of a cardholder and G^{id} is the set of all behavioral patterns of the cardholder with id. Figure 7.5 illustrates an example of the visualization of 49 time-related features obtained that use a cardholder's transactions in December and January and the window size $p = 50$. We can see that time-related curves are often different in different months, which means that a cardholder's transaction behaviors are variable with seasons. Based on every cardholder's normal feature set, we can obtain the set of all normal features for each group

$$G_f = \cup id \in j G^{\mathrm{id}} \ \forall j \in V.$$

In the real world, it is a difficult job to classify these normal feature sets to specific behavioral patterns. The reason is that the definitions of behavioral patterns may be obscure when they are concluded by using human domain knowledge. However, it is more convenient to use a clustering method to solve this unsupervised learning problem, which can automatically organize high-level abstract knowledge. For example, G_l represents all normal feature sets of the low consumption group. Then, for each group $j \in V$, we carry out the cluster method k-means over G_j and thus obtain a set of clusters $B_j = \{b_1, b_2, \ldots, b_k\}$ where k is the number of different behavioral patterns and preset up by hand. For example, B_l is the behavioral pattern set of the low consumption group. Each cluster can be thought of as the specific behavioral patterns of group j. In other words, those aggregated transactions in a fixed cluster are of similar features.

In the previous step, we have obtained several specific behavioral patterns from those aggregated transactions for each group. In each group, we have several normal behavioral patterns, but we cannot still predict the incoming transaction due to the lack of abnormal features. Hence, in this step, we first collect all abnormal features from the three groups and form an abnormal feature set

$$F = \cup_{\mathrm{id} \in V} F^{\mathrm{id}}.$$

For each b_i, F, and their labels, we utilize random forest to train a classifier c_i. Random forest is one of the state-of-the-art ensemble methods. This method can produce a classifier that is constructed by combing several different independent-base classifiers. This technique is known as bagging, or bootstrap aggregation, which has a significantly lower risk of overfitting. By using multiple trees based on a majority voting on the individual predictions, we reduce the error rate and variance of a classifier that is more accurate than a single-base classifier. After training, we obtain a set of classifiers for each group

$$Cj = \{c1, \ldots, ck\}, \quad j \in V.$$

Here, each classifier can be viewed as a profile of a single behavioral pattern.

Next, the classifier set Cj will be assigned to each cardholder in group j. For example, the classifier set C_l will be assigned to cardholder u where $u \in l$ and Cu^l are denoted as the classifier set of u. Thus, each group member has many specific profiles from a similar group. By using group profiles instead of using individual profiles, we enrich a cardholder's behavioral patterns, some of which may not occur in his/her historical transactions but may happen in the future. Finally, for each cardholder u in group j, our method will choose the most suitable classifier from set Cu^j as the cardholder's recent profile. This can always keep the trends of the cardholder's transaction behaviors and the outdated behaviors can be forgotten.

To the best of our knowledge, the True label of a transaction in the test dataset has never been used to update the profile of the cardholder. We note that the True label information is useful because it can reflect the changes of a cardholder's transaction behaviors indirectly. Hence, our proposed method uses a feedback mechanism to update the profile of each cardholder when a new transaction comes. Each cardholder u in group j has a set $Cu^j = \{c_1, c_2, \ldots, c_k\}$. A rating score will be assigned to each classifier, and the cardholder's profile is represented as a 2-tuple $<r_i, c_i>$, where:

(1) c_i is one of the behavioral patterns in set Cu^j;
(2) r_i is one of the rating scores of the classifier c_i.

Figure 7.6 illustrates the framework of the proposed fraud detection method. In the last stage, we can see that a priority queue is used to choose a classifier with the highest rating score, which is highlighted as the gray block. Once the method produces a wrong prediction, it considers that the recent transactions cannot conform to the newest profile of the cardholder. The True label of the incoming transaction will be used to change the rating score of the classifier and our method tries to find out the most suitable classifier as the newest profile of the cardholder. Hence, we propose a feedback mechanism for updating the rating score. The incoming transaction inconsistent with the newest profile will be input to each classifier, and the classifier c_i will be rewarded (i.e., $r_i = r_i + 1$) if it predicts correctly, else it will be punished (i.e., $r_j = r_j - 1$). By using this feedback mechanism, the next transaction can be predicted by a classifier c^* such that r^* is the highest rating score in $\{r_1, r_2, \ldots, r_k\}$.

Clearly, for each cardholder, our method derives several behavioral patterns from the group including him/her, and dynamically

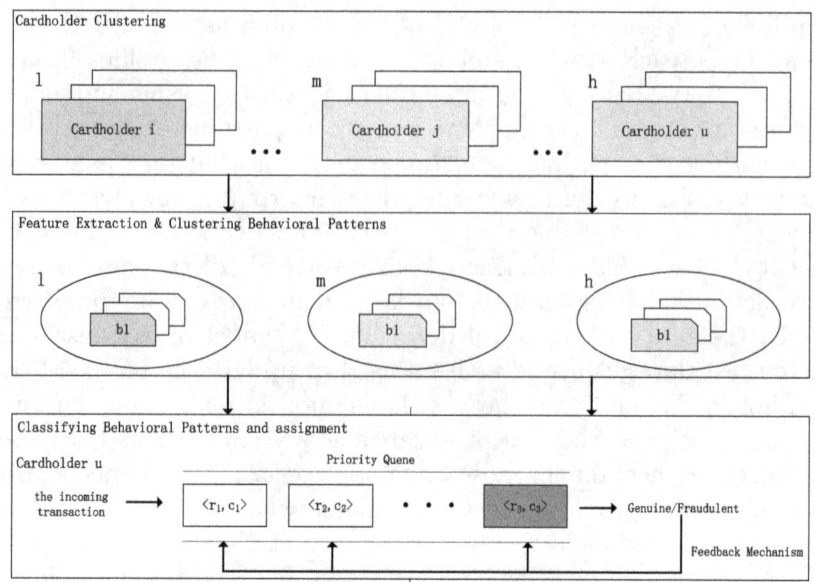

Figure 7.6   Framework of the proposed fraud detection method [31].

chooses the most suitable classifier as his/her recent profile. In this way, the feedback mechanism makes our online method have the ability to adapt to the cardholder's transaction behaviors.

7.6.2   *Transaction fraud detection based on total order relation and behavior diversity*

An important way of detecting fraud is to extract the behavior profiles (BPs) of users based on their historical transaction records, and then to verify if an incoming transaction is a fraud or not given their BPs. Markov chain models are popular to represent the BPs of users, which is effective for those users whose transaction behaviors are stable relatively. However, with the development and popularization of online shopping, it is more convenient for users to consume via the Internet, which diversifies the transaction behaviors of users. Therefore, Markov chain models are unsuitable for the representation of these behaviors. In this section, we propose a logical graph of BP (LGBP) which is a total order-based model to represent the logical relation of attributes of transaction records. Based on LGBP and users' transaction records, we can compute a path-based transition probability from an attribute to another one. At the same time, we define an information entropy-based diversity coefficient to characterize the diversity of transaction behaviors of a user. Also, we define a state transition probability matrix to capture the temporal features of transactions of a user. Consequently, we can construct a BP for each user and then use it to verify if an incoming transaction is a fraud or not.

The main idea of BP is that different users can have different personalized behaviors due to their different identities, different incomes, different motivations, and so on.

Definition 7.1 (Transaction Record): A transaction record r consists of m attribute values, i.e., $r = \{a_1, a_2, \ldots, a_m | a_1 \in A_1, a_2 \in A_2, \ldots, a_m \in A_m\}$ where $A_i = \{a_1^i, a_2^i, \ldots, a_{n_i}^i\}$ is the set of values of the ith attribute and $n_i = |A_i|$.

Given a user u, her/his transaction log is a set of her/his transaction records in a period and denoted as $L_u = \{r_1^u, r_2^u, \ldots, r_{n^u}^u\}$ in which $n^u = |L_u|$.

For example, Table 7.1 lists six transaction records of a user who bought goods. Transaction record r_1^u means that the user bought a good of daily supply (DS) at Shanghai Jiading (SJ) at night (NI), its price is in (0, 200] Chinese Yuan, and it is shipped to Anhui Xuancheng (AX).

Note that we preprocess some information in the original records. For example, the goods are classified and transaction time is divided

Table 7.1　Example of transaction log [32].

Transaction records	Transaction_ time	Transaction_ location	Category_ of_good	Amount	Shipping_ address
		Transaction attributes			
r_1^u	NI	SJ	DS	$(0, 200]$	AX
r_2^u	MO	SJ	SS	$(0, 200]$	SJ
r_3^u	AF	AX	DS	$(0, 200]$	AX
r_4^u	MO	SJ	EP	$(500, 1000]$	SJ
r_5^u	MO	SJ	SS	$(0, 200]$	SJ
r_6^u	NI	SJ	DS	$(0, 200]$	SJ

into four segments. Any two original records are different since their transaction time is different, but some records in L_u are possibly equal because their transaction times are put into the same segment or their goods belong to the same category. These equal records are all kept in L_u to characterize the user's behavior. To represent some equations conveniently, we denote R_u as the set of all different records in L_u. R_u is a set and L_u is a multiset. In Table 7.1, every transaction record has five attributes: *transaction_ time*, *transaction_location*, *category_of_good*, *amount*, and *shipping_ address*, where *transaction_time*={Early Morning: [0, 6], Morning: (6, 12], Afternoon: (12, 18], Night: (18, 24]}, and *amount* $= \{(0, 200],$ $(200, 500], (500, 1000], (1000, \infty)\}$.

Some attributes in each record are dependent on the related operations (events) executed in the system. For example, *transaction_location* can be previous to *category_of_good* because a user can select goods only after s/he logins. Note that transaction time and location are recorded once s/he logins. Then, the amount of goods is obtained. At last, the user submits the shipping address. Also, some attributes are related to a user's behavior habit. For example, it is often the morning or afternoon when a user logs in at the office, while it is often the evening when s/he logs in at home. Therefore, we assume that *transaction_time* is previous to *transaction_location*. Without loss of generality, we let $A_1 \prec A_2 \prec \cdots \prec A_m$ in this section.

Based on the total order relation and the transaction log of a user, we can construct a logic graph of BP (LGBP) for the user, which represents the dependent relations of all attribute values of this user's records and covers all transaction records. First, we abstract all attribute values occurring in the transaction records of user u as follows:

$$A_1^u = \{a \in A_1 | \exists r \in R_u : a \in r\}$$

$$A_2^u = \{a \in A_2 | \exists r \in R_u : a \in r\}$$

$$\cdots$$

$$A_m^u = \{a \in A_m | \exists r \in R_u : a \in r\}.$$

Obviously, $A_1^u \subseteq A_1$, $A_2^u \subseteq A_2, \ldots$, and $A_m^u \subseteq A_m$. Without loss of generality, we denote $A_i^u = \{a_1^i, a_2^i, \ldots, a_{n_i^u}^i\}$ in which $n_i^u = |A_i^u|$ for each $i \in \{1, 2, \ldots, m\}$.

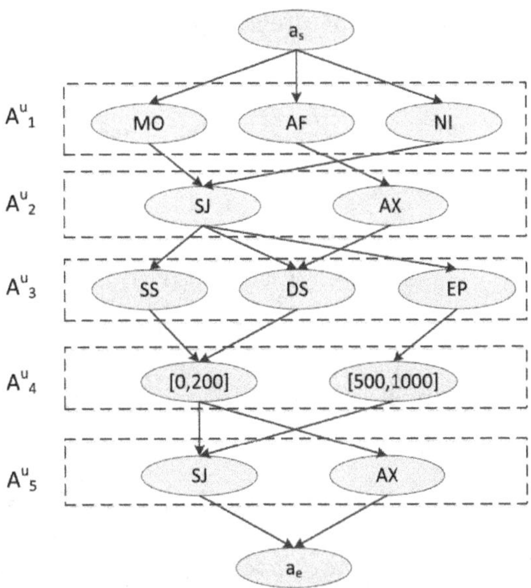

Figure 7.7   LGBP of a user whose transaction log is listed in Table 7.1 [32].

Definition 7.2 (LGBP): Let $L_u = \{r_1^u, r_2^u, \ldots, r_{n_u}^u\}$ be the transaction log of user u. The LGBP of u is a directed acyclic graph $G_u = (V_u, E_u)$, where:

(1) $V_u = \{a_s, a_e\} \cup A_1^u \cup A_2^u \cup \cdots \cup A_m^u$ in which a_s and a_e are the two special nodes that represent the start and end of a transaction;
(2) $\forall a \in A_1^u, (v_s, a) \in E_u$;
(3) $\forall a \in A_m^u, (a, v_e) \in E_u$;
(4) $\forall i \in \{1, 2, \ldots, m - 1\}, \forall a \in A_i^u, \forall a' \in A_{i+1}^u : (a, a') \in E_u$ if and only if $\exists r \in R_u: a \in r \bigwedge a' \in r$.

Figure 7.7 shows the LGBP of a user whose transaction log is listed in Table 7.1.

Definition 7.3 (Prepaths): Let $G_u = (V_u, E_u)$ be the LGBP of user u. $\forall \in V_u$, prepaths(v) is the set of all directed paths from node a_s to node v in G_u.

Definition 7.4 (Postnodes): Let $G_u = (V_u, E_u)$ be the LGBP of u. $\forall v \in V_u$, postnodes(v) is the set of nodes that are directly reached from v in G_u.

For example, there are five directed paths from node a_s to $(0, 200]$ in Figure 7.7

$$\sigma_1 = a_s \cdot \text{MO} \cdot \text{SJ} \cdot \text{SS} \cdot (0, 200]$$

$$\sigma_2 = a_s \cdot \text{MO} \cdot \text{SJ} \cdot \text{DS} \cdot (0, 200]$$

$$\sigma_3 = a_s \cdot \text{AF} \cdot \text{AX} \cdot \text{DS} \cdot (0, 200]$$

$$\sigma_4 = a_s \cdot \text{NI} \cdot \text{SJ} \cdot \text{SS} \cdot (0, 200]$$

$$\sigma_5 = a_s \cdot \text{NI} \cdot \text{SJ} \cdot \text{DS} \cdot (0, 200].$$

Nodes SJ and AX in A_5^u are the postnodes of $(0, 200]$ in Figure 7.7, i.e., $\text{postnodes}((0, 200]) = \{\text{SJ}, \text{AX}\}$.

Definition 7.5 (Path-Based Probability Transition Matrix): Let $G_u = (V_u, E_u)$ be the LGBP of user u. $\forall v \in V_u$, M_v is a $|prepaths(v)| \times |\text{postnodes}(v)|$ matrix where $\forall \sigma \in prepaths(v)$, $\forall v' \in \text{postnodes}(v)$

$$M_v(\sigma, v') = P(v \rightarrow v'|\sigma)$$

which is the transition probability from v to v' under the condition that v is reached via σ.

For example, node $(0, 200]$ in Figure 7.7 has five directed paths from a_s: $\sigma_1 - \sigma_5$, and has two postnodes: SJ and AX. Therefore, we have

$$M_{(0,200]} = \begin{pmatrix} P((0, 200] \rightarrow \text{SJ}|\sigma_1) & P((0, 200] \rightarrow \text{AX}|\sigma_1) \\ P((0, 200] \rightarrow \text{SJ}|\sigma_2) & P((0, 200] \rightarrow \text{AX}|\sigma_2) \\ P((0, 200] \rightarrow \text{SJ}|\sigma_3) & P((0, 200] \rightarrow \text{AX}|\sigma_3) \\ P((0, 200] \rightarrow \text{SJ}|\sigma_4) & P((0, 200] \rightarrow \text{AX}|\sigma_4) \\ P((0, 200] \rightarrow \text{SJ}|\sigma_5) & P((0, 200] \rightarrow AX|\sigma_5) \end{pmatrix}$$

Here, we propose a method to calculate the path-based transition probability matrix for each node. We first introduce a diversity coefficient ω_u to reflect the diversity of transaction behaviors of a user u. In other words, the greater the value of ω_u, the higher the probability of conducting a transaction that never took place in the historical records of the user. Referring to the information entropy [37], we use the following equation to represent diversity:

$$\omega_u = - \sum_{i \in R_u} P(r) \times \log_k P(r)$$

where $P(r)$ is the probability of record r occurring in L_u and is calculated by the frequency of r in L_u, U is the set of all users, and

$$\kappa = \max_{u \in U}\{|R_u|\}$$

Table 7.2 illustrates five different values of ω_u if the user u has six transaction records, and we consider five different cases of these records. For example, Case 2 means that r_2 occurs three times in the six records, and r_1, r_3, and r_4 occur once, respectively. Hence, $\omega_u = 0.35$ for Case 2 where we let $\kappa = 32$. The value of ω_u becomes greater if the diversity of transaction records of a user is more abundant.

Given a directed path σ in the LGBP of user u, we use the following equation to represent the frequency of σ occurring in all transaction records. Note that σ occurs in a record r if and only if all nodes (except for a_s) in σ are in r:

$$f(\sigma) = |\{r \in L_u | \forall v \in \#(\sigma)/\{a\}_s : v \in r\}|.$$

In (3), $\#(\sigma)$ is the set of all nodes in σ. Considering the diversity of transaction behaviors of user u, we use the following equation to calculate the transition probability from v to v' under the condition

Table 7.2 Illustration of different values of diversity under different distributions of records [32].

	r_1	r_2	r_3	r_4	r_5	r_6	ω_u
Case1	1	1	1	1	1	1	1
Case2	1	3	1	1	0	0	0.35
Case3	3	3	0	0	0	0	0.2
Case4	5	1	0	0	0	0	0.13
Case5	6	0	0	0	0	0	0

that v is reached from a_s via σ:

$$P(v \to v'|\sigma) = \begin{cases} (1 - \omega_u) \times \dfrac{f(\sigma v')}{f(\sigma)} & f(\sigma) \neq 0 \\ 0 & f(\sigma) = 0 \end{cases}$$

If (4) has no coefficient $1 - \omega_u$, then we have that

$$\sum_{v' \in \text{postnodes}(v)} P(v \to v'|\sigma) = \sum_{v' \in \text{postnodes}(v)} \frac{f(\sigma v')}{f(\sigma)}$$

$$= \frac{\sum_{v' \in \text{postnodes}(v)} f(\sigma v')}{f(\sigma)}$$

$$= \frac{f(\sigma)}{f(\sigma)} = 1.$$

This means that in the future, the user cannot conduct a new transaction that never took place in her/his historical records, which contradicts the fact. Therefore, we use a diversity coefficient to represent the probability that a user conducts a new transaction.

$f(\sigma) = 0$ means that there is no record r in L_u such that

$$\forall v'' \in \#(\sigma)/\text{as} : v'' \in r.$$

Hence, the transition probability from v to v' under σ should be equal to zero, i.e., $P(v \to v'|\sigma) = 0$ if $f(\sigma) = 0$ in (4).

For example, in the five paths $\sigma_1 - \sigma_5$ from the node a_s to node $(0, 200]$ in Figure 7.7, σ_1 corresponds to r_2^u and r_5^u, σ_3 corresponds to r_3^u, σ_5 corresponds to r_1^u and r_6^u, but σ_2 and σ_4 do not correspond to any record. Therefore, we can obtain the path-based transition probability matrix of the node $(0, 200]$ as follows:

$$M_{(0,200]} = \begin{array}{c} \\ \sigma_1 \\ \sigma_2 \\ \sigma_3 \\ \sigma_4 \\ \sigma_5 \end{array} \begin{array}{c} \text{SJ} \qquad\quad \text{AX} \\ \begin{pmatrix} 1 - \omega_u & 0 \\ 0 & 0 \\ 0 & 1 - \omega_u \\ 0 & 0 \\ \frac{1-\omega_u}{2} & \frac{1-\omega_u}{2} \end{pmatrix} \end{array}$$

$P((0, 200] \to \text{SJ}|\sigma_1) = 1 - \omega_u$ due to $f(\sigma_1) = 2$ and $f(\sigma_1\text{SJ}) = 2$.
$P((0, 200] \to \text{AX}|\sigma_1) = 0$ due to $f(\sigma_1) = 2$ and $f(\sigma_1\text{AX}) = 0$.

$P((0, 200] \to \text{SJ}|\sigma_4) = P((0, 200] \to \text{AX}|\sigma_4) = 0$ due to $f(\sigma_4) = 0$. One can easily understand others.

Next, we define the state transition probability matrix to capture the temporal features of transactions of a user.

Definition 7.6 (State Transition Probability Matrix): Let $X = \{C_1, C_2, \ldots, C_N\}$ be the set of categories of goods. The good category in the transaction at time t is denoted by q_t. The state transition probability matrix with respect to user u is denoted as $T_u = [\tau_{ij}]$, where

$$\tau_{ij} = P(q_{t+1} = C_j | q_t = C_i), \quad 1 \leq i, j \leq N.$$

Specifically,

$$P(q_{t+1} = C_j | q_t = C_i) = \frac{f(C_i \to C_j)}{f(C_i)}$$

where

$$f(C_i) = |\{r \in L_u / \{r_{n_u}^u\} | C_i \in r\}|$$

and

$$f(C_i \to C_j) = |\{\{r, r'\} \subseteq L_u | C_i \in r \wedge C_j \in r'\}|.$$

Note that r and r' are the two consecutive transactions in L_u such that r occurs before r'. Therefore, we only compute the transition probability of two goods categories in two consecutive transactions. For example, in Table 7.1, there are three categories of goods: DS, SS, and EP. The transition probability of DS and SS that are in two consecutive transactions r_1^u and r_2^u can be calculated as follows:

$$P(q_2 = \text{SS}|q_1 = \text{DS}) = \frac{1}{2} = 0.5$$

and then, we can obtain the state transition probability matrix of Table 7.1 as follows:

$$T = \begin{array}{c} \\ \text{DS} \\ \text{SS} \\ \text{EP} \end{array} \begin{array}{ccc} \text{DS} & \text{SS} & \text{EP} \\ \left(\begin{array}{ccc} 0 & 0.5 & 0.5 \\ 1 & 0 & 0 \\ 0 & 1 & 0 \end{array} \right). \end{array}$$

Obviously, $\sum_{j=1}^{N} \tau_{ij} = 1$ for each $i \in \{1, \ldots, N\}$. In what follows, we use $C(r)$ to represent the category of the good occurring in transaction r.

Definition 7.7 (Behavior Profile): Let $L_u = \{r_1^u, r_2^u, \ldots, r_{n_u}^u\}$ be the transaction log of user u. $\mathrm{BP}_u = (V_u, E_u, M_u, T_u, \omega_u)$ is the BP of u, where:

(1) $G_u = (V_u, E_u)$ is the LGBP of u;
(2) $M_u = \{M_v | v \in V_u\}$ is the set of path-based transition probability matrices of all nodes in G_u;
(3) T_u is the state transition probability matrix w.r.t. u, and
(4) ω_u is the diversity coefficient of u.

For each user, we can construct a BP based on her/his transaction log. In what follows, we propose a method to detect if a transaction record is acceptable by a BP.

Then, we propose the algorithm to compute the recognition degree of a transaction record by a given BP [32]. Let $\mathrm{BP}_u = (V_u, E_u, M_u, T_u, \omega_u)$ be the BP of user u and $r = \{a_1, a_2, \ldots, a_m\}$ be an arbitrary record where $\forall i \in \{1, 2, \ldots, m\}$: $a_i \in A_i$. We denote $\sigma_r = a_0 \cdot a_1 \ldots a_m \cdot a_{m+1}$ as the virtual path corresponding to r, and denote $\sigma_r^i = a_0 \cdot a_1 \ldots a_{i-1}$ as the prefix of σ_r with length i, where $a_0 = a_s$ and $a_{m+1} = a_e$.

If $r \in L_u$, we know that $f(\sigma_r^i) \neq 0$ and thus $P(a_{i-1} \rightarrow a_i | \sigma_r^i) = 0$, $\forall i \in \{1, 2, \ldots, m\}$.

Hence, we can use the following equation to calculate the recognization degree of r by BP_u:

$$\beta(r, \mathrm{BP}_u) = \prod_{i=1}^{m} P(a_{i-1} \rightarrow a_i | \sigma_r^i) = \prod_{i=1}^{m} M_{a_{i-1}}(\sigma_r^i, a_i).$$

The above-mentioned conclusion implies that the recognization degree of a transaction represents the probability of the transaction in history. If $r \notin L_u$, then we know that $f(\sigma_r) = 0$. Two cases are leading to $f(\sigma_r) = 0$. One is that $\forall a \in r$: $a \in V_u$, but $\exists i \in \{1, 2, \ldots, m\}$: $f(\sigma_r^i) \neq 0 \wedge f(\sigma_r^{i+1}) = 0$. Another one is that $\exists a \in r$: $a \notin V_u$. For the latter, we still have that $\exists i \in \{1, 2, \ldots, m\}$: $f(\sigma_r^i) \neq 0 \wedge f(\sigma_r^{i+1}) = 0$. The two cases both result in $P(a_{i1} \rightarrow a_i | \sigma_r^i) = 0$, where $i \in \{1, 2, \ldots, m\}$. Hence, if we calculate the recognization degree of r by BP_u, then $\beta(r, \mathrm{BP}_u) = 0$. However, if we measure the degree to which a transaction that never took place in the historic records is similar to the historic behavior, we do not hope that its recognization degree is 0. Therefore, $P(a_{i-1} \to a_i | \sigma_r^i)$ is assigned by ω_u instead of 0 for the case of $r \notin L_u$. For the next calculation, we should update σ_r^{i+1} since $f(\sigma_r^{i+1}) = 0$. $\sigma_r^{i+1} = \sigma_r^i a_i$ is replaced by $\sigma_r^{i+1} = \sigma_r^i v_{\max}$ such that

$$M_{a_{i-1}}(s_r^i, v_{\max}) = \max_{v \in \text{postnodes}(a_{i-1})} \{M_{a_{i-1}}(\sigma_r^i, v)\}.$$

Algorithm 7.1 Calculation of Recognition Degree

Input: A user's BP $BP_u = (V_u, E_u, \mathcal{M}_u, \mathcal{T}_u, \omega_u)$ and
a transaction record $r = \{a_1, a_2, \ldots, a_m\}$ where
$\forall i \in \{1, 2, \ldots, m\}$: $a_i \in A_i$;
Output: The recognition degree β of r by BP_u;

1 $a_0 := a_s$;
2 $\sigma := a_0$;
3 $\beta := 1$;
4 **for** $(i:=1; i \le m; i{+}{+})$ **do**
5   **if** $M_{a_{i-1}}(\sigma, a_i) \ne 0$ **then**
6      $\beta := \beta \times M_{a_{i-1}}(\sigma, a_i)$;
7      $\sigma := \sigma \cdot a_i$;
8   **else**
9      $\beta := \beta \times \omega_u$;
10   select node $v_{\max}$ that satisfies $M_{a_{i-1}}(\sigma, v_{\max}) = \max_{v \in postnodes(a_{i-1})}\{M_{a_{i-1}}(\sigma, v)\}$;
11      $\sigma := \sigma \cdot v_{\max}$;
12   **end**
13 **end**

The above-mentioned equation guarantees $f(\sigma_r^{i+1}) = f(\sigma_r^i v_{\max}) \ne 0$. The above process can clearly describe the process of calculating the recognition degree of a transaction. Then, we compute the reorganization degree, we can use the following equation to calculate the acceptance degree of r by BP_u:

$$\varphi(r, \mathrm{BP}_u) = \beta(r, \mathrm{BP}_u) \times P(q_{n^u+1} = C(r) | q_{n^u} = C(r_{n^u}^u))$$

Next, we give a method to decide if an incoming transaction is legal or not based on acceptance degree. We calculate the acceptance degrees of the latest k transaction records and then obtain their mean φ_k. For an incoming transaction r, we calculate its acceptance degree φ. We use the following equation to evaluate the illegality of this transaction:

$$(\varphi_k - \varphi)/\varphi_k \geq \text{Threshold}.$$

If $(\varphi_k - \varphi)/\varphi_k \geq$ threshold, then this transaction is thought of as a fraud, else it is legal.

7.6.3 *Improved TrAdaBoost and its application to transaction fraud detection*

AdaBoost is a boosting-based machine learning method under the assumption that the data in training and testing sets have the same distribution and input feature space. It increases the weights of those instances that are wrongly classified in a training process. However, the assumption does not hold in many real-world datasets. Therefore, AdaBoost is extended to transfer AdaBoost (TrAdaBoost) that can effectively transfer knowledge from one domain to another. TrAdaBoost decreases the weights of those instances that belong to the source domain but are wrongly classified in a training process. It is more suitable for the case that data are of different distribution. Can it be improved for some special transfer scenarios, e.g., the data distribution changes slightly over time? We find that the distribution of credit card transaction data can change with the changes in the transaction behaviors of users, but the changes are slow most of the time. These changes are yet important for detecting transaction fraud since they result in a so-called concept drift problem. To make TrAdaBoost more suitable for the abovementioned case, we, thus, propose an improved TrAdaBoost (ITrAdaBoost). It updates (i.e., increases or decreases) the weight of a wrongly classified instance in a source domain according to the distribution distance from the instance to a target domain, and the calculation of distance is based on the theory of reproducing kernel Hilbert space [33].

ITrAdaBoost is to find a classifier $H(x)$: $x \to y$ that has a high performance of classification on a testing set. When the training data that have the same distribution with the testing data are scarce, some data from another domain (or some outdated data in the same domain) can be used to enrich the training set in a target domain. Therefore, the training data of ITrAdaBoost come from both source and target domains. Generally, data distributions between the two domains are different.

Algorithm 7.2 Merge   Process

Input: $S_1, S_2, \ldots, S_k$, classifier $h(x)$, threshold T
Output: A group of sections

1 $Q := \{S_1, S_2, \ldots, S_k\}$;
2 **while** $Q \neq \emptyset$ **do**
3   select an element S from Q;
4   train a classifier h over S;
5      $Q := Q - \{S\}$;
6      $Q' := Q$;
7   **while** $Q' \neq \emptyset$ **do**
8   select an element S' from Q';
9          $Q' := Q' - \{S'\}$;
10   compute the error rate θ of $h(x)$ on S';
11   **if** $\theta < T$ **then**
12             $S := S \cup S'$;
13             $Q := Q - \{S'\}$;
14   **end**
15   **end**
16   output a section S;
17 **end**

Formally, we denote $X^T = \{x_1^T, x_2^T, \ldots, x_m^T\}$ and $\{X^S = x_1^s, x_2^s, \ldots, x_n^s\}$ as the training data instances coming from the target and source domains (without considering category labels of data), respectively. Y is denoted as the finite set of category labels. In fact, for each data instance $x \in X^T \cup X^S$, there is a category label corresponding to it, which is denoted as $c(x)$. Therefore, the training set (with category labels) is denoted as $\{(x, c(x)) | x \in X^T \cup X^S, c(s) \in Y\}$.

Next, we calculate the distance between an instance in the source domain and the whole target domain.

First, we fine-grainedly divide X^S into k parts: $S_1, S_2, \ldots$, and S_k, where $1 < k \leq n$. Note that the dataset can be divided according to different factors, such as time. We then merge those parts that have the same distribution into a section, and finally, $S_1, S_2, \ldots$, and S_k are merged into $\mathcal{D}$ sections. Algorithm 7.2 describes a merge process. If the time complexity of training a classifier $h(x)$ is O_1 and the time complexity of computing the error rate on a section by $h(x)$ is O_2, then the time complexity of Algorithm 7.2 is $O(k \cdot (O_1 + k \cdot O_2))$ in the worst case. In our experiments, we select the decision stump as a classifier. Its time complexity is $O(l*n^2 * \log n)$, and the time complexity of each decision by decision stump is $O(\log n)$ [thus, the time complexity of computing the error rate on a section is on average $O((n/k) \log n)$], where l is the dimension of each data sample and n is the number of data samples in a training set. Thus, the time complexity of Algorithm 7.2 is $O((k*(l*n^2*\log n+k\cdot((n/k)\log n)) = O(k*l*n^2*\log n)$.

For each section $X_i^S \subseteq X^S (i \in \{1, 2, \ldots, \mathcal{D}\})$, we let $n_i = |X_i^S|$. Then, the distribution distance between X_i^S and X^T can be computed via (5) and is described as follows:

$$D^2(X_i^S, X^T) = \mathrm{MMD}_l^2[F, X_i^S, X^T]$$

$$= \frac{2}{n_i} \sum_{l=1}^{\frac{n_i}{2}} k(x_{2l-1}^S, x_{2l}^S) + \frac{2}{m} \sum_{j=1}^{\frac{m}{2}} k(x_{2j-1}^T, x_{2j}^T)$$

$$- \frac{2}{n_i} \sum_{l=1}^{\frac{n_i}{2}} k(x_{2l-1}^S, x_{2l}^T) - \frac{2}{m} \sum_{j=1}^{\frac{m}{2}} k(x_{2j-1}^T, x_{2j}^S)$$

$\forall x \in X_i^S$, and we use $D(X_i^S, X^T)$ to represent the distance between x and X^T, i.e., $D(x, X^T) = D(X_i^S, X^T)$.

After computing the distribution distance, we introduce the mechanism of updating weights in ITrAdaBoost.

After the tth iteration, the weight of instance $x \in X_i^S \subseteq X^S$ can be computed as follows:

$$\omega_i^{t+1} = \begin{cases} \omega_i^t \cdot \beta^{\lfloor h_t(x)-c(x) \rfloor}, & D(X_i^S, X^T) > d \\[2mm] \omega_i^t \cdot [\beta \cdot (1 + e^{D(x,X^T)})]^{-\lfloor h_t(x)-c(x) \rfloor} \\[2mm] D(X_i^S, X^T) \leq d \end{cases}$$

where

$$\beta = \frac{\theta_t}{1 - \theta_t}$$

and θ_t is the error rate produced by the weak learner on X^T in the tth iteration

$$\theta_t = \sum_{i=1}^{m} \frac{\omega_i^t \cdot |h_t(x_i^T) - c(x_i^T)|}{\sum_{i=1}^{m} \omega_i^t}$$

The weight of instance x in X^T can be updated as follows:

$$\omega_i^{t+1} = \omega_i^t \cdot \beta^{-\lfloor h_t(x) - c(x) \rfloor}$$

Algorithm 7.3 ITrAdaBoost

Input: X^T and X^S, weak learning algorithm,
      the maximum number of iterations N;
Output: The final classifier $H(x)$;
1 **Initialize**: The initial weight vector

$$w^1 = (w_1^1, w_2^1, \dots, w_{m+n}^1),$$

w^1 can be initialized as $w_i^1 = \frac{1}{m+n}$, $i = 1, 2, \dots, m+n$.
2 **for** $t = 1, t < N, t++$ **do**
3 | Set

$$p^t = \frac{w^t}{\sum_{i=1}^{m+n} w_i^t}$$

4 | Call the weak learning algorithm over X^T and X^S and
      then produce a base weak learner: $h_t(x) \to \{0, 1\}$;
5 | Calculate the error rate of $h_t(x)$ on X^T by Eq. 9;
6 | Calculate the coefficient of $h_t(x)$ by Eq. 11;
7 | Set $\beta = \frac{\theta_t}{1 - \theta_t}$ and then update the weight of each
      training data as follows:
8 | **if** $x \in X^T$ **then**
9 | | Update its weight by Eq. 10;
10 | **else**
11 | | Update its weight by Eq. 8;
12 | **end**
13 **end**
14 Return a strong classifier:

$$H(x) = sign\left[\sum_{t=1}^{N} \alpha_t \cdot h_t(x)\right];$$

When an instance in a source domain is wrongly classified, we first decide whether its distribution is similar to the distribution of instances in a target domain. If the distribution distance is bigger than the threshold d, then we think that the distribution of data in the source domain is dissimilar to the distribution of the instance in the target domain, or else they are similar. Note that d is a super parameter, and its value is decided by experiments. If they are dissimilar, we decrease their weight to weaken their influence in the next iteration. The weight is decreased by multiplying a factor that is less than 1. If they are similar, this means that the error of the weak learner makes it wrongly classified, and thus, we increase its weight in the next iteration. The weight is increased by multiplying a factor that is greater than 1.

Each iteration produces a weak learner and the coefficient of the tth weak learner can be computed as follows:

$$\alpha_t = \frac{1}{2} \log \frac{1 - \theta_t}{\theta_t}$$

Algorithm 7.3 realizes ITrAdaBoost. We first compute all distribution distances before executing Algorithm 7.3, and these distances are used in the step of updating weights in Algorithm 7.3. Therefore, the time complexity is $O(N * (O_1 + O_2))$, where N is the maximum number of iterations, O_1 is the time complexity of producing a weak classifier, and O_2 is the time complexity of computing the error rate in the target domain.

Theorem 7.1 *Let* $x \in X_i^S$, $z \in X_j^S (i \neq j \leq k)$, $s \in X^T$, *and* d *be the threshold of distribution distance. If* $D(x, X^T) < D(z, X^T) \leq d$, *and* x, z, *and* s *are wrongly classified in the tth iteration, then*

$$\frac{\omega_z^{t+1} - \omega_z^t}{\omega_z^t} < \frac{\omega_x^{t+1} - \omega_x^t}{\omega_x^t} < \frac{\omega_s^{t+1} - \omega_s^t}{\omega_s^t}$$

Theorem 7.1 means that if an instance in a source domain is wrongly classified, the increase rate of its weight is less than the increase rate of the weights of the wrongly classified instances in a target domain. Besides, the more the similarity between the distribution of an instance in a source domain and that of a target domain, the larger the increase rate of its weight.

For transaction fraud detection, one simple approach is to train a model by using the historical transaction data and then judge the legality of an incoming transaction via the model. This approach is based on an assumption that the training data and incoming data are of the same distribution. However, the assumption does not hold in the real world since users' transaction behaviors generally change with time, leading to the so-called concept drift problem.

Concept drift [38] is a phenomenon where users change their transaction behavior over time due to an unstable external environment such as goods prices. In other words, their current transaction behavior pattern may be different from their historical pattern. Therefore, it is unreasonable to train a model using history transaction data directly. An alternative way is to update the training data using a window-sliding method with a forgetting mechanism [39]. However, it takes a basic assumption that the data distribution is changeable over time, i.e., data have become useless for predicting the current behavior when they are getting too old. However, the transaction behaviors of users do not necessarily completely drift. Some previous transaction behaviors may reappear after some time. Therefore, history data are still of potential value for training a model. The best way is to automatically select useful transaction data and filter out the useless ones when training a model.

In this section, we introduce a transaction fraud detection method based on ITrAdaBoost. First, the historical transaction data are divided into two parts: source domain and target domain. The data in the target domain arc thought of as having the same distribution with the incoming transaction data. For example, the data in the target domain can be the most recent transaction data or the transaction data that have a similar external environment with the current transaction. Transaction data in the source domain generally are generated before a relatively long period, and thus, many of them tend to have different distributions in comparison with the incoming transactions. The purpose of our fraud detection method based on ITrAdaBoost is to transfer knowledge from a source domain to a target one by increasing the influence of the useful data and decreasing the influence of the valueless data. Our method of computing distance can better evaluate the usefulness of data.

The framework of our fraud detection method is shown in Figure 7.8. Case$_1$, ..., and Case$_n$ represent n different situations of concept drift. For example, we can use the transaction data produced in the most recent month or week as the target domain and the data produced in other months or weeks as the source domain. If we want

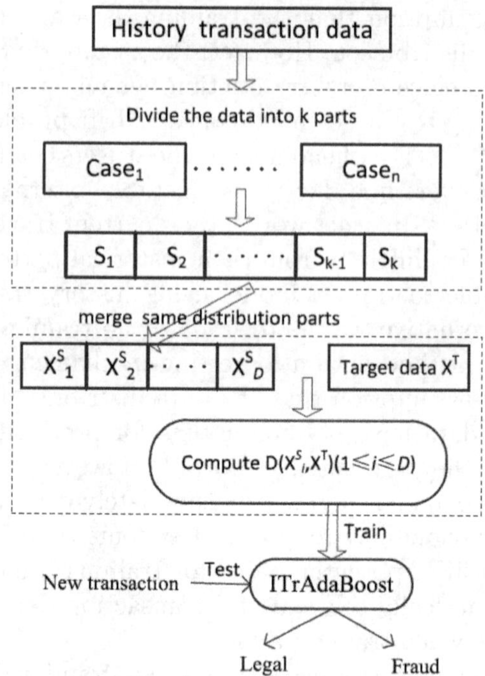

Figure 7.8　Framework of fraud detection by ITrAdaBoost [33].

to predict the transaction behavior of users at weekends, we can use the transaction data produced in all previous weekends as the target domain and others in the working days as the source domain.

7.6.4　*Deep representation learning with full center loss for credit card fraud detection*

Credit card fraud detection is an important study in the current era of mobile payment. Improving the performance of a fraud detection model and keeping its stability is very challenging because users' payment behaviors and criminals' fraud behaviors are often changing. In this section, we focus on obtaining deep feature representations of legal and fraud transactions from the aspect of the loss function of a deep neural network. Our purpose is to obtain better separability and discrimination of features so that it can improve the performance of our fraud detection model and keep its stability. We propose a new kind of loss function, full center loss (FCL), which considers both distances and angles among features and, thus, can comprehensively supervise the deep representation learning [34].

We present a deep neural network as our representation learning model, mapping the original features of transactions into deep representations for identifying fraud transactions accurately. Intuitively, the learned deep representations should maximize their intraclass compactness and interclass separability simultaneously. FCL integrates two different aspects of optimization objectives (or losses). The first aspect is about the distance between deep representation and class center, named distance center loss (DCL). DCL can stress the intraclass compactness. The second aspect is an optimized softmax loss (SL) with a maximum angle that can promote the deep representations of samples from different classes so that the interclass separability is improved. We call our optimized SL as angle center loss (ACL).

Building an effective credit card fraud detection model consists of some essential steps which significantly influence the detection. The first step is feature engineering that aims at extracting informative features of users' transaction behaviors. After feature engineering, a classifier can be trained as a binary classification task. However, if the class imbalance problem is not considered, the learned classifier will tend to identify most of the fraud transactions as genuine ones. The reason is that almost all classifiers have a default assumption of a balanced dataset, and thus, the learned decision boundary tends to bias toward the class with more samples. Hence, dealing with the class imbalance problem has become an indispensable step before training a fraud detection model. A fraud transaction detection model, as a binary classifier, can be trained with a relatively balanced dataset after handling the class imbalance problem. There are many machine learning methods, and the latest neural network architectures make a deep representation learning model not only deeper with much more layers but also easier for model training. These advanced architectures significantly enhance the ability of complex non-linear mapping of a deep representation learning model. On the other hand, the ingeniously designed loss functions can supervise the process of deep representation so that the final model can obtain an ideal result.

As shown in Figure 7.9, the fraud transaction detection model in this section is composed of two parts: the deep neural network layers

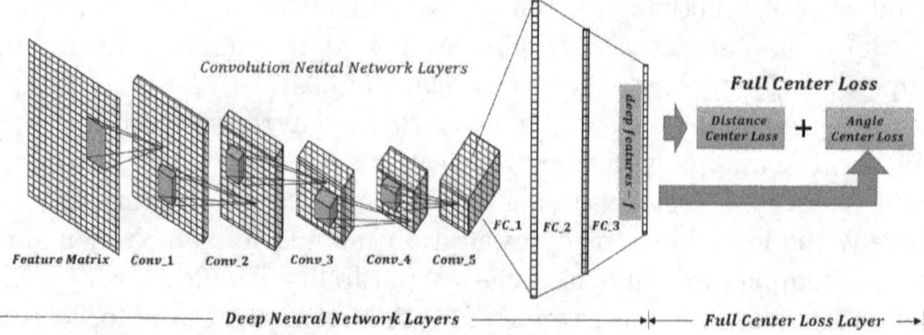

Figure 7.9   The deep representation learning framework [34].

(e.g., convolution neural network (CNN) layers) for obtaining separable and discriminative representations, and the fully center loss layer for supervising the model training. The key is to optimize the loss function so that the quality of those learned deep features and the performance of fraud transaction detection are enhanced. The loss function is to supervise the training of deep convolution neural network layers that project the original feature space of transactions into a deep feature space. The goal is that the transactions from the same class can be compact as fully as possible and the transactions from different classes can be separated as fully as possible. For this goal, the FCL combines two different aspects of losses: ACL for addressing the separability of transactions from different classes and DCL for addressing the compactness of transactions from the same class.

ACL is an improved SL, which is specially designed for credit card fraud detection as a binary classification problem. It can enhance the classification ability compared to the softmax function. Meanwhile, the advantage of the simplicity of the SL is still retained in ACL. DCL is originally proposed in Ref. [40] and is to measure the aggregation of deep features of each class.

FCL can be formulated as follows:

$$L_{\text{Full}} = \sum_{i=1}^{m} (L_{A\_i} + \alpha L_{D\_i})$$

where α is a hyperparameter to trade off these two losses and m denotes the size of minibatch samples for training our deep representation learning model. A detailed explanation of every loss is shown in the following.

In general, the ideal deep features should keep intraclass compactness and interclass separability as much as possible. Although the SL of the normal CNN model is very simple and performs well in many classification applications, it is not too effective to generate discriminative features. When using the original SL to solve a binary class problem, the posterior probabilities of the learned deep representation f_i of an input sample x_i with label 0 or 1 can be written as

$$P0 = \frac{e^{W_0^T f_i + b_0}}{e^{W_0^T f_i + b_0} + e^{W_1^T f_i + b_1}}$$

$$P1 = \frac{e^{W_1^T f_i + b_1}}{e^{W_0^T f_i + b_0} + e^{W_1^T f_i + b_1}}$$

where (W_0, b_0) and (W_1, b_1) are weights and bias of the softmax layer in CNN corresponding to class 0 and 1, respectively. f_i is the output of the last fully connected layer. $p0$ and $p1$ are the posterior probabilities of f_i belonging to classes 0 and 1, respectively. If an input deep representation f_i has the label y_i, then the original SL of deep representation f_i can be reformulated as follows:

$$L_{\text{softmax}\_i} = -\log\left(\frac{e^{W_{y_i}^T f_i + b_{y_i}}}{e^{W_{y_i}^T f_i + b_{y_i}} + e^{W_{\tilde{y}_i}^T f_i + b_{y_i}}}\right)$$

$$= -\log\left(\frac{1}{1 + e^{\left(W_{ji}^T - W_{y_i}^T\right) f_i + \left(b_{y_i} - b_{y_i}\right)}}\right)$$

where $\tilde{y}_i$ denotes another class different from y_i in the binary classification.

We design two constraints for the original SL to keep the angular separability of instances from different classes. First, following the modified SL in [33], we normalize $||\boldsymbol{W}|| = ||\boldsymbol{W}_{y_i}|| = ||\boldsymbol{W}_{\tilde{y}_i}|| = 1$ and set the biases $||b_{y_i}|| = ||b_{\tilde{y}_i}|| = 0$ to maintain the angular boundary. This can guarantee that the value of SL just depends on the norm value of deep representations f_i and the angles between $\boldsymbol{W}_i$ and f_i. Therefore, the modified SL of the deep feature vector f_i can be written as

$$L_{\text{modified}\_i} = -\log\left(\frac{e^{||f_i||\cos\theta_{y_i}}}{e^{||y_i||\cos\theta_{y_i}} + e^{||f_i||\cos\theta_{\tilde{y}_i}}}\right)$$

$$= -\log\left(\frac{1}{1 + e^{-||f_i||(\cos\theta_{y_i} - \cos\theta_{\tilde{y}_i})}}\right)$$

where $0 \leq \theta_{y_i}, \theta_{\tilde{y}_i} < 2\pi$, θ_{y_i} denotes the angle between vectors $\boldsymbol{W}_{y_i}$ and f_i, and $\theta_{\tilde{y}_i}$ denotes the angle between vectors $\boldsymbol{W}_{\tilde{y}_i}$ and f_i.

To minimize the value of L_{modified_i}, intuitively, two optimizations should be taken into account. On the one hand, θ_{y_i} should be decreased, and $\theta_{\tilde{y}_i}$ should be increased. On the other hand, the value of $||f_i||$ should be enlarged since we have already constrained $||\boldsymbol{W}|| = 1$. Because the value range of $||f_i||$ is closely related to the DCL, we put more focus on the feasible optimization measure to make θ_{y_i} smaller than $\theta_{\tilde{y}_i}$ as much as possible. Ideally, instances from the same class are closely distributed on both sides of their corresponding $\boldsymbol{W}_{y_i}$. Hence, $\boldsymbol{W}_{y_i}$ can be regarded as the angle center of each class instance, and thus, we name this loss as ACL.

To obtain a stable classification performance, the learned deep representations of instances from different classes should keep separability as fully as possible. However, the modified SL is only able to directly minimize the angles between f_i and its corresponding $\boldsymbol{W}_{y_i}$. Therefore, we design another stronger constraint, i.e., $\boldsymbol{W}_{y_i}$ and $\boldsymbol{W}_{\tilde{y}_i}$, are in opposite directions: $\boldsymbol{W} = \boldsymbol{W}_{y_i} = -\boldsymbol{W}_{\tilde{y}_i}$. Finally, ACL with deep representation f_i can be reformulated as

$$L_{A-i} = -\log\left(\frac{1}{1 + e^{-2||f_i||\cos\theta_{y_i}}}\right)$$

$$= -\log\left(\frac{1}{1 + e^{-2W^T f_i}}\right)$$

$$= \log\left(1 + e^{-2W^T f_i}\right)$$

Based on the above description, it is easy to infer that with the decreasing of ACL, the deep representation f_i will gradually get close to $\boldsymbol{W}_{y_i}$, and thus, the learned representations from different classes will gradually be separated in opposite directions since $\boldsymbol{W}_{y_i}$ and $\boldsymbol{W}_{\tilde{y}_i}$ are always in opposite directions.

Though we apply these stronger constraints to the original SL, ACL retains the superiorities of the original SL. Therefore, it can still be easily optimized with gradient computation and backpropagation. When we replace $\cos\theta_{y_i}$ with $\boldsymbol{W}$ and f_i, the derivative of ACL concerning $\boldsymbol{W}$ and f_i can still be easily computed, just like the original SL.

DCL is mainly responsible for the separability of the learned deep representations from different classes. As for the compactness of intraclass deep representations, we adopt the center loss [40] in Euclidean space, which can be measured by the distance from an instance to its corresponding center. The center loss of deep representation f_i can be formulated as follows:

$$L_{D\_i} = \frac{1}{2}||f_i - c_{yi}||_2^2$$

where c_{y_i} denotes the corresponding class center of f_i with label y_i.

As the original center loss directly uses the Euclidean distance, we name it DCL. It has been proven that CNNs supervised by DCL are trainable and can be optimized through the standard stochastic gradient descent (SGD) method [40]. When training a model, the distance center of every class is computed by averaging the learned deep representations in the class in Euclidean space. A scalar γ is adopted to limit the updating speed of the distance centers to avoid large perturbations caused by a few mislabeled samples. Therefore, following the definition in [40], the updated equation of c_{y_i} can be formulated as

$$\frac{\partial L_{D\_i}}{\partial f_i} = f_i - c_{y_i}$$

$$\Delta c_j = \frac{\sum_{i}^{m} \delta(y_i = j) \cdot (\boldsymbol{c}_j - \boldsymbol{f}_i)}{1 + \sum_{i}^{m} \delta(y_i = j)}$$

$$\boldsymbol{c}_j' = \boldsymbol{c}_j - \gamma \cdot \Delta \boldsymbol{c}_j$$

where $\delta(\text{condition}) = 1$ if the condition is satisfied, otherwise $\delta(\text{condition}) = 0 \cdot c_j'$ is the center of class j after updating, and the hyperparameter γ is limited in the range $[0,1]$.

Combing ACL and DCL, the learning details of our proposed fraud detection model can be summarized as in Algorithm 7.4. Figure 7.10 shows the idea of FCL visually. a_center_0 and a_center_1 denote the centers of classes 0 and 1 in angel space, respectively. a_center_0 and a_center_1 are always in two opposite directions for the best angle separation. d_center_0 and d_center_1 denote the centers of classes 0 and 1 in Euclidean space, respectively. When training a model, each training sample and the related centers (distance center and angle center) will be pulled closer gradually.

Algorithm 7.4 DeepRepresentations Learning With FCL

Require: Training data set of transactions $X = \{x_i\}(i \in \{1, 2, \ldots, m\})$ and the learned deep representations $F = \{f_i\}$ corresponding to X. Initialized parameters θ_c in convolution-based deep representation learning layers. The initialized parameters W and $\{c_k\}(k = 0, 1)$ of angle center loss and distance center loss. Hyperparameters α, γ and the learning rate μ_t. The number of iterations t is initialized by 0.

Ensure: The learned parameters θ_c, W and c_k.

1: **repeat**
2:    $t = t + 1$;
3:    Compute FCL $L^t_{Full} = \sum_{i=1}^{m} L^t_{A\_i} + \alpha L^t_{D\_i}$;
4:    Compute the backpropagation error $\dfrac{\partial L^t_{Full}}{\partial f^t_i} = \dfrac{\partial L^t_{A\_i}}{\partial f^t_i} + \alpha \dfrac{\partial L^t_{D\_i}}{\partial f^t_i}$;
5:    Update W: $W^{t+1} = W^t - \mu_t \dfrac{\partial L^t_{Full}}{\partial f^t_i} = W^t - \mu_t \dfrac{\partial L^t_{A\_i}}{\partial f^t_i}$;
6:    Update c_k: $c_k^{t+1} = c_k^t - \gamma \, \Delta c_k^t$;
7:    Update θ_c: $\theta_c^{t+1} = \theta_c^t - \mu_t \sum_i^N \dfrac{\partial L^t_{Full}}{\partial f^t_i} \dfrac{\partial f^t_i}{\partial \theta_c^t}$;
8: **until** Parameters converge

FCL can supervise the deep representation learning model from both distance and angle so that the yielded model can enhance the intraclass compactness and interclass separation. Especially, ACL can directly separate learned representations of different classes in opposite directions. At last, we summarize the state-of-the-art loss functions used in the deep representation learning methods and compare them with ours over two big datasets. We also demonstrate that our model has better performance stability [34].

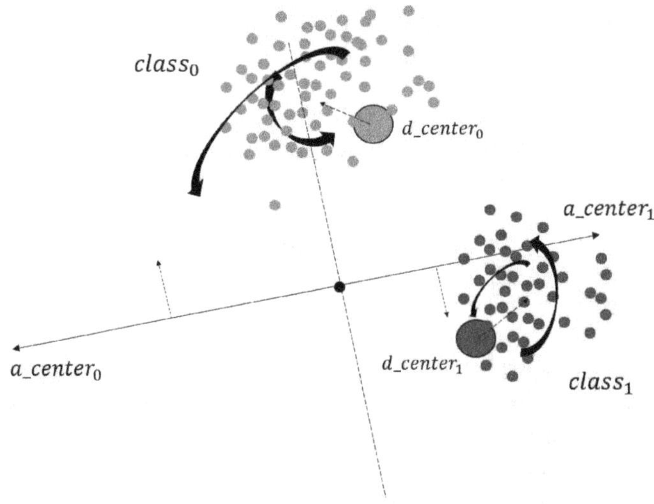

Figure 7.10 Idea of our FCL that consists of ACL and DCL [34].

7.7 Chapter Summary

The measurement of credit risk has not yet formed a mature model in the world. International mainstream credit risk measurement methods and models also have their own advantages and disadvantages. In general, to build a credit model with high accuracy and generalization capabilities, you must have sufficient basic data and good data mining techniques. In China, the construction of the credit information system started late. As data mining technology is continuously applied to credit evaluation, using automated analysis techniques, through the integration of individual transactions and behavioral data modeling, completing credit evaluation, improving credit accuracy, integrating user data precipitated by many enterprises, and thus building a unified and improved credit system, can further protect the security of all parties involved in online transactions and reduce the risk degree of transactions.

References

[1] Wang, C. Comparative Study on National Risk Assessment Index System. *Research on Economics and Management*, (6): 51–55 (2008).

[2] Zhao, X. Y. *Analysis of Mechanism and Research of Application on Credit Derivatives*, Tianjin University of Finance and Economics, (2008).

[3] Fishman. Financial Intermediaries as Facilitators of Information Exchange between Lenders and Reputation Formation by Borrowers. *International Review of Economics and Finance*, 18(2): 301–305 (2009).

[4] Anthony, S. *Credit Risk Measurement: New Approaches to Value at Risk and Other Paradigms*, John Wiley Sons, pp. 12–56, (1999).

[5] Feng, J. Y. *The Development of Modern Credit Risk Management Models and Their Comparative Study*, Tianjin, China: University of Science and Technology of China, (2007).

[6] Xiong, D. Y. *Credit Risk Theory and Application Research*, Shanghai, China: Fudan University, (2002).

[7] An, H. International Transmission Mechanism and Empirical Analysis of Modern Financial Crisis: A Case Study of Asian Financial Crisis. *Research on Financial and Economic Issues*, (8): 45–48 (2004).

[8] Xu, W. B., Zhang, Y. C., and Huang, J. X. A Review on the Sovereign Credit Rating Models of the Three Biggest Rating Agencies. *Studies of International Finance*, 10: 26–33 (2009).

[9] Chen, X. N. The Experience and Enlightenment of American Credit Service System. *Macroeconomics*, (1): 57–60 (2005).

[10] Hammer, P. L., Kogan, A., and Lejeune, M. A. Modeling Country Risk Ratings Using Partial Orders. *European Journal of Operational Research*, 175(2): 836–859 (2006).

[11] Pinheiro, A. C. and Moura, A. *Segmentation and the Use of Information in Brazilian Credit Markets. Credit Reporting Systems and the International Economy*, Boston: MIT Press, (2003).

[12] Agostino, C. and Cvitani, J. Credit Risk Modeling with Misreporting and Incomplete Information. *International Journal of Theoretical and Applied Finance*, 12(2): 1–29 (2009).

[13] Oral, M., Kettani, O., Cosset, J. C. *et al.* An Estimation Model for Country Risk Rating. *International Journal of Forecasting*, 8(4): 583–593 (1992).

[14] Zadeh, L. A. Outline of a New Approach to the Analysis of Complex Systems and Decision Processes. *IEEE Transactions on Systems, Man and Cybernetics*, SMC-3(1): 28–44 (1973).

[15] Alain, D. J., Craig, M., and Elisabeth, S. The Supply and Demand-Side Impacts of Credit Market Information. *Journal of Development Economics*, 93(2): 173–188 (2010).

[16] Kobrin, S. Assessing Political Risk Overseas. In *Multinational Enterprise in Transition: Selected Readings and Essays*, London, UK: Darwin Press, pp. 59–68 (1986).

[17] Leland, H. E. Predictions of Default Probabilities in Structural Models of Debt. *The Journal Of Investment Management*, 2(2): 5–20 (2004).

[18] Zadeh, L. A. *Fuzzy Sets and Fuzzy Information-Granulation Theory*, Beijing: Beijing Normal University Press, (2005).

[19] Xu, J. P. and Wu, W. *Multiple Attribute Decision Making*, Beijing: Tsinghua University Press, (2006).

[20] Estes, R. J. Economies in Transition: Revisiting Challenges to Quality of Life. *Handbook of Social Indicators and Quality of Life Research*, Springer, Dordrecht, pp. 433–457, (2012).

[21] Kou, G., Lou, C. W., Peng, Y. *et al.* DMCDM: A Dynamic Multi Criteria Decision Making Model for Sovereign Credit Default Risk Evaluation. *Journal of Management Sciences in China*, 15(4): 81–87 (2012).

[22] Phua, C., Lee, V., Smith, K. *et al.* A Comprehensive Survey of Data Mining-Based Fraud Detection Research. arXiv preprint arXiv:1009.6119, (2010) https://arxiv.org/abs/1009.6119.

[23] Sherman, E. Fighting Web Fraud. *Newsweek*, (2002) https://www.elibrary.ru/item.asp?id=4479228.

[24] Ghosh, S. and Reilly, D. L. Credit Card Fraud Detection with a Neural-Network. In *Proceedings of the Twenty-Seventh Hawaii International Conference on System Sciences*, IEEE, HI, USA, pp. 621–630 (1994).

[25] Kokkinaki, A. I. On Atypical Database Transactions: Identification of Probable Frauds Using Machine Learning for User Profiling. In *Proceedings of Knowledge and Data Engineering Exchange Workshop*, IEEE, Newport Beach, USA, pp. 107–113 (1997).

[26] Shen, A., Tong, R., and Deng, Y. Application of Classification Models on Credit Card Fraud Detection. In *International Conference on Service Systems and Service Management*, IEEE, Chengdu, China, pp. 1–4 (2007).

[27] Tian, L. Q. and Lin, C. Evaluation Mechanism for User Behavior Trust Based on DSW. *Journal of Tsinghua University: Science and Technology*, 50(5): 763–767 (2010).

[28] Fan, L. J., Wang, S. Z., and Liu, W. Evaluation Method Based on Human Trust Mechanism for Mobile E-commerce Trust. *Computer Science*, 39(1): 190–192 (2012).

[29] Zhang, S., Lu, X., and Wang, B. A Trust Evaluation Model Behaviors Based in Electricity Market. In *Third International Conference on Electric Utility Deregulation and Restructuring and Power Technologies, DRPT 2008*, IEEE, pp. 561–566, (2008).

[30] Wang, Y. and Wong, A. K. C. From Association to Classification: Inference Using Weight of Evidence. *IEEE Transactions on Knowledge and Data Engineering*, 15(3): 764–767 (2003).

[31] Jiang, C. J., Song, J. H., Liu, G. J. *et al.* Credit Card Fraud Detection: A Novel Approach Using Aggregation Strategy and Feedback Mechanism. *IEEE Internet of Things Journal*, 5(5): 3637–3647 (2018).

[32] Zheng, L. T., Liu, G. J., Yan, C. G. *et al.* Transaction Fraud Detection Based on Total Order Relation and Behavior Diversity. *IEEE Transactions on Computational Social Systems*, 5(3): 796–806 (2018).

[33] Zheng, L. T., Liu, G. J., Yan, C. G. *et al.* Improved TrAdaBoost and Its Application to Transaction Fraud Detection. *IEEE Transactions on Computational Social Systems*, 7(5): 1304–1316 (2020).

[34] Li, Z. C., Liu, G. J., Jiang, C. J. *et al.* Deep Representation Learning with Full Center Loss for Credit Card Fraud Detection. *IEEE Transactions on Computational Social Systems*, 7(2): 569–579 (2020).

[35] Hartigan, J. A. and Wong, M. A. Algorithm as 136: A K-Means Clustering Algorithm. *Journal of the Royal Statistical Society*, 28(1): 100–108 (1979).

[36] Lee, C. H., Lin, C. R., and Chen, M. S. Sliding-Window Filtering: An Efficient Algorithm for Incremental Mining. In *Proceedings of the ACM International Conference on Information and Knowledge Management*, ACM, Atlanta, GA, USA, pp. 263–270 (2001).

[37] Carter, T. *An Introduction to Information Theory and Entropy*, Ed. Fe, S., CiteSeer, Santa Fe, (2007).

[38] Wang, X., Kang, Q., Zhou, M. *et al.* A Multiscale Concept Drift Detection Method for Learning from Data Streams. In *Proceedings of the IEEE CASE*, Munich, Germany, pp. 786–790 (August 2018).

[39] Klinkenberg, R., Renz, I., and Ag, D. B. Adaptive Information Filtering: Learning in the Presence of Concept Drifts. AAAI, Menlo Park, CA, USA, Technical Report WS-98-05, pp. 33–40, (1998).

[40] Wen, Y., Zhang, K., Li, Z. *et al.* A Discriminative Feature Learning Approach for Deep Face Recognition. In *Proceedings of the European Conference On Computer Vision (ECCV)*, Cham, Switzerland: Springer, pp. 499–515, (2016).

Chapter 8

Case Study

8.1 Introduction

The function and performance requirements of online transaction systems are represented by the interaction of business software, so it is necessary to design software architecture that is business process-oriented, to correctly reflect the processing logic and behavior dependency and to achieve the aim that the execution of business software is consistent with the functional requirements of the business process. In the process of design and implementation, it is necessary to consider the running environment of the software, design-related interfaces, and interaction protocols. Based on the architecture and interface design, the functional predictability analysis and related test methods of the business process are studied to analyze the functional predictability of business software. The online transaction software system is a kind of typical human–computer interaction system. Therefore, it is necessary to integrate the software behavior and user behavior to form an overall system behavior pattern, to describe the online behaviors of online transaction software systems completely and accurately. In this chapter, several practical cases are modeled and analyzed formally, and some key properties of online transaction systems are verified.

8.2 Internet Open Trading Protocol

Internet Open Trading Protocol (IOTP) is an open standard for Internet trading, which is expected to evolve into one of the central building blocks for developing e-commerce on the Internet. It describes the content, format, and sequences of messages that are passed among the participants in electronic trade, and provides an interoperable framework for e-commerce [1–4]. IOTP defines nine transactions: Authentication, Deposit, Withdrawal, Purchase, Refund, Value Exchange, Customer Care, Enquiry, and Ping. The purchase transaction is carried out for the purchase of goods or services using certain payment methods. In this section, we model and analyze it as an example to illustrate the applicability of LPNs [5–10]. The introduced method can also be applied to the analysis of other trade scenarios.

8.2.1   *IOTP purchase transaction*

Figure 8.1 depicts a possible sequence of messages exchanged between the parties in a Purchase transaction. IOTP defines six trading roles: Consumer (C), Merchant (ME), Payment Handler (PH), Delivery Handler (DH), Merchant Customer Care Provider, and Payment Instrument Customer Care Provider. C receives and pays for the goods or services. ME is legally responsible for providing the goods or services and receives the benefit of the payment made. PH physically receives the payment from C on behalf of ME. DH physically

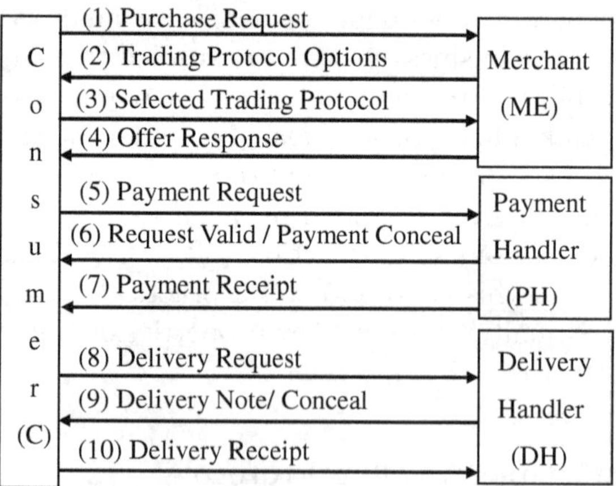

Figure 8.1   The procedure of cooperative actions in a Purchase transaction [6].

delivers the goods or services to C on behalf of ME. Merchant Customer Care Provider is involved with customer dispute negotiation and resolution on behalf of the Merchant. Payment Instrument Customer Care Provider resolves problems with a particular payment instrument (e.g., an entity for resolving problems with e-cash). For simplicity, we do not consider the last two trading roles.

The messages exchanged between C and ME are involved with a payment brand and a payment protocol. When C decides to buy goods from ME, it sends a Purchase Request to ME. ME then starts the Purchase transaction upon receiving the Purchase Request. ME offers a list of Trading Protocol Options to C. The options include a list of payment brands (e.g., Visa Credit) that are accepted by ME and the correspondent payment methods available. C selects a payment brand and method among the options offered by ME, and responds to ME. ME uses the selection from C and related information to create and send an Offer Response to C. The Offer Response contains the details of goods or services such as payment amount and delivery instructions.

The messages exchanged between C and PH aim to resolve the problems with the payment in the transaction. After checking the payment messages contained in the Offer Response, C sends a Payment Request to PH. PH checks the messages provided (such as a signature) in the Payment Request. If the messages are valid, the payment is carried out via the exchange of Payment Protocol Data between them. PH sends a Payment Response that includes the payment receipt and an optional signature after the payment exchanges are performed. This provides C with receipt of the transaction.

The exchanges between C and DH are involved with the delivery of the goods or services. C checks the delivery information in the Offer Response and uses the payment receipt as authorization in the Delivery Request sent to DH. DH starts or schedules the delivery, and sends a delivery note in the Delivery Response to C. The delivery of the goods might be physical or digital. Finally, C sends a Receipt of Delivery to DH upon receiving the goods. Note that the actual delivery of goods and receipt of delivery are outside the scope of IOTP in the phase of delivery. In this transaction, we separate each communication event into two parts: sending and receiving actions [10].

8.2.2　*Labeled workflow net model for purchase transactions*

An e-commerce system usually includes many cooperative entities called participants. The Labeled Petri Net (LaPN) model of the system is composed of all participants' LaPN models, called an interorganizational LaPN (ILaPN). The communication among the LaPNs is implemented based on the network conditions. That is, they share the messages in Ψ. In the following, suppose that the e-commerce system contains n participants. Let $\mathbb{N} = \{1, 2, \ldots, n\}$.

For the example in Figure 8.1, LaPN_c, modeling the trading process of Consumer C, is shown in Figure 8.2. Some *Inner* actions are

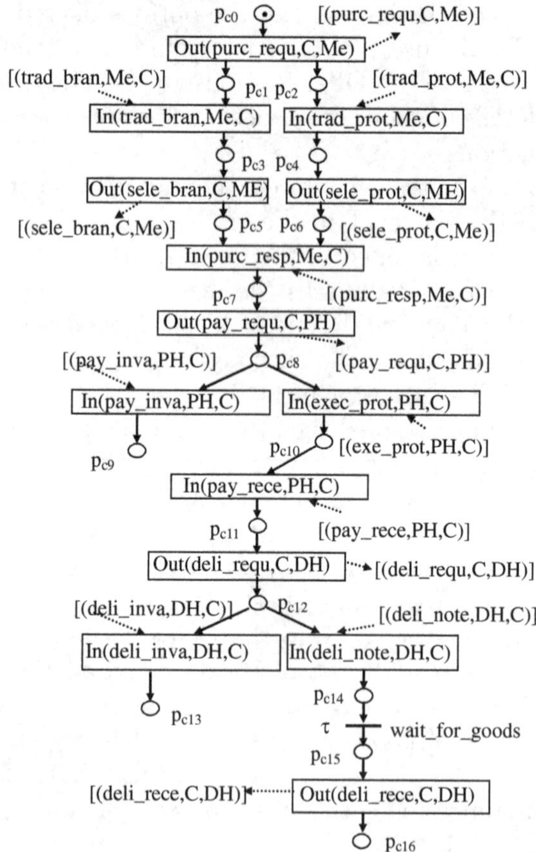

Figure 8.2　LaPN_c modeling of the trading process of Consumer C [6].

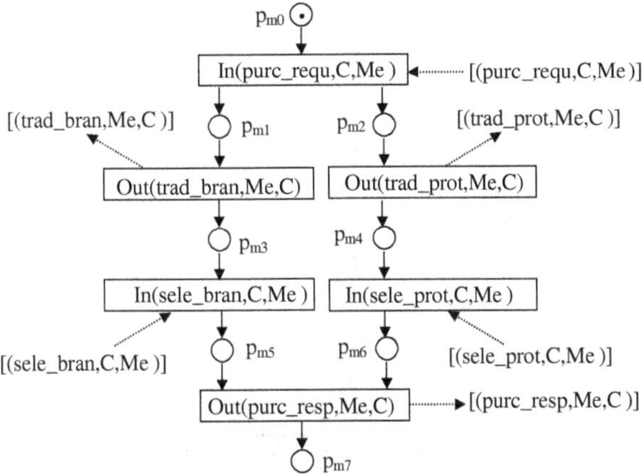

Figure 8.3 LaPN$_{me}$ modeling of the trading process of Merchant [6].

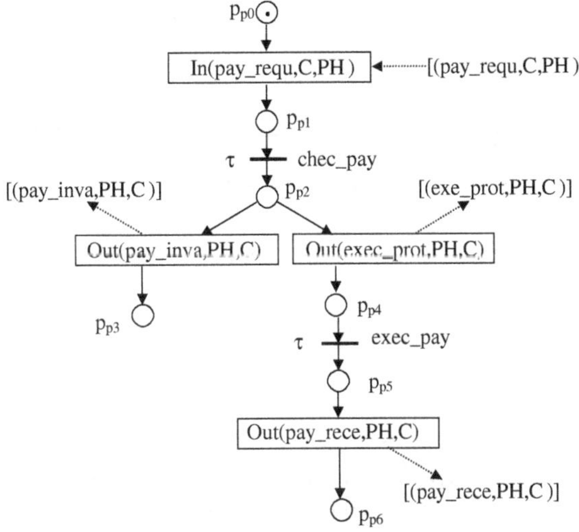

Figure 8.4 LaPN$_{ph}$ modeling of the trading process of PH [6].

omitted (e.g., auditing the payment receipt) as they are not involved with the other partners. An *Inner* action is labeled with τ and has an identifier, e.g., *wait_for_goods*. The process ends when one of the places p_{c9}, p_{c13}, and p_{c16} has a control token.

LaPNs are dependent on network conditions only. The trading processes of ME, PH, and DH are modeled in Figures 8.3–8.5 by

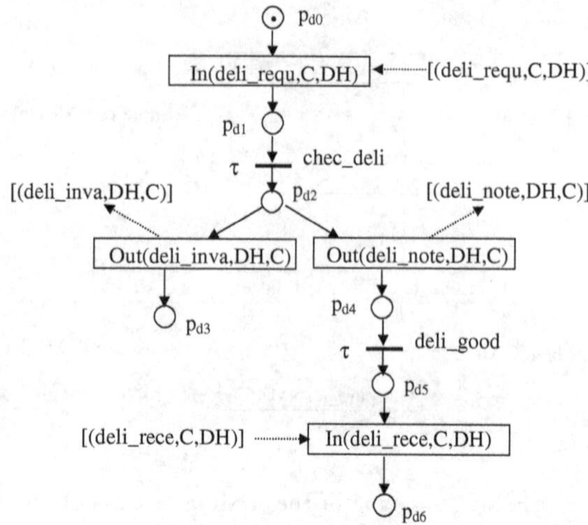

Figure 8.5　LaPN$_{dh}$ modeling of the trading process of DH [6].

LPN$_{me}$, LPN$_{ph}$, and LPN$_{dh}$, respectively. The ILaPN model of the example is composed of four LaPNs. In Figure 8.3, $M_0^{(m)}(p_{m0}) = 1$. ME receives a purchase request from C by firing transition *In(purc_requ*, C, ME). Upon firing transitions *Out(trad_bran*, ME, C) (or *Out(trad_prot*, ME, C)) and *In(sele_bran*, C, ME) (or *In(sele_prot*, C, ME)), ME sends to C trading protocol options, and receives the selected protocols from C, respectively. Then ME sends a purchase response to C by executing *Out(purc_resp*, ME, C).

In Figure 8.4, if the message about the payment request from the Consumer is invalid after firing *In(pay_requ*, C, PH) and *chec_pay*, PH executes *Out(pay_inva*, PH, C). Otherwise, it makes the payment according to the selected payment protocol through firing *Out(exec_prot*, PH, C) and *exec_pay*. Then the payment receipt is sent to C by firing *Out(pay_rece*, PH, C). In Figure 8.5, once receiving the delivery request from C by firing *In(deli_requ*, C, DH), DH checks its validity via firing *chec_deli*. If its authenticity is verified, the purchased goods are delivered by executing *Out(deli_note*, DH, C) and *deli_good*, and then a delivery receipt of the goods is received from C through performing *In(deli_rece*, C, DH). Otherwise, the delivery request is rejected by firing *Out(deli_inva*, DH, C).

8.2.3 *Analysis of transaction properties*

Assume that $<$ILaPN, $G_f>$ is not blocked in this section, we analyze the obligations of participants to ensure that a common goal is achieved. Also, if some partners cannot achieve an individual goal after cooperation ends, the accountability of implemented actions is investigated based on the collected proofs to settle disputes between participants.

(1) Obligation analysis

The common goals defined in G_f can ensure that the profit of each cooperative partner is not jeopardized. However, it is by no means excluded that partners get out of the cooperation prematurely once they obtain their private goals, before any of the common goals are achieved. To avoid this from happening, $\forall \sigma \in$ L($<$ILaPN, $M_0>$), if $\sigma \notin$ L($<$ILaPN, $G_f>$), some partners are obliged to take specific follow-up actions such that the cooperation approaches a common goal in G_f.

When a partner is under an obligation, it means that "if so-and-so actions have been taken by this partner, s/he must continue with so-and-so actions". In LPNs, however, taking any action changes control conditions. The change specifies explicitly that the specific continuation actions must be carried out by the partners under the obligation. The common goal set G_f of all cooperative parties includes all success linkage goals and regular abort goals. One of the common goals should be achieved once starting to run a protocol. Therefore, at least one of the parties is responsible for taking an enabled In/Out action if a common goal cannot be obtained. This concept can be formalized as follows.

In Figure 8.3, ME is responsible for firing $Out(trad\_bran$, ME, C) and $Out(trad\_prot$, ME, C) concurrently after executing action $In(purc\_requ$, C, ME). However, in Figure 8.4, PH is responsible for firing selectively action $Out(pay\_inva$, PH, C) or $Out(exec\_prot$, PH, C) after performing actions $In(pay\_requ$, C, PH) and τ. $\forall i \in \mathbb{N}$, if $LaPN_i$ is under no obligation, a common goal of the e-commerce protocol modeled by the ILaPN can thus be achieved.

With respect to the example modeled in Figures 8.2–8.5, for $M(p_{c16}) = 1$, $M(p_{m7}) = 1$, $M(p_{p6}) = 1$, $M(p_{d6}) = 1$, $M_0(p_{c0}) = 1$, $M_0(p_{m0}) = 1$, $M_0(p_{p0}) = 1$, $M_0(p_{d0}) = 1$, we have $M \in G_f$ and $M \in R(M_0)$. If C is under the obligation of firing sequence $\sigma^{(c)} = Out(purc\_requ, \text{C}, \text{ME})^{\circ} ((In(trad\_bran, \text{ME}, \text{C}) \circ Out(sele\_bran, \text{C}, \text{ME}))\| (In(trad\_prot, \text{ME}, \text{C}) \circ Out(sele\_prot, \text{C}, \text{ME}))) \circ In(purc\_resp, \text{ME}, \text{C}) \circ Out(pay\_requ, \text{C}, \text{PH}) \circ In(exec\_prot, \text{PH}, \text{C}) \circ In(pay\_rece, \text{PH}, \text{C}) \circ Out(deli\_requ, \text{C}, \text{DH}) \circ In(deli\_note, \text{DH}, \text{C}) \circ \tau \circ Out(deli\_rece, \text{C}, \text{DH}) \in L(< Z_c, \Gamma_{P \to Pc}(M) >)$; ME is responsible for firing sequence $\sigma^{(m)} = In(purc\_requ, \text{C}, \text{ME}) \circ ((Out(trad\_bran, \text{ME}, \text{C}) \circ In(sele\_bran, \text{C}, \text{ME})) \| (Out(trad\_prot, \text{ME}, \text{C}) \circ In(sele\_prot, \text{C}, \text{ME}))) \circ Out(purc\_resp, \text{ME}, \text{C}) \in L(<Z_{me}, \Gamma_{P \to Pm}(M)>)$; PH is under the obligation of firing sequence $\sigma^{(p)} = In(pay\_requ, C, PH) \circ \tau \circ Out(exec\_prot, \text{PH}, \text{C}) \circ \tau \circ Out(pay\_rece, \text{PH}, \text{C}) \in L(< Z_{ph}, \Gamma_{P \to Pph}(M) >)$; and DH is duty bound to fire sequence $\sigma^{(d)} = In(deli\_requ, \text{C}, \text{DH}) \circ \tau \circ Out(deli\_note, \text{DH}, \text{C}) \circ \tau \circ In(deli\_rece, \text{C}, \text{DH}) \in L(<Z_{dh}, \Gamma_{P \to Pdh}(M)>)$, then M is achieved on the basis of Theorem 3.5 after their obligations are performed. In fact, $\sigma^{(c)}$, $\sigma^{(m)}$, $\sigma^{(p)}$, and $\sigma^{(d)}$ are the projection sequences of $\sigma \in L(<\text{ILPN}_{pt}, M>)$ on LPN_c, LPN_{me}, LPN_{ph}, and LPN_{dh}, respectively, where σ is the parallel combination of sequences $\sigma^{(c)}$, $\sigma^{(m)}$, $\sigma^{(p)}$, and $\sigma^{(d)}$.

(2) Accountability and proofs

Accountability comes into question when a party denys the receipt of a document, a commitment, or receipt of payment. Accountability is a piece of evidence against such denials. Moreover, in this section, we assume that the communication system is safe, i.e., (a) the message sent is bound to result in its receipt on the other side and (b) receiving a message is bound to be a result of sending it by the other side. Therefore, we consider no cases where a message sent by a partner is lost and received by a wrong partner on the network. Since some partners may not continue a follow-up action in $\sigma \in L(<\text{ILaPN}, G_f>)$, each cooperation party has to provide evidence to verify accountability. According to the evidence, any third-party (the arbitrator) can prove that some Out actions have been carried out on a partner's side or some In actions cannot be performed as some required messages from the other sides are not sent to the network. For this purpose, therefore, each partner and the communication system must collect proofs.

In fact, since the network conditions of an ILaPN contain all messages sent by each partner and they are preserved throughout the life cycle of a case; their origins are provable utilizing the digital signatures of the corresponding senders. Consequently, an *Out* action is provable based on the messages in Ψ. Concerning *In* actions, however, participants must depend on the network conditions and the control progress sequence appearing on their side for reasoning the non-repudiatable proofs of their partners. Moreover, under the assumption that the communication system is safe, each message sent by partners can be received by a correspondent receiver once being sent by a partner.

In the Purchase transaction, if there is an action sequence $\sigma \in \mathrm{L}(<\mathrm{ILaPN}_{pt},\ R(M_0)>)$ such that $(M_0,\ \Psi_0)[\sigma > (M, \Psi)$, and $\Psi = \{[(purc\_requ, \mathrm{C}, \mathrm{ME})],\ [(trad\_bran, \mathrm{ME}, \mathrm{C})],\ [(trad\_prot, \mathrm{ME}, \mathrm{C})],\ [(sele\_bran, \mathrm{C}, \mathrm{ME})],\ [(sele\_prot, \mathrm{C}, \mathrm{ME})]\}$, then it is non-repudiatable that ME executes action $Out(trad\_bran, \mathrm{ME}, \mathrm{C})$ in terms of ME's digital signature on message $[(trad\_bran, \mathrm{ME}, \mathrm{C})]$. Furthermore, C can claim that ME has received C's purchase request by means of the network conditions. According to the ILaPN model and the above network conditions, any third-party can decide the occurrence sequences $\sigma^{(c)} = Out(purc\_requ, \mathrm{C}, \mathrm{ME})\ \circ\ ((In(trad\_bran, \mathrm{ME}, \mathrm{C})\ \circ\ Out(sele\_bran, \mathrm{C}, \mathrm{ME}))\ ||\ (In(trad\_prot, \mathrm{ME}, \mathrm{C})\ \circ\ Out(sele\_prot, \mathrm{C}, \mathrm{ME})))$ in LaPN_c, and $\sigma^{(m)} = In(purc\_requ, \mathrm{C}, \mathrm{ME})\ \circ\ (Out(trad\_bran, \mathrm{ME}, \mathrm{C})\ ||\ Out(trad\_prot, \mathrm{ME}, \mathrm{C}))$ in LaPN_{me}. If actions $In(sele\_bran, \mathrm{C}, \mathrm{ME})$ and $In(sele\_prot, \mathrm{C}, \mathrm{ME})$ are not executed in LaPN_{mc}, ME is responsible for firing them. Otherwise ME is under the obligation of firing $Out(sele\_bran, \mathrm{C}, \mathrm{ME})$. Therefore, if $\sigma \notin \mathrm{L}(<\mathrm{ILaPN}, G_f>)$ and the cooperation makes no progress, some partner must be held responsible for firing a follow-up action. Therefore, a common goal in G_f is achieved when no partner is under obligation.

The graphical representation of an LaPN is suitable for describing the overall structure of a local specification comprehensibly on a partner's side, while its formal definition of a component can be used to provide precise abstraction. The accountability and obligations can be well analyzed based on the proposed LaPN models and languages. If no partner is under obligation, a common goal is achieved. This means that each partner under obligation is enforced to perform a follow-up action for the progress in cooperation and achievement of a common goal. This is a type of security we need in open networks that cannot be controlled centrally. The network conditions and dependency concepts are used to resolve interaction problems among parties. Moreover, the obligations of each partner can be analyzed based on LaPN languages and the non-blocking property. It is demonstrated that the obligations and accountability can be handled efficiently based on LaPNs.

8.3   Process Defects in the Integration of Multi-participants

E-commerce and online shopping with a third-party payment platform (TPP) has rapidly developed recently, and encountered many fault tolerance and security problems by users. The causes of these problems include malicious behavior and imperfect business processes. The latter lead to the emergence of security vulnerabilities and loss of user funds which have become more and more serious these past few years [11–15]. E-commerce sites require the unity of data flow, control flow, and fund flow, the model must be able to reflect them and help one verify the transaction properties. In addition to potential system crashes and accompanying message failures, one has to deal with the security flaws of an e-commerce business process. As a distributed application on the web, e-commerce business processes are complex and loosely coupled.

The new security issues of e-commerce business processes are at the design level and application level. The most pressing challenge is how to ensure the correctness and reliability of a transaction process in the conceptual model phase so that defects and logic errors can be detected before the implementation of an e-commerce system. If errors are found after the e-commerce system is implemented, irreparable damage may be caused, and compensation for the errors and modification of the program of an e-commerce system can be extremely costly. This section offers a complete methodology for modeling and validating an e-commerce system with a TPP from the viewpoint of a business process. Its usage enables a designer to identify errors early in the design process and correct them before the deployment phase. To demonstrate the applicability and feasibility of the methodology, we have modeled and validated a real-world e-commerce business process and discovered the problems that cause the violation of transaction properties [16].

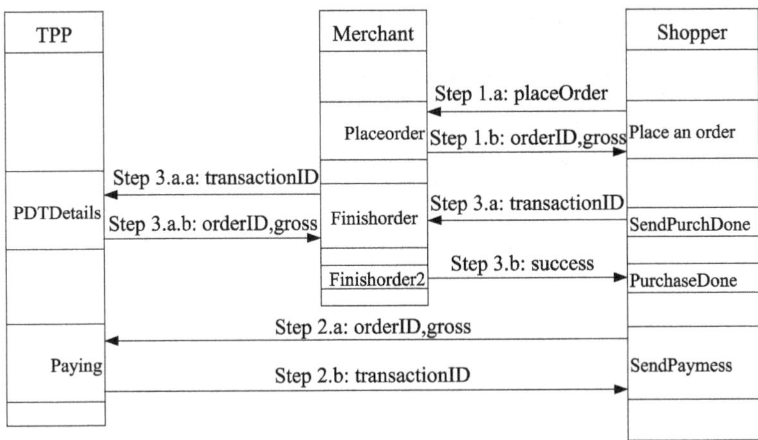

Figure 8.6   The business process of an e-commerce system [16].

The purpose of this section is to guarantee the correctness and reliability of an e-commerce business process before the e-commerce system is implemented to avoid irreparable damage and huge maintenance cost. To do so, a conceptual model must be constructed first. We construct a real-world e-commerce business process based on the distributed transaction system described in Ref. [11].

Figure 8.6 shows the workflow of an e-commerce system with a Shopper, Merchant, and TPP. Firstly, Shopper makes an order and sends Step 1.a to invoke Merchant's API — placeorder, and the order information is inserted into a database, including *gross* and *orderID*. Since the order is unpaid, its state is set to *Pending*. Then Step 1.b passes the order information to Shopper and redirects his/her browser to TPP for paying according to the order information. Payment details are recorded by TPP and *transactionID* is returned in Step 2.b. When the payment is finished, Shopper's browser calls API finishOrder of Merchant to finalize the invoice in Step 3.a. Here, the pseudo-code of the function is presented in Table 8.1 to highlight the part of its functionality which interests us. Furthermore, using *transactionID*, it makes a call to API PDTDetails of TPP in Step 3.a.a to obtain the payment details by Step 3.a.b. Then it finds the order from its database based on the *orderID* in the payment details. Once the order is founded and its state is *Pending*,

Table 8.1   Key functionalities of the business process in Figure 8.6 [16].

Merchant/Placeorder: orderID=InsertPendingOrder ()
Merchant/Finishorder:
tnDetails=wCall_PDTDetails(transitionID); /*resulting in Step 3.a.a and Step 3.a.b*/
orderID=GetOrderIDField(tnDetails);
order=LoadOrderByID(orderID);
if (order≠null) and (order.state==Pending)
order.state = Paid;

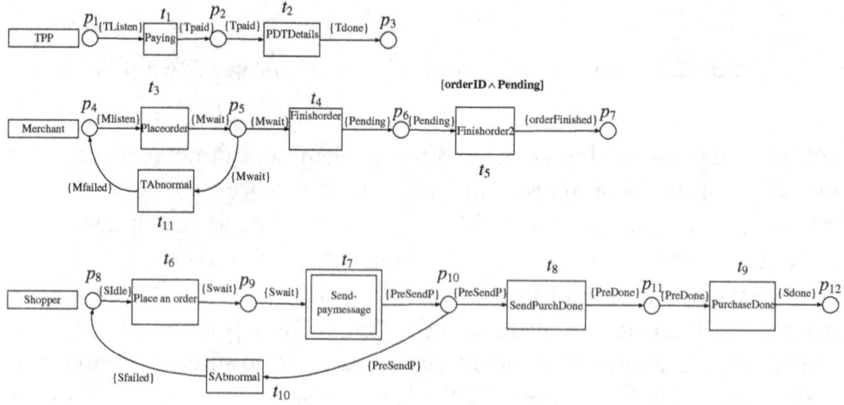

Figure 8.7   Control flow of EBPN of the example [16].

the state is set to *Paid* and a confirmation is passed to Shopper through Step 3.b.

During the trading process, communication takes place among Merchant, TPP, and Shopper. They are used to coordinate the internal states of Merchant and TPP. They are more complex than bilateral interactions between a browser and a server. Together with site failures, unilateral transaction abortion, and fraudulent behaviors, guaranteeing fund security of these systems is very difficult. We will use this case to illustrate our methodology.

Figure 8.7 shows the control flows of the above case, and Figure 8.8 shows its data flow. Figure 8.9 shows the complete EBPN.

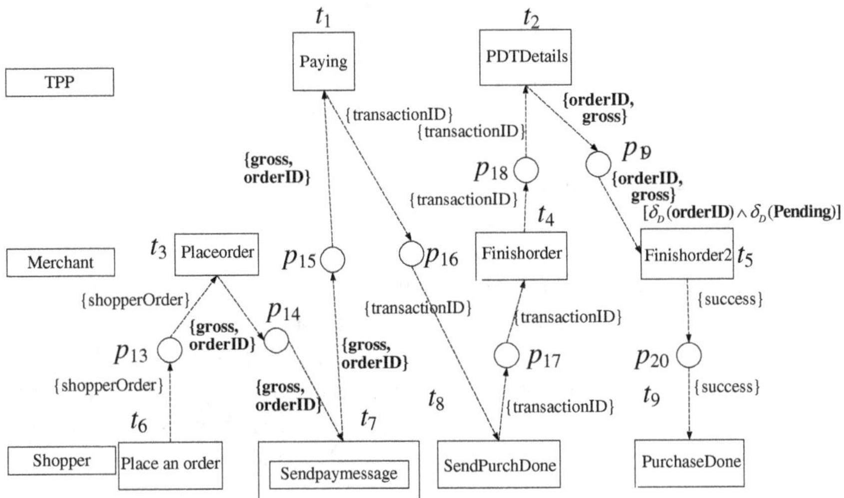

Figure 8.8   Data flow of EBPN of the example [16].

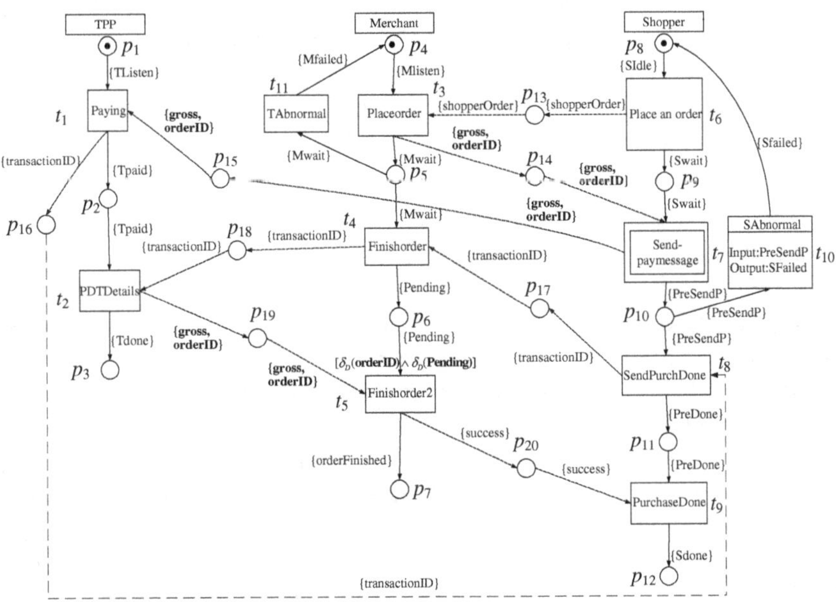

Figure 8.9   Complete EBPN of the example [16].

In this case, $\{orderID, gross\} \in S$, and we make them bold on the graph; t_7 is the key transition, and it is a rectangle with two borders to distinguish with other transitions. Initially, p_1, p_2, and p_3 have one token, respectively, with the type of *TListen*, *MListen*, and *SIdle* representing that Shopper, Merchant, and TPP are ready to conduct a transaction. The initial marking is $M_0 = [p_1(TListen), p_4(MListen), p_8(SIdle)]$.

Every transition in control flows represents the API or operation event of three parties. For example, t_6 in Figure 8.7 represents that a client makes an order on his/her web browser. $t_1 - t_5$ are open APIs of the Merchant website and TTP. For control flows of an e-commerce system, trading events of each party must be organized in order. Meanwhile, potential system crashes and accompanying message failures must be considered. Hence, we must consider the possibility of abnormal events such as canceling the transaction unilaterally and site failure. This means that each party must reach the correct conclusion, even facing failures [17, 18].

Places in control flows represent the states of three parties. For example, Merchant first processes the request of an order from Shopper (t_3, Placeorder). After firing t_3, it is at the state of *MWait* (p_5 has one token with the type of *MWait*). If t_4 can fire, it will transmit a *Pending* token to p_6. Meanwhile, t_{11} can also fire, making Merchant at the state *MFailed*. t_5 has a predicate $[\delta_D(orderID) \wedge \delta_D(gross)]$. When $\delta_D(orderID) \wedge_D (Pending) = \mathbf{T}$ and $M \xrightarrow{t_5}$ under a data state $\wedge = <M, \alpha> = <M, (\beta, \delta_D)>$, t_5 can fire, and after firing t_5, Merchant is at the terminated state *orderFinished*.

Figure 8.10 has 55 data states and 12 terminated data states. In the terminated data states, only $<M_9, \alpha_9>$ completes the transaction and does not violate the transaction consistency. In $<M_9, \alpha_9>$, $p_3(TDone)$ represents that TPP has finished the payment. $p_7(orderFinished)$ represents that Merchant has finished the order, and $p_{12}(Sdone)$ represents that Shopper has bought the ordered item successfully. $<M_{16}, \alpha_{16}>$, $<M_{31}, \alpha_{31}>$, and $<M_{32}, \alpha_{32}>$ violate the transaction consistency.

At $<M_{16}, \alpha_{16}>$, we know that $M_{16}(p_3) = $ TDone, $M_{16}(p_7) = $ orderFinished, and $M_{16}(p_{12}) = $ Sdone. Thus, all three parties have finished the transaction, i.e., TTP is at the paid state, the finished-transaction state of Merchant is reached, and the finished-order

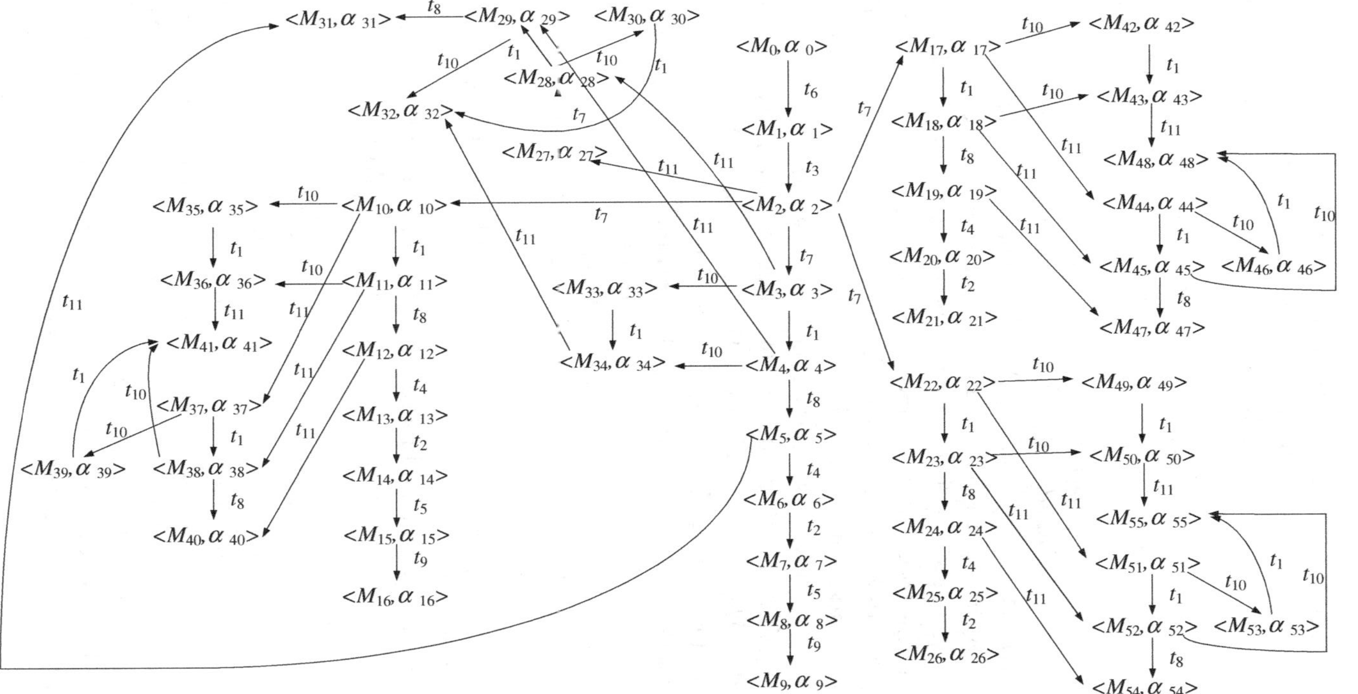

Figure 8.10   Reachability data state graph of EBPN of the example [16].

state of Shopper is reached, but $\exists gross \in \beta \cap S$, $\delta_D(gross) = \mathbf{F}$, i.e., *gross*$\mathbf{F}$. $<M_{16}, \alpha_{16}>$ does not satisfy Condition 1 of Definition 3.29. At $<M_{31}, \alpha_{31}>$, $\exists M_{31}(p_2) = TPaid$, i.e., TTP is at the paid state and has removed the money from Shopper to Merchant, but $\exists M_{31}(p_4) = MFailed$, i.e., Merchant does not reach the state of finished-transaction, and Shopper will not receive goods forever. Thus, $<M_{31}, \alpha_{31}>$ does not satisfy Condition 2 of Definition 3.29. At $<M_{32}, \alpha_{32}>$, $\exists M_{32}(p_2) = TPaid$, i.e., TTP is at the paid state, but $\exists M_{32}(p_4) = MFailed$, i.e., Merchant does not reach the state of finished-transaction, and $\exists M_{32}(p_8) = SFailed$, i.e., the finished-order state of Shopper is not reached. The situation of $<M_{32}, \alpha_{32}>$ is similar to $<M_{31}, \alpha_{31}>$. Their only difference is that Shopper is at the state of failure too, but the fund of Shopper has been lost. Thus, $<M_{32}, \alpha_{32}>$ does not satisfy Condition 2 of Definition 3.29 either. Other terminated data states do not complete the transaction, but they do not violate the transaction consistency either.

By analyzing the three illegal data states $<M_{16}, \alpha_{16}>$, $<M_{31}, \alpha_{31}>$, and $<M_{32}, \alpha_{32}>$, we reveal that the cause of $<M_{16}, \alpha_{16}>$ is that the logic of API finishOrder does not check the data element *gross*, i.e., the predicate on t_5 lacks some validation criterion; The causes of $<M_{31}, \alpha_{31}>$ and $<M_{32}, \alpha_{32}>$ are the potential system abnormalities and accompanying message failures. Then we can specify the adjustment strategies as follows:

(1) For the missing predicate, add a check data element *gross* to it, i.e., $[\delta_D(orderID) \wedge \delta_D(Pending) \wedge \delta_D(gross)]$.
(2) For abnormal events, add a rollback mechanism at transition t_{12}, which can guarantee that a user's fund is not lost.

After adjustment, the integrity of EBPN is shown in Figure 8.11, and its RD with the description is given in Figure 8.12. The e-commerce business process in Figure 8.11 can deal with potential data inconsistencies and abnormal events, and thus guarantees the transaction consistency of the case. Because the problem discovered via the above validation has been already corrected, once any failure caused by abnormal events appears, the rollback mechanism is turned on to ensure the security of funds.

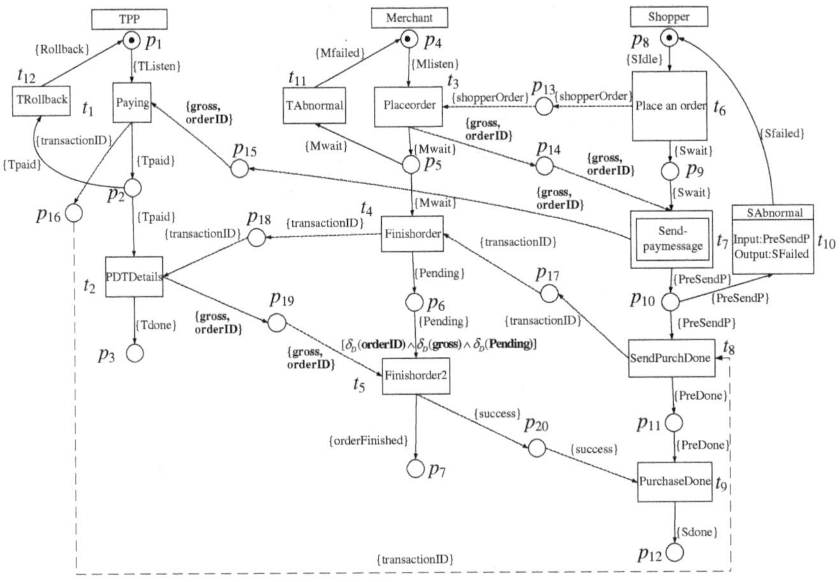

Figure 8.11   Adjusted EBPN [16].

8.4   Malicious Behavior Patterns in the Integration of Multi-participants

At the requirement analysis and design levels, we need to explicitly identify whether the online shopping systems can be resistant to the possibly malicious behavior patterns, and such patterns can be found in many public threat libraries [11,19–29]. This section focuses on the online shopping business process that consists of three parties: Shopper, Merchant, and TPP, and verifies it by formal methods at the conceptual modeling phase from the application-level viewpoint. The basic idea is: initially, to construct the functional model according to design specification; then, to choose one malicious behavior pattern and translate it to a malicious behavior model according to the functional model; next, to synthesize them for establishing an online shopping business process able to handle malicious behavior scenario; at last, verify it and determine whether the online shopping business process can withstand such a malicious behavior pattern. The framework is shown in Figure 8.13 [30, 31].

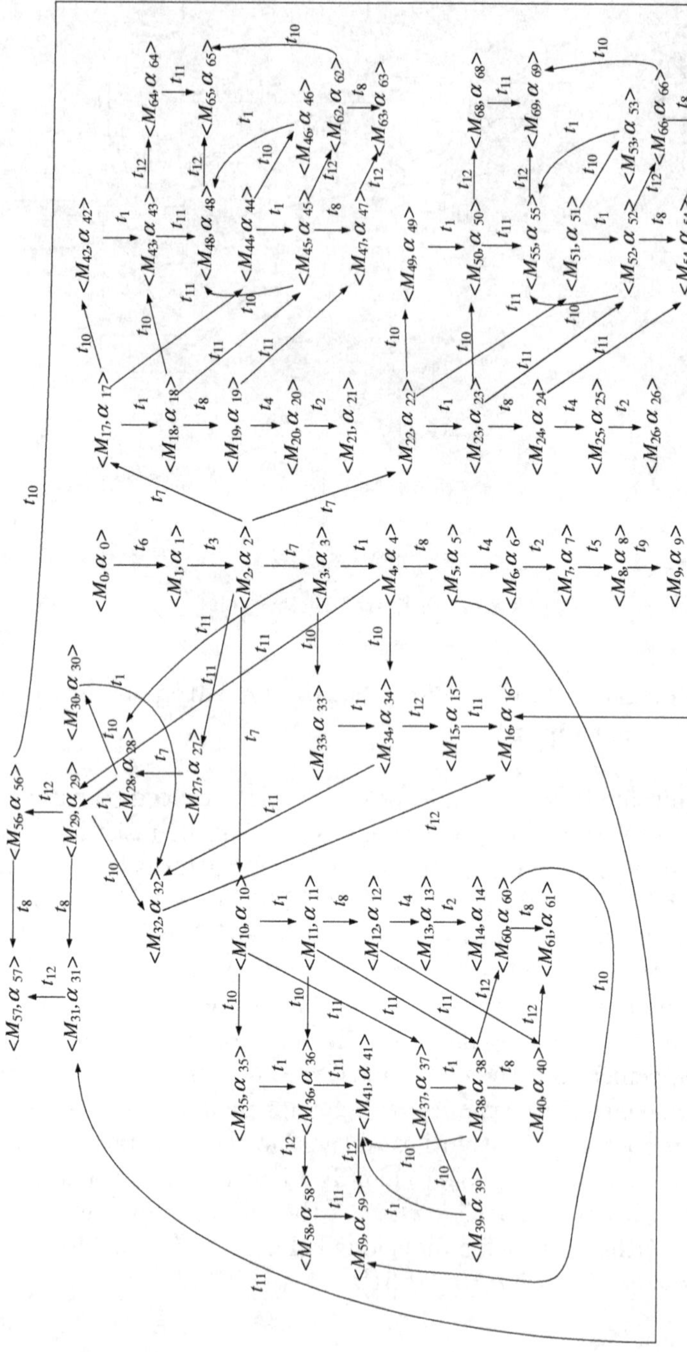

Figure 8.12   Reachability data state graph of the adjusted EBPN[16].

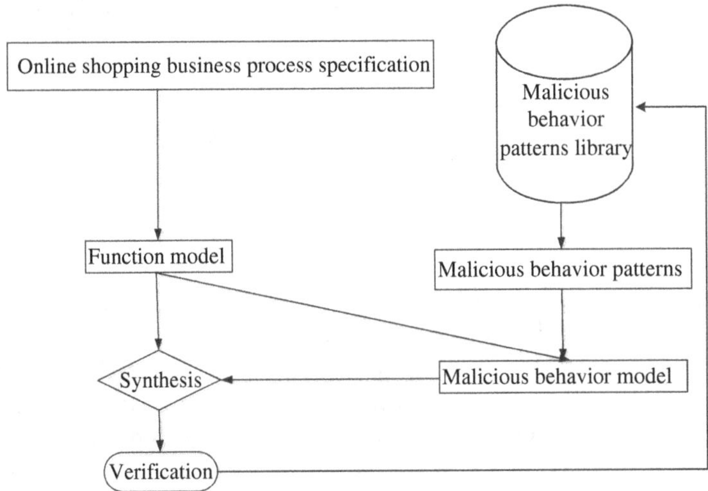

Figure 8.13   Framework of the proposed solution [30].

First, according to the malicious behavior model, a malicious behavior sequence of attackers is constructed. As the malicious behavior sequence is not a complete executable sequence in the composed EBPN, second, we analyze the composed EBPN with the malicious behavior sequence and derive the relation graph of the malicious behavior sequence and its related transitions, which is called Transition Dependency Graph (TDG). Third, by using EBPN's dynamic properties, we determine whether the sequence can be executed to the end. If yes, the malicious behavior pattern in the system is feasible. Otherwise, the system can withstand such an attack.

Definition 8.1 Given $EN_1 = (P_1, T_1; F_1, D_1, W_1, S_1, G_1)$ is a functional model of an online trading system, and $EN_2 = (P_2, T_2; F_2, D_2, W_2, S_2, G_2)$ is a malicious behavior model constructed according to EN_1. A **client malicious behavior sequence** of EN_2 is a transition sequence $\sigma = t_i t_j, \ldots, t_k$, where $t_i, t_j, \ldots, t_k \in T_2$, $i, j, k \in \mathbb{N}^+$. σ is the transition set of σ, and $|\sigma|$ is the length of σ.

Definition 8.2 Given $EN = EN \odot EN_2 = (P, T; F, D, W, S, G)$ is a composed EBPN with malicious behavior pattern considered, where EN_1 and EN_2 are a functional model and malicious behavior model, and $\sigma = t_i t_j \ldots t_k$ is a client malicious behavior sequence in EN_2.

A TDG of *EN* and σ can be defined as a three-tuple $TDG(EN, \sigma) = (B, E; L)$, where

(1) B is the set of nodes in $TDG(EN)$, $B \subseteq T$, $\sigma \subset B$;
(2) E is the set of arcs, $E = \{(b_i, b_j)|b_i, b_j \in B, \exists p_k \in P \to (b_i, p_k), (p_k, b_j) \in F$ or $b_i b_j$ is a subsequence of $\sigma\}$; and
(3) $L: E \to P$, where if $(b_i, p_k), (p_k, b_j) \in F$, $L(b_i, b_j) = p_k$; Else $L(b_i, b_j) = \varnothing$.

A TDG is used to intuitively portray the relationships among transitions. It is a directed graph reflecting the structural properties of an EBPN statically. Special operations of key transitions in client malicious behavior sequences are considered according to the specific malicious behavior patterns, such as tampering with some key trading parameters. If t_i is a transition in a client malicious behavior sequence, and t_i is a key transition, according to the specification of a malicious behavior pattern, it sets the value of d_i to **T** or **F**. Then we use the notation $t_i\{d_i\}$ or $t_i\{d_i\mathbf{F}\}$ to represent the value of the token with the type of d_i produced by it. Then, the complete client malicious behavior sequences attached to operation descriptions are obtained.

Definition 8.3 Given $EN_1 = (P_1, T_1; F_1, D_1, W_1, S_1, G_1)$ is a functional model of an online trading system, and $EN_2 = (P_2, T_2; F_2, D_2, W_2, S_2, G_2)$ is a malicious behavior model constructed according to EN_1. A client malicious behavior sequence of EN_2 is a transition sequence $\sigma = t_i t_j \ldots t_k$. Then, A **complete client malicious behavior sequence** of EN_2 is a sequence $\rho = (t_i \Sigma_i)(t_j \Sigma_j) \ldots (t_k \Sigma_k)$, $(t_i \Sigma_i)$, Σ_i is called an operation of t_i. If $t_i \in \sigma$ is a key transition, then $\Sigma_i = \{s\xi | s \in S' \subset S_2, \in \{\mathbf{T}, \mathbf{F}, \varnothing\}\}$, else $\Sigma_i = \varnothing$. $|\rho|$ is the length of ρ.

Here, $(M, \delta_D) \xrightarrow{t\Sigma}$ means that t is fired according to its operation Σ at (M, δ_D). If t is a key transition, when t fires, the token with the type of key trading parameters produced by firing t would be assigned with only one value, i.e., ξ, and a data state (M', δ'_D) is produced, not a state set Γ, because Σ defines the data allocation after firing t, i.e.,

$$(M', \delta'_D) = (M', \forall s \in \{W(t, p)|p \in t^\bullet\} \cap S \to \delta'_D(s) \in \xi \text{ and } s\xi \in \Sigma$$
$$\wedge \forall d \in \{M(p) - \{W(t, p)|p \in t^\bullet\} \cap S\} \to \delta'_D(d) = \delta_D(d))$$

Due to the problem of state explosion, $RD(EN)$ may be infinity as an EBPN with an initial data may have an infinite number of reachability data states. Hence, we construct $RD(EN)$ according to $TDG(EN, \sigma)$ and ρ. Its construction algorithm is as follows:

Algorithm 8.1: Constructing a $\mathcal{RD}(EN)$ according to $TDG(EN, \sigma)$ and ρ [30]

Input: The composed EBPN $EN = (P, T; F, D, W, S, G)$, (M_0, δ_{D0}), the complete client malicious behavior sequence $\rho = t_i \Sigma_i t_j \Sigma_j \ldots t_k \Sigma_k$, $TDG(EN, \sigma) = (B, E; L)$.
Output: R(EN), "YES" or "NO".

---

1. Let (M_0, δ_{D0}) be the root node, and mark it with "New";
2. $B_l = \{t_i\}$;
3. **While** "New" nodes exist and $|\rho| \neq 0$**Do**
4.   Choose an arbitrary "New" node as (M, δ_D);
5.   **If** $\forall t \in B_l : \neg(M, \delta_D) \xrightarrow{t}$
6.   Marking (M, δ_D) as "Terminated node", and go to step 2;
7.   **Endif**
8.   **If** $\exists t \in B_l$ and t is a transition in ρ and $(M, \delta_D) \xrightarrow{t}$ **Then**
9. $(M', \delta'_D) = (M, \delta_D) \xrightarrow{t\Sigma}$;
10.   **If** (M', δ'_D) exist in R(EN) **Then**
11.   Create a directed edge from (M, δ_D) to (M', δ'_D), and mark the edge labeled with t;
12.   **Endif**
13.   **Else** Create a new node (M', δ'_D), create a directed edge from (M, δ_D) to (M', δ'_D), and mark the edge labeled with t;
14.   **Endif**
15.   Mark (M', δ'_D) with "New" and remove mark "New" of (M, δ_D);
16. $B_l = B_l \cup \{t'|t'$ is successor node of $t\} - \{t\}$;
17.   Remove $t\Sigma$ from the beginning of ρ;
18.   **Endif**
19.   **Else Foreach** $\forall t \in B_l$ and $(M, \delta_D) \xrightarrow{t}$ **Do**
20. $(M', \delta'_D) = (M, \delta_D) \xrightarrow{t\Sigma}$;
21.   **Executing Step** 10–16;
22.   **Endforeach**
23.   **Endif**
24. **Repeat**
25. **If** $|\rho| = 0$ **Then** output "YES" **Else** output "NO";

Using Algorithm 8.1, we can determine whether a client malicious behavior sequence can be executed successfully. If the output is "YES", the malicious behavior pattern in the system is feasible. Otherwise, the malicious behaviors of clients will not succeed, and the system can withstand such an attack.

We have applied our approach to the modeling and verification of a real-world online shopping business process. Based on the assumption that the business process is at the conceptual design phase, our purpose is to identify whether it is resistant to known malicious behavior patterns. In our procedure, at process design time, we need to verify the entire malicious behavior patterns in the malicious behavior pattern library to make the software design provably secured from the known malicious behavior patterns at the conceptual design phase. First, we briefly introduce the business process and then demonstrate a complete process of its modeling and verification against a typical malicious behavior pattern.

As Figure 8.14 shows, three parties including TPP, Merchant, and Shopper, as well as data exchange among them are described. The business process adopts an HTTP message that TPP uses to notify Merchant of payment status, which is called Instant Payment Notification (*ipn*). This message is shown in Step 2.a.a, which is sent immediately after Shopper makes the payment through Step 2.a. Using this notification method, Merchant needs to specify an *ipn* handler URL and embeds the URL in Step 1.b. Then, the message redirects Shopper's browser to TPP through Step 2.a. When TPP invokes this handler through Step 2.a.a, the argument list is signed.

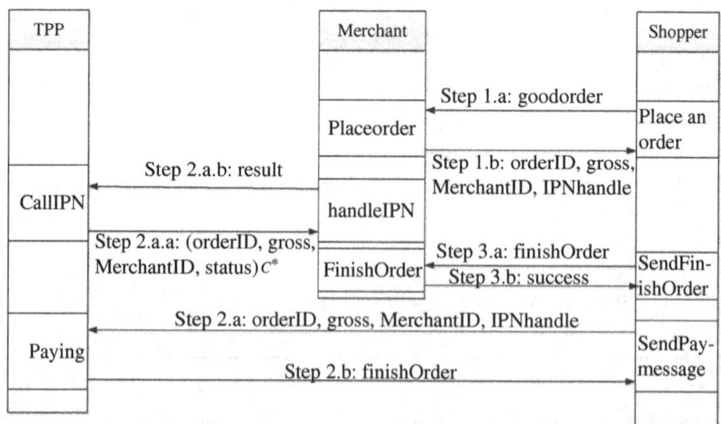

Figure 8.14   The business process of an online shopping system [30].

Merchant's handler verifies the signature, order data, and payment data in *ipn*, and then the order status is updated. The key functionalities of handleIPN are shown in Table 8.2. In this system, a malicious user can achieve his/her malicious purpose through some complex malicious behaviors.

Figure 8.15 is the schematic diagram of the malicious behavior pattern. It has "begin" and "end" nodes representing a complete malicious behavior process. A rectangle and its text mean an operation. The directed arcs represent the orders of operations, and the labels on the arcs mean how many times the malicious user carries out the process. In this example, first, the malicious user changes the message in Step 2.a by setting its *orderID* to be empty and setting *IPNHandler* to be his/her. This change delivers the TPP's IPN message to the malicious user via Step 2.a.a. This action gives him/her an *ipn* message signed by the TPP, which consists of the argument list (*orderID*= empty, *gross*, *merchantID*, *status*) and a signature C^*.

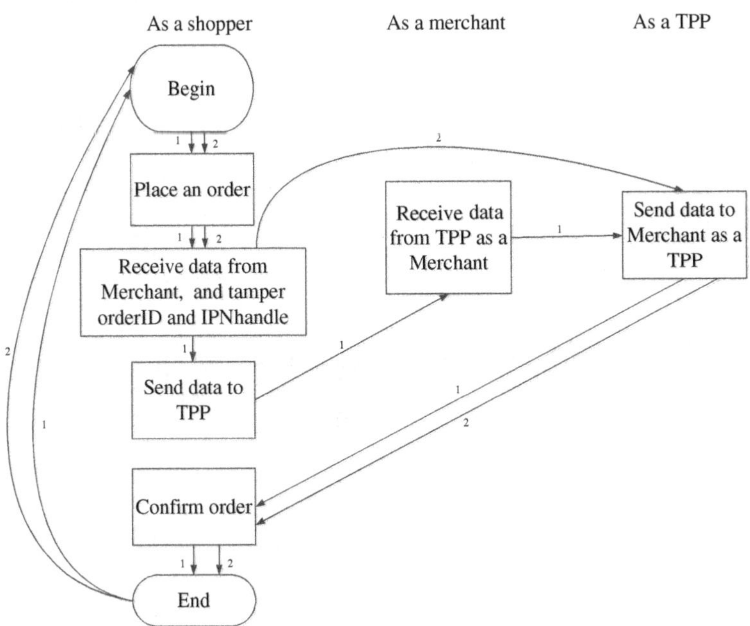

Figure 8.15   Multiple checkouts with one payment [30].

By replaying this message, the malicious user can check out an arbitrary number of orders with the same prices. Each time, all he/she needs to do is to place a new order by Step 1.a, set the order's ID as the browser cookie *ORDER_ID*, then call Merchant's IPN-handler with the arguments in Step 2.a, and finally call Merchant's finishOrder by Step 3.a. In this example, the malicious user plays all three roles: Shopper, Merchant, and TPP. Note that the malicious user also changes his/her browser cookie before he/she calls Merchant's handleIPN as a TPP. Therefore, it is a hybrid of TPP behaviors and browser behaviors. This is a new and complicated case in online shopping systems nowadays where an attacker plays three roles and calls APIs in arbitrary orders, which results in the fund loss of Merchant. Therefore, we need a formal mechanism to determine whether an online shopping system can withstand this type of malicious behavior.

Then, we can model the business process using EBPN. The operation events of Shopper, as well as APIs of TPP and Merchant, are depicted by transitions in an EBPN. As Figure 8.16 shows, the operation "Place an order" of Shopper is represented by t_1, and the phrase

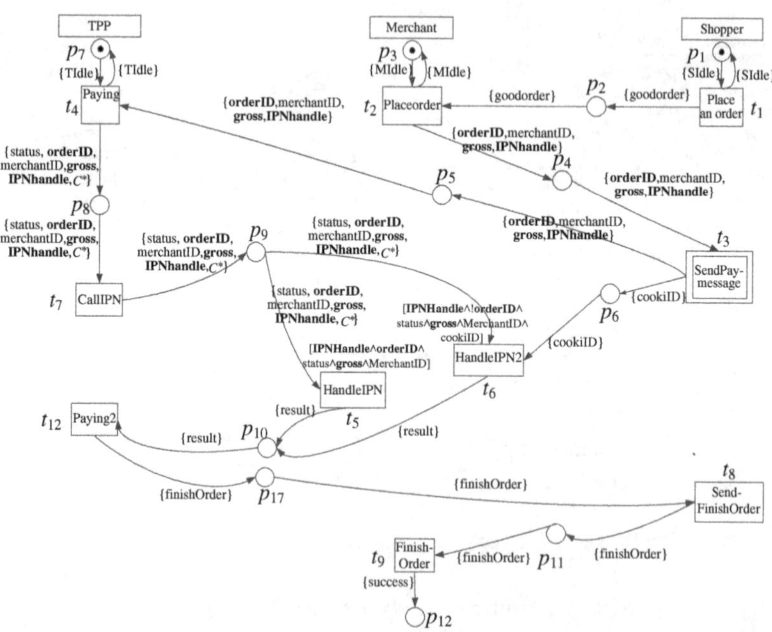

Figure 8.16   The EBPN depicting the business process of Figure 8.14 [30].

Table 8.2   Key functionalities of the business process in Figure 8.14 [30].

```
handleIPN(){
order = LoadOrderByID(orderID);
if (order==null || order.status≠PAID) exit;
if (merchantID ≠ Merchant) exit;
if (gross ≠ order.gross) exit;
order.status = PAID;}
loadOrderByID(orderId){
if (orderId is empty)
orderId = COOKIE['ORDER_ID'];}
```

in it is used to signal its function. t_2 is an API of Merchant, representing the function of processing an order from Shopper. p_2 is a data transfer channel between them. In Figure 8.16, p_1, p_3, and p_7 are the initial places of Shopper, Merchant, and TPP, respectively, and they are linked with three transitions: t_1, t_2, and t_4 via two contrary arrows, and this means that three parties are always ready to start a new transaction. The initial data state is $(M_0, \delta_{D0}) = ([p_1(Sidle), p_3(MIdle), p_7(TIdle)])$. Two predicates are added to t_5 and t_6 for describing the validation criteria in Table 8.2, and different implementations caused by the validation criteria are depicted by the conditional selection and join structures through p_9, t_5, t_6, and p_{10}, and parallel branch and join structures are used to depict the access operation of cookies through t_3, p_5, p_6, p_9, and t_6. In Figure 8.16, t_3 is the key transition, and {*orderID, gross, IPNhandle*} is the set of key trading parameters. The malicious behavior model corresponding to the malicious behavior pattern in Figure 8.15 is expressed in Figure 8.17. t_1, t_3, and t_8 are legal transitions in the functional model, while t_{10} and t_{11} are the malicious behaviors that are used to play Merchant and TPP by malicious users. Note that the marks of legal places and transitions in Figure 8.17 are consistent with those in Figure 8.16. In Figure 8.17, t_3 and t_{10} are the key transitions, and the key trading parameters are the same as those in Figure 8.16.

After the functional model and malicious behavior model are constructed, we need to synthesize them to verify whether the malicious behavior pattern can be implemented successfully in the functional model. We synthesize the two models of Figures 8.16 and 8.17 to obtain the composed EBPN as shown in Figure 8.18.

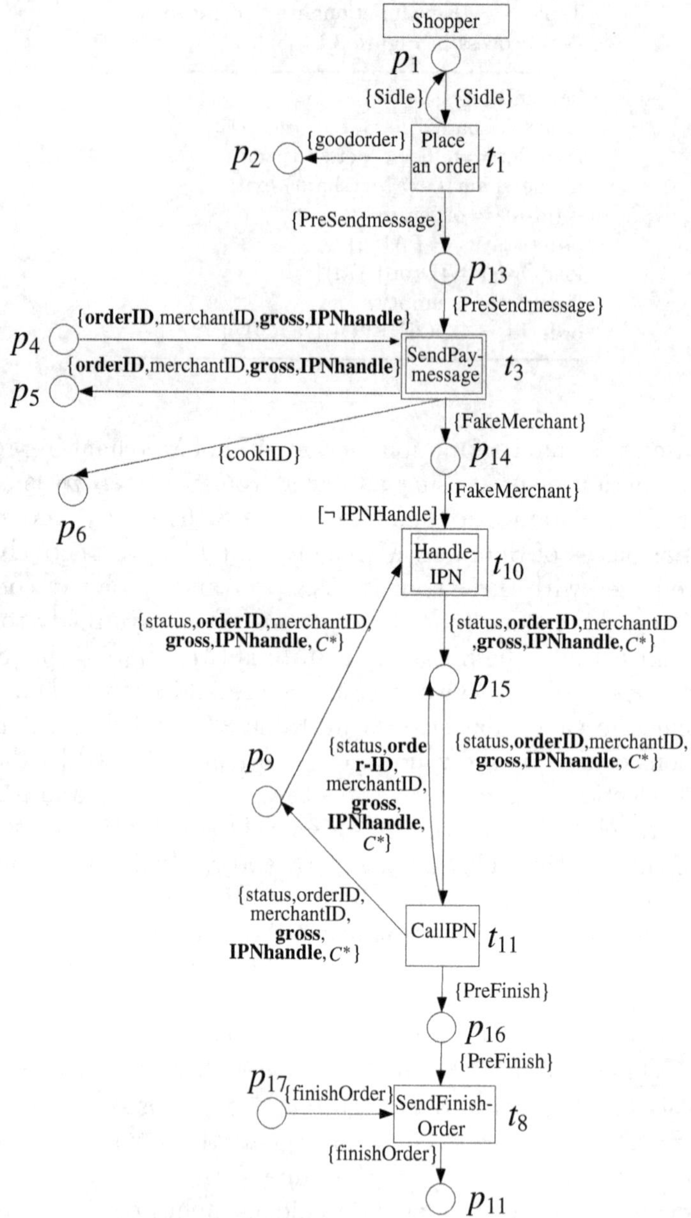

Figure 8.17   The EBPN of the malicious behavior pattern in Figure 8.15 [30].

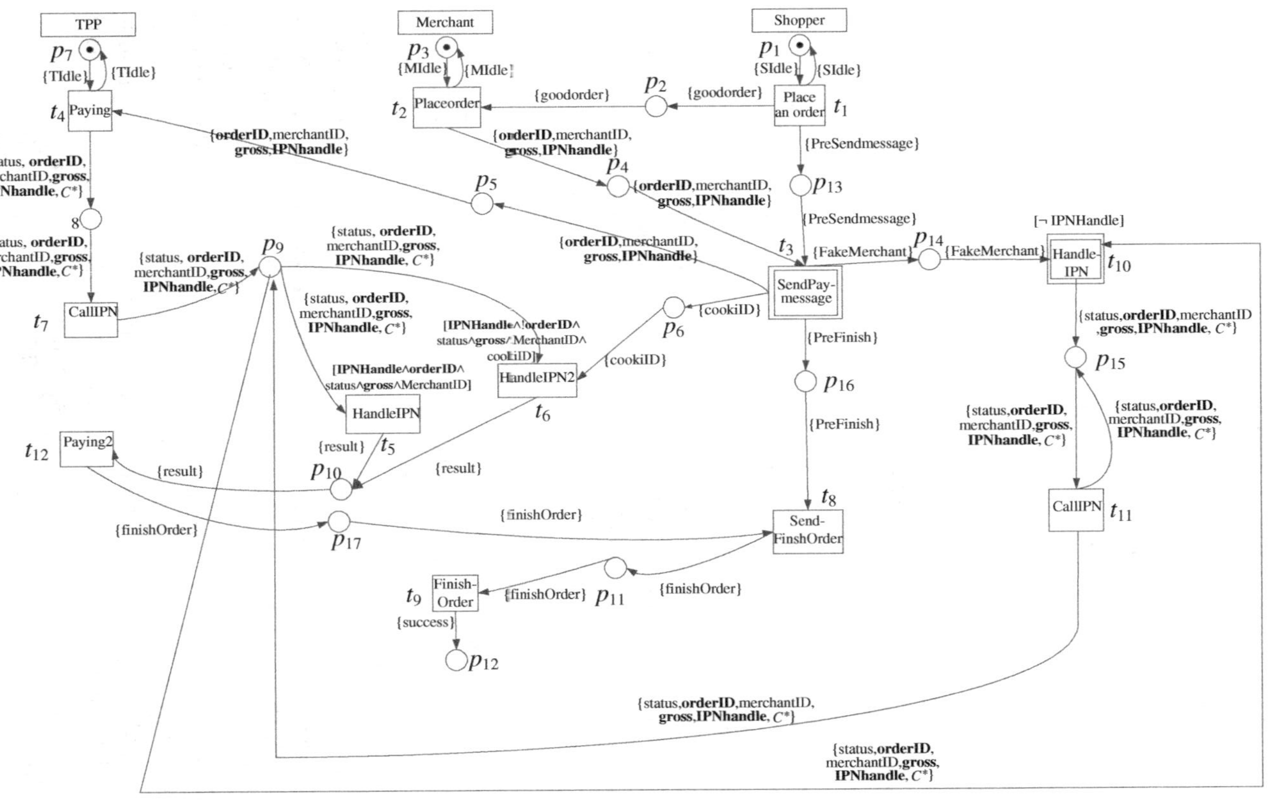

Figure 8.18 The composed EBPN integrating malicious behavior pattern [30].

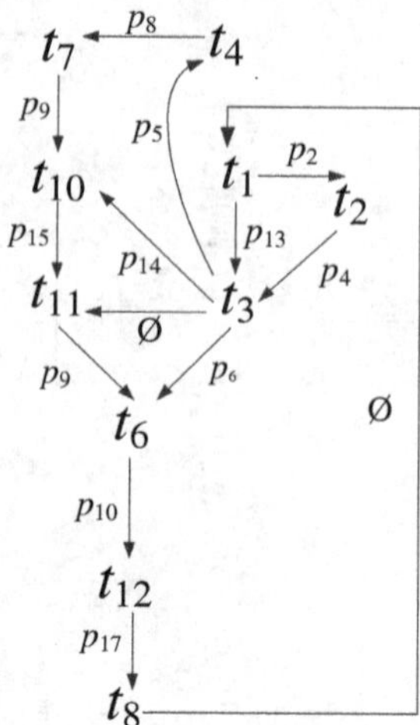

Figure 8.19   The TDG of Figure 8.18 and σ [30].

For the malicious behavior pattern of Figures 8.15 and 8.17, it is easy to construct the CMBS $\sigma = t_1 t_3 t_{10} t_{11} t_8 t_1 t_3 t_{11} t_8$. Then, according to Definition 8.3, the CCMBS of Figure 8.18 is $\rho = t_1 t_3 \{orderID\emptyset,\ IPNhandle\mathbf{F}\}\ t_{10} \{IPNhandle\} t_{11} t_8 t_1 t_3 t_{11} t_8$. Using Algorithm 8.1, the TDG of the model in Figure 8.16 and σ is shown in Figure 8.19. The R(EN) based on TDG and ρ is shown in Figure 8.20. ρ can be executed successfully, and the output is "YES". Thus, we know that the online trading system cannot withstand an attack of multiple checkouts with one payment.

By analyzing the R(EN) based on TDG and ρ, a business process and the corresponding malicious behavior model, we find that after "Receive data from Merchant and tamper orderID and IPNhandlethe", TPP accepts the argument (orderID = empty, gross, merchantID, status) and transfers it to handleIPN at Step 2.a.a. Then handleIPN of Merchant accepts it and returns a result. That is the problem as handleIPN of Merchant should not accept it. It is worth noting that the problem is caused by transition t_5 and t_6 corresponding to the function LoadOrderByID in Table 8.2. It is a heavily used utility function in online shopping systems and is usually called in many situations, e.g., when handling a TPP's request or handling a browser's request. Therefore, it is designed to be generic. However, a typical request from the browser does not contain the *orderID* field in

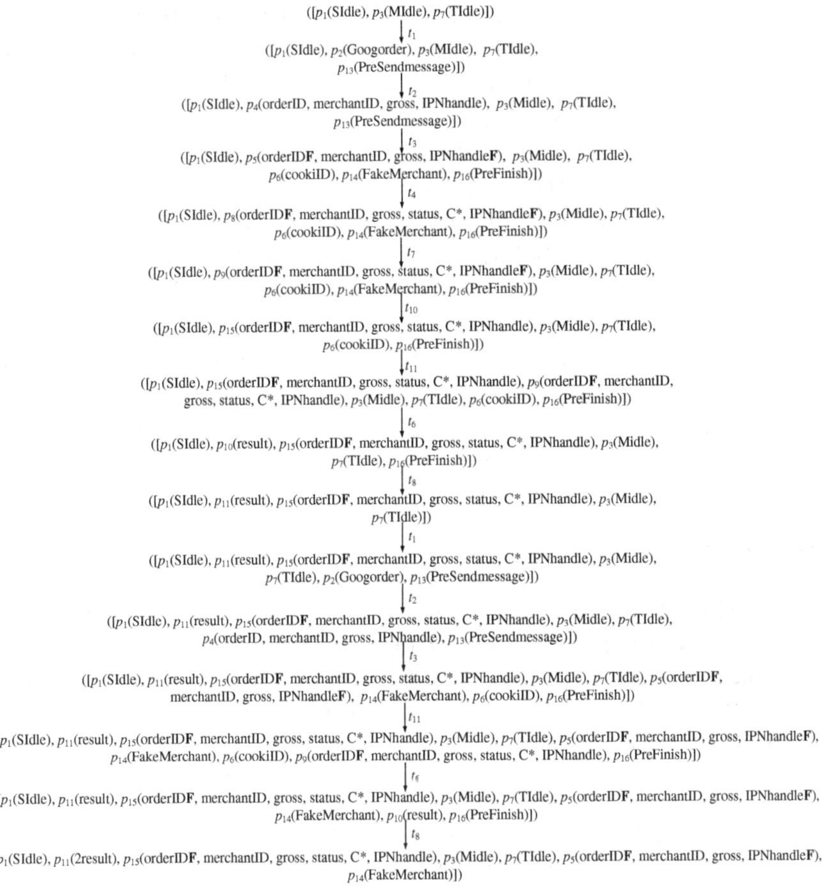

Figure 8.20   R(EN) based on TDG and ρ [30].

the request URL. In this situation, loadOrderByID(empty) would be called, and the *orderID* is retrieved from a cookie named ORDER_ID. Therefore, this generic design turns out to be problematic. Changing this generic design can resolve such a security issue.

8.5   Chapter Summary

The current online transaction system requires the unification of control flow and data flow. The formal model and methods must be able to depict these properties and verify the transaction properties of the e-commerce system. At the same time, in the face of the complex, open, and dynamic network environment, corresponding modeling technology, and corresponding verification methods are needed to deal with the complex malicious behaviors of some malicious users. Based on the theoretical basis of the previous chapters, this chapter conducts a complete study on three typical cases, namely the IOTP, the real case of integration of multi-participants, and the process defects caused by the behavior risk. Using the methods proposed in this chapter, the soundness and non-blocking of online transaction business processes are analyzed and verified. This chapter analyzes and detects the logical defects of the business process itself, and proposes a framework to deal with the problems of malicious behavior patterns and illegal behaviors in the open network environment.

References

[1] Burdett, D. Internet Open Trading Protocol-IOTP. RFC 2801. IETF Trade Working Group Version 1.0., (April 2000).

[2] Burdett, D., Eastlake, D., and Goncalves, M. *Internet Open Trading Protocol*, NY, USA: McGraw-Hill, (2000).

[3] Ouyang, C., Kristensen, L. M., and Billington, J. An Improved Architectural Specification of the Internet Open Trading Protocol. In *Proceedings of the 3rd Workshop and Tutorial on Practical Use of Coloured Petri Nets and the CPN Tools*, DAIMI PB, Aarhus, Denmark, pp. 115–133 (2001).

[4] The Internet Engineering Task Force — IETF. http://www.ietf.org/.

[5] Du, Y. Y. and Jiang, C. J. Verifying Functions in Online Stock Trading Systems. *Journal of Computer Science and Technology*, 19(2): 203–212 (2004).

[6] Du, Y. Y., Jiang, C. J., and Zhou, M. C. A Petri Net-Based Model for Verification of Obligations and Accountability in Cooperative Systems. *IEEE Transactions on Systems, Man, and Cybernetics, Part A: Systems and Humans*, 39(2): 299–308 (2009).

[7] Du, Y. Y., Jiang, C. J., Zhou, M. C., and Fu, Y. Modeling and Monitoring of E-Commerce Workflows. *Information Sciences*, 179(7): 995–1006 (2009).

[8] Du, Y. Y., Jiang, C. J., and Zhou, M. C. A Petri Net Based Correctness Analysis of Internet Stock Trading Systems. *IEEE Transactions on Systems, Man, and Cybernetics Part C*, 38(1): 93–99 (2008).

[9] Du, Y. Y., Jiang, C. J., and Zhou, M. C. Modeling and Analysis of Real-Time Cooperative Systems Using Petri Nets. *IEEE Transactions Systems, Man, and Cybernetics Part A*, 37(5): 643–654 (2007).

[10] Du, Y. Y. *Research on Petri Net Modeling Theory and Analysis Technology of E-Commerce System*, Shanghai, China: Tongji University, (2003).

[11] Wang, R., Chen, S., Wang, X. F. *et al.* How to Shop for Free Online–Security Analysis of Cashier-as-a-Service Based Web Stores. In *32th IEEE Symposium on Security and Privacy (S&P)*, IEEE, Oakland, USA, pp. 465–480 (2011).

[12] Asokan, N., Schunter, M., and Waidner, M. Optimistic Protocols for Fair Exchange. In *4th ACM Conference on Computer and Communication Security*, Zurich, Switzerland: ACM Press, pp. 8–17 (April 1997).

[13] Chen, E., Chen, S., Qadeer, S. *et al.* Securing Multiparty Online Services via Certification of Symbolic Transactions. In *36th IEEE Symposium on Security and Privacy (S&P)*, IEEE, San Jose, USA, pp. 833–849 (2015).

[14] Chen, E., Chen, S., Qadeer, S. *et al.* A Practical Approach to Protocol-Agnostic Security for Multiparty Online Services. Technical Report (MSR-TR-2014-72), Redmond, WA, USA: Microsoft Research, (2014).

[15] Sun, F. Q., Xu, L., and Su, Z. D. Detecting Logic Vulnerabilities in E-Commerce Applications. In *21st Network and Distributed System Security Symposium (NDSS)*, Internet Society, San Diego, USA, pp. 1–16 (2014).

[16] Yu, W. Y., Yan, C. G., Ding, Z. J., Jiang, C. J. *et al.* Modeling and Validating E-commerce Business Process Based on Petri Nets. *IEEE Transactions on Systems, Man, and Cybernetics: Systems*, 44(3): 327–341 (2014).

[17] Katsaros, P. A Roadmap to Electronic Payment Transaction Guarantees and a Colored Petri Net Model Checking Approach. *Information and Software Technology*, 51(2): 235–257 (2009).

[18] Katsaros, P. *et al.* Colored Petri Net Based Model Checking and Failure Analysis for E-Commerce Protocols. In *Proceedings of the 6th Workshop and Tutorial on Practical Use of Coloured Petri Nets and the CPN Tools*, DAIMI PB, Aarhus, Denmark, pp. 267–283 (2005).

[19] Swiderski, F. and Snyder, W. *Threat Modeling*, O'Reilly Media, Inc., Sevastopol, CA, USA, (2009).

[20] Xu, D. and Nygard, K. E. Threat-Driven Modeling and Verification of Secure Software Using Aspect-Oriented Petri Nets. *IEEE Transactions on Software Engineering*, 32(4): 265–278 (2006).

[21] Bhargavan, K., Fournet, C., and Gordon, A. D. Modular Verification of Security Protocol Code by Typing. In *Proceedings of the 37th Annual*

ACM Symposium on Principles Programming Languages (SIGPLAN-SIGACT), ACM, New York, NY, USA, pp. 445–456 (2010).

[22] Ray, I. Failure Analysis of an E-Commerce Protocol Using Model Checking. In *Proceedings of the 2nd International Workshop on Advanced Issues of E-Commerce, Web-Based Information Systems*, IEEE, Milpitas, CA, USA, pp. 176–183, (2000).

[23] Hoglund, G. and McGraw, G. *Exploiting Software: How to Break Code*, Delhi, India: Pearson Education India, (2004).

[24] Viega, J. and McGraw, G. *Building Secure Software*, Tokyo, Japan: Ohmsha, (2006).

[25] Garner Group. Available at http://www.securityinnovation.com.

[26] Neumann, P. Principled Assuredly Trustworthy Composable Architectures. In *SRI International, Computer Science Laboratory*, Menlo Park, USA, SRI Project 11459, Contract N66001-01-C-8040, (December 2004).

[27] Ana, S. and Marjan, K. Enterprise Architecture Patterns for Business Process Support Analysis. *The Journal of Systems and Software*, 84(9): 1480–1506 (2011).

[28] Antonio, R., Óscar, C., Antonio, F. *et al.* Payment Frameworks for the Purchase of Electronic Products and Services. *Computer Standards and Interfaces*, 34(1): 80–92 (2012).

[29] Christian, W., Michael, M., Andreas, S. *et al.* Model-Driven Business Process Security Requirement Specification. *Journal of Systems Architecture*, 55(4): 211–223 (2009).

[30] Yu, W. Y., Yan, C. G., Ding, Z. J., Jiang, C. J. *et al.* Modeling and Verification of Online Shopping Business Processes by Considering Malicious Behavior Patterns. *IEEE Transactions on Automation Science and Engineering*, 13(2): 647–662 (2016).

[31] Yu, W. Y., Yan, C. G., Ding, Z. J., Jiang, C. J. *et al.* Analyzing E-Commerce Business Process Nets via Incidence Matrix and Reduction. *IEEE Transactions on Systems, Man, and Cybernetics: Systems*, 48(1): 130–141 (2016). DOI: 10.1109/TSMC.2016.2598287.

Index

CPSIA information can be obtained
at www.ICGtesting.com
Printed in the USA
LVHW050934021221
704785LV00001B/7

9 789811 241161